Defence Budgeting
Recent Perspective

DEFENCE BUDGETING
Recent Perspective

Major (Retd.) S.K. Sharma

PRASHANT PUBLISHING HOUSE

DELHI-110094

Published by :

Prashant Publishing House

C-34, 28 Foota Road, Gali-3,

West Karwal Nagar, Delhi-110094

Phone : 011-22963970, Mob. : 9810396373

e-mail.: prashantpublishinghouse@gmail.com

DEFENCE BUDGETING

(Recent Perspective)

First Published 2013

ISBN 978-93-80565-36-1

PRINTED IN INDIA

Published by Mr. R.K. Jha M/s Prashant Publishing House and Published at H.S. Offset House Press, Delhi.

Preface

A military budget (or military expenditure), also known as a defense budget, is the amount of financial resources dedicated by an entity (most often a nation or a state), to raising and maintaining an armed forces. Military budgets often reflect how much an entity perceives the likelihood of threats against it, or the amount of aggression it wishes to employ. It also provides an idea of how much finances could be provided for the upcoming year. The size of a budget also reflects the entity's ability to fund military activities, with factors including the size of that entity's economy, other financial demands on that entity, and the willingness of that entity's government or people to fund such military activity. Generally excluded from military expenditures is spending oninternal law enforcement and disabled veteran rehabilitation.

The strategic defence plan specifies the required outputs of defence at the highest level as well as the macro envisaged resource allocation to defence over an extended period. The defence programmes, in turn, specify outputs in the form of objectives at the next lower level as well as planned allocations to the programme managers for producing these outputs. This must now be converted into business plans where specific activities for reaching these objectives are specified and accurately costed from zero in terms of the required inputs. These business plans are done at unit level (including directorates or sections at headquarters) and are in turn the basis for the performance agreements between the programme managers and unit commanders/section chiefs as well as for service agreements directly negotiated. The same considerations as discussed in the previous paragraph on performance and service agreements at the next higher level are valid for these agreements.

The Union Budget 2012-13, presented to the Parliament on March 16, 2012 hiked the defence outlays to Rs. 1,93,407.29 crore (US$ 40.44 billion1). This represents a growth of 17.63 per cent over the previous year's outlays – one of the highest increases in recent years excluding that for 2009-10 when the budget was increased by over 34 per cent, mostly to accommodate the pay hikes caused by the implementation of the recommendations of the Sixth Central Pay Commission. The increase in the latest defence budget was made possible by the expansionary fiscal policy adopted by the government in general. Further, although the increase looks impressive at first glance, it is not however driven by the modernisation needs as much as by manpower needs.

China's Defence Budget 2012 announced in the first week of March 2012 significantly draws global and regional attention in that China has shot through its defence expenditure over the $ 100 billion mark, making China's military expenditure at the global level, second only to that of the United States, even though there exists a wide differential between the two.In terms of global concerns, China's hikes in defence expenditures in 2012 military budget come under sharper scrutiny when China's defence hikes are placed in the context of a sharp drop in United States defence budget by about $ 380 billion necessitated by US Congressional mandates. Though President Obama has reiterated that the Asia Pacific regional military posture of the United States would not be in the purview of budgetary cuts because of the new US strategic pivot to Asia Pacific, what cannot be ruled out is that in case of a sudden Middle East contingency, the United States would be forced to redirect US Forces from its strengthened posture against a fast militarily rising China.

This book makes an interesting reading for historians, defence and policy analysts, researchers and general readers alike.

—Editor

Contents

1

Management of Defence Budgeting

A major lacuna in defence planning and implementation has been lack of financial commitment for the Plan period. Financially, the defence plans are treated more as annual plans rather than composite five years plan. There is a rush to spend the annual capital budget by the end of the financial year since the amount not spent has to be surrendered. In FY 2004-05, the previous government had proposed to institute a non-lapsable Defence Modernisation Fund of Rs 25,000 crore. This was a long awaited reform in the defence-finance mechanism as budgeted capital expenditure worth thousands of crores was surrendered year after year. However, the new government, being of the view that there are no provisions in the budgetary rules and regulations to carry forward unspent funds for three years, has done away with this reform. It needs to be pointed out that a similar procedure was being followed in the 1930s and 1940s. The provisions invoked at that time need to be studied carefully and could be used as a precedent. Action should be taken expeditiously to revive the Defence Modernization Fund.

Otherwise, funds earmarked for capital expenditure on an annual basis will continue to lapse, leading to lack of systematic defence preparedness. In the Revenue Budget, there is a need to include incentives to save and reduce annual maintenance expenditure without adversely affecting operational efficiency. It is also necessary to exploit the increasing domestic industrial capability to support the existing infrastructure and thus reduce maintenance costs and enhance the quality of maintenance.

The development of human resources must keep pace with the modernisation of the armed forces so that new, state-of-the-art equipment can be optimally exploited by well trained and motivated soldiers, sailors and airmen. The age profile of military personnel, particularly in the Army, and the age of commanders at battalion and brigade levels needs to be looked into. Currently, a soldier has to serve for 15 to 17 years to earn his pension. When he retires, besides the lifelong pension that has to be paid, a trained individual is lost to the nation. Similarly, while there is a shortage of approximately 14,000 officers, most officers retire in rank of Lieutenant Colonel or Colonel at the age of 52-54 years when they still have years of productive life ahead though they are no longer fit for active combat.

Innovative measures need to be adopted to reduce the effects of the current national loss on this account. The best method would be to institute a procedure of 'lateral induction" under which both officers and personnel below officer rank can be transferred to central police and paramilitary forces (CPMFs). The colour (active) service of jawans should be reduced to 7-10 years with no pension liability after which the volunteers are transferred to the BSF, CRPF, ITBP, CISF and other such forces. Similarly, the Shipping Corporation of India, National Port Trust and other such maritime organisations can fruitfully employ Naval personnel. Ex-servicemen will be expected to serve in these organisations till superannuation, after which they would be entitled to pension. This will improve the age profile of the Services, provide trained manpower to the CPMFs, ensure productive long-term employment for a large number of trained men till superannuation, and also reduce the pension bill of the Central Government. The Army should increase the recruitment of Short Service Officers to make up its shortfall. Induction of these officers to the CPMFs after five years of service will improve junior leadership and effectiveness of these forces in internal security and counter insurgency operations.

THE STATE DEFENCE CONCEPT

The goal of the State Defence Concept is to define the guidelines for strengthening and improving the defence system in accordance with Latvia's geopolitical situation and Latvia's obligations to the collective security of the North Atlantic Treaty Organisation (hereinafter – NATO), of which Latvia is preparing to become a full member in the middle of 2004. The Concept determines the basic strategic principles that will guide the implementation of the tasks associated with state defence and is the basis for planning the development of the National Armed Forces (hereinafter – NAF). The State Defence Concept is formulated on the basis of Analysis of Endangerment to the State, the Military Risk Analysis and forecasted trends in the development of international security. The state's defence policy and strategy have been formulated to avert possible threats. The Constitution of the Republic of Latvia [Satversme], the National Security Concept and Foreign Policy Concept and other regulations adopted by the Republic of Latvia determine principles, goals, tasks and legal mechanisms of state defence.

Latvia's regulations and action plans related to state defence are updated in accordance with the basic principles of the State Defence Concept. The goal of the State Defence Concept is to define the guidelines for strengthening and improving the defence system in accordance with Latvia's geopolitical situation and Latvia's obligations to the collective security of the North Atlantic Treaty Organisation (hereinafter – NATO), of which Latvia is preparing to become a full member in the middle of 2004. The Concept determines the basic strategic principles that will guide the implementation of the tasks associated with state defence and is the basis for planning the development of the National Armed Forces (hereinafter – NAF).

The State Defence Concept is formulated on the basis of Analysis of Endangerment to the State, the Military Risk

Analysis and forecasted trends in the development of international security. The state's defence policy and strategy have been formulated to avert possible threats. The Constitution of the Republic of Latvia [Satversme], the National Security Concept and Foreign Policy Concept and other regulations adopted by the Republic of Latvia determine principles, goals, tasks and legal mechanisms of state defence. Latvia's regulations and action plans related to state defence are updated in accordance with the basic principles of the State Defence Concept.

SECRET SECTOR IN DEFENCE PRODUCTION

The Government of India has been reiterating its commitment to achieve the much-publicised target of procuring 70 per cent of its defence requirements from indigenous sources by 2010. Despite its best efforts over the last two decades, India is nowhere near that figure as yet. The Government is well aware of the emergence of private sector as a vibrant and dynamic force, especially in information technology, service sector and manufacturing fields. It has come to realise that self reliance would remain a pipe dream if it continued to bank on public sector alone. One of the objectives mentioned in the new defence procurement procedure is to achieve self-reliance in defence equipment. But the whole procedure is silent about the role of the private sector and no worthwhile initiatives have been proposed to integrate its potential in India's quest for self reliance.

In addition to economic factors, defence industry is generally considered to be an instrument of national sovereignty and pride. Defence industry comprises of all industrial undertakings engaged in the production of hardware and services for use by the defence forces. The origin of the Indian defence industry can be traced to the establishment of Gun and Shell Factory at Cossipore in 1801. At the time of the Independence, India had 16 Ordnance Factories, established by the British to produce low tech items. Bharat Electronics Ltd was the first Defence Public Sector Undertaking (DPSU) established in 1954 to manufacture electronic equipment for the forces. Today, India has 39 Ordnance Factories and eight DPSU.

The Industrial Policy Resolution of 1956 divided industry into three parts:-

- Schedule A: Basic industries which are the preserve of the state, including defence and heavy engineering.
- Schedule B: Industries in which private industry was allowed to operate.
- Schedule C: All other industries.

Manufacture of components, assemblies and sub-assemblies was thrown open to the private sector in 1991. With a view to promote defence-industry partnership, the Ministry of Defence constituted six Joint Task Forces in collaboration with Confederation of Indian Industry in 1998. Consequent to their recommendations, the Government opened defence production to the private sector in January 2002. It allowed 100 percent private equity with 26 percent Foreign Direct Investment (FDI). It was a major policy change. Subsequently, the Department of Industrial Policy and Promotion issued detailed guidelines for the issuance of licence for the production of arms and ammunition.

The Kelkar Committee, constituted in 2004, made many radical recommendations. The Government has accepted a majority of them but their implementation has lacked earnestness and focus. The Department of Industrial Policy & Promotion (DIPP), in consultation with Ministry of Defence, has so far issued 37 letters of intent for the manufacture of various types of defence hardware which include armoured and combat vehicles, radars, electronic warfare equipment, warships, submarines, avionics, military aircraft, safety and ballistic products, armaments and ammunition.

Despite the above measures, there has been no discernible change in the ground situation. Only a handful of India's top companies are involved in small value defence contracts. The private sector has to remain content with the supply of some low-tech items to the public sector. Its supplies to DPSU and

Ordnance Factories grossed over Rs. 1200 crores and Rs. 1900 crores respectively last year. Whereas these figures signify the contribution made by the private sector, they also highlight the fact that the private sector continues to be merely an outsourcing base for the public sector.

DEFENCE AND ECONOMIC PROCESS

The defence sector has a major share of the budget in most countries. The perceived adverse effects of higher defence spending on economic growth are due to the following:

- Purchase by the defence sector of domestic goods, or the use of foreign exchange to purchase imported goods.
- The government sector shows no measurable productivity increases. Thus, an enlargement in defence spending shifts resources from the productive sector to the non-productive sector.
- A shift of resources to defence reduces the resources available for the rest of the economy and in particular "crowds out" private investment as well as diverts skilled workers from civilian sectors.

The dominant view among economists has been that defence is a drag on economic growth. A contrary view was brought out strongly for the first time in a study of developing countries on this topic by Benoit in 1973. Of the favourable effects of defence spending, Benoit lists many, of which the following seem relevant for the Indian situation: Security effects—To the extent that the military provides security to the country, it enables an atmosphere conducive to investment and long-term planning decisions.

Training effects—Military manpower receives training even at the rudimentary level and this can be beneficial if the recruits come in substantial numbers from the subsistence economy and if the military programmes introduce people to 'modern' methods and social skills and general inculcation of 'national' values.

Infrastructure effects—The military may create infrastructure, such as roads, airports, docks and communications, which can be used by the civilian sector, especially 'up country'.

Consumable effects—The services provide substantial numbers of people with food, clothing, shelter and medicines. They also engage in 'civic action' programmes and in 'hearts and minds' campaigns. The existing research by and large seems to indicate that certain groups of developing countries derive positive benefits from military spending. The sustainability of the defence budget is a function of the health of the economy. A glaring example of this in recent times has been the inability of the Soviet Union to sustain high levels of defence spending in superpower competition with the USA, in the face of a faltering economy. Defence expenditure in India has benefited from higher growth rates in the recent past. In real dollar terms, the Indian defence budget has more than doubled in the past decade. The ratio of defence expenditure to GDP is well below 3% today, which is a healthy sign. On the flip side, internal security is adversely impacted by social and economic backwardness and regional balance issues seems to be needed for the sustainability both of growth-fostering reformist economic policies as well as a stronger defence.

Military Work Force

The human resource dimension of defence economics is a relatively neglected field. US studies dominate the theoretical, empirical, and policy literature on military manpower. Two issues have been pre-eminent. First, studies of conscription versus an all-volunteer force. Second, the concern with downsizing and its implications for military manpower. In India, the structure of military manpower has changed little since British times. Reliance continues on a large, conventional force with over 1.3 million men in uniform in the armed forces and another nearly 1.7 million paramilitary personnel with about 400,000 of these in organisations directly performing a defence role. In addition, entities like the Border Roads Organization (employing about a lakh) and defence civilians (estimated to be of the order of another four lakhs) perform a support role. There probably is a case for looking at overall numbers in the context of modernization; even the Chinese People's Liberation Army has apparently made conscious manpower reductions in recent times. Putting a price to the manpower input into defence would also be instructive in taking a call on these issues.

Arms Control and Trade

Arms imports by India in the 2001-05 period are estimated at over $9 billion at constant 1990 prices. Defence markets are large, government regulated, and generally non-transparent in their functioning. Economic factors are relevant in understanding and dealing with defence markets. For example, the post-Cold War situation and disarmament in NATO and in the former Warsaw Pact countries has made their defence contractors seek export sales to compensate for declining domestic procurement. As a result, disarmament in one part of the world might actually promote arms exports, regional arms races, and possibly instability elsewhere in the world. Similarly, major technical advances result in new products and fuel demand from buyers who need to "catch up."

The Indian Context

Issues relating to arms imports are important for India, which has only a 30% rate of self-reliance in arms procurement, despite a sizable arms industry. By their very nature, arms import deals tend to involve large amounts of money, and are politically highly sensitive. It is possible to work out the costs and benefits of a procurement alternative in quantitative terms, and such exercises should be encouraged, so that better decisions are made. The putting in place a new, more transparent Defence Procurement Procedure in India in 2006 has drawn attention to the issue of "offsets". As the arms trade takes place in a buyers' market, it follows that arms importing countries are in a dominant position to extract compensatory investment. The new procedure in India requires direct offsets of 30% of the value of the contract to be made for all defence capital contracts of over Rs 300 crores. This is expected, according to the Defence Minister, to result in gains for the country of over Rs 45,000 crores ($10 billion) in investments over the Eleventh Plan period (2007-12). The limited international research on the subject, however, tends to cast doubt on the net benefits of defence offsets to national economies. As has been pointed out in this context, "there are no free lunches."

DEFENCE MECHANISM AND INDUSTRY

Strategic motivations apart, indigenous arms production efforts have been justified on the economic grounds that (a) It will spur generalized industrialisation by means of spill-over or spin-off effects; and; (b) It will permit foreign-exchange earnings. The reference point for determining the value of any defence-industry relationship is its contribution to the ability of the defence forces to meet their key responsibilities. Joint production or collaborative ventures should be expected to lead to cost savings and greater scales of output. But international collaboration is only one form of work sharing: alternative forms are licensed production and offsets; these also need to be evaluated as alternatives.

Economics of Defence Production

A substantial defence production capability has been developed in India, and inevitably some of the issues that surround defence industries in other parts of the world are relevant for India. Efficiency issues exist. The recent award of two $20 million contracts for rocket launchers to be used in the Pinaka missile system to the Indian engineering companies Tata Power and Larsen & Toubro is noteworthy in this context, since it is the first time that private-sector Indian companies have been appointed as prime contractors on a defence project. We should also be concerned that while two decades back, an estimated 40% of weapons and equipment requirements was met by outright imports, today this figure is around 70%. In the case of India's Defence Research and Development Organisation (DRDO), the development time taken is in many cases said to be so long that before an item reaches the prototype stage, the specifications and performance parameters aimed at are obsolete by contemporary standards. Such things are known to happen in more advanced countries also.

The Economics of Insurgency and Extremism

Left wing extremism in India happens to have arisen in the most backward regions of the country, lending support to the argument that economic solutions in terms of raising the levels of development and improving economic prospects for the unemployed have to be a major factor in arriving at long-term solutions to the conflict. At the same time, it has been estimated that "10-20% of development funds" in militancy affected areas in India end up in the hands of the insurgents, major investments committed to the resource-rich but less developed states of central India are at risk due to insurgent attacks on economic targets.

Defence Technology

Technological advances occur today at a breathtaking pace. Economists can contribute in helping identify least cost solutions consistent with security imperatives, using the potential offered by technological changes. The trends outlined are part of the global landscape today, and for the Indian defence forces, it is only a question of whether they will allow the changes to pass them by or will seek to stay ahead of the curve by factoring them into defence strategies. We can begin here and now. The rapidly evolving global scenario will have no mercy on laggards. Would it be prudent to deny ourselves the benefit of information, techniques and analysis that are currently available? Don't we want to squeeze the maximum "bang for the buck", so that the best decisions on strengthening of national security can be made, for any given level of resources allocated? These are the questions that we need to reflect upon. In the answer to these questions lies the road ahead.

DEFENCE ECONOMICS DIRECTION

Defence economics, field of national economic management concerned with the economic effects of military expenditure, the management of economics in wartime, and the management of peacetime military budgets.

OPPORTUNITIES DEPARTED: THE COST OF WAR

There is no such thing as an inexpensive war. First, there is the human cost in loss of life and in the physical and psychological maiming of healthy people. While the personal cost of such loss is immeasurable, the economic cost to society can be estimated. This measure was first proposed by a French economist, Jean-Baptiste Say, in 1803. He asserted the principle that war costs more than its direct expenses, for it also costs what its casualties (military and civilian) would have earned throughout their lifetimes if they had never participated in war. Second, war has economic costs arising from the destruction of buildings, productive farmlands and forests, public services such as waterworks, electricity-generating and distribution systems, roads, bridges, harbours, and airfields, and all manner of personal and corporate property such as homes, possessions, factories, machinery, vehicles, and aircraft. War, therefore, destroys physical capital that has been created by previous economic activity.

Reconstruction after war is a particular economic burden because the finance, imported capital goods, and labour used in reconstruction merely restore the losses a country has sustained, rather than adding to the stock of capital available to its economy. Thus, even if it manages to restore all its physical losses, it uses scarce resources that would otherwise have been available for extending and improving economic activity. As most wars since 1945 have occurred in the Third World, some of the world's poorest countries have suffered the most from the economic losses of war.

War also costs a great deal in goods and services to create the weapons of war and to supply the people engaged in the war effort. The diversion of these goods and services—which range from the metals and chemicals transformed into weapons to the food, clothing, and shelter for the armed forces—reduces current civilian consumption, which lowers the population's living standards. Metal used to make a tank cannot be used to build bridges, fuel used to transport military supplies cannot be used on school buses, cement used to construct ammunition dumps cannot be used in house construction. This constitutes the opportunity cost of war—that is, the extent to which the economy foregoes the opportunity to commit these resources to alternative peaceful uses.

The opportunity cost of war is also felt in the future. In addition to allocating resources to consumption (the satisfaction of current needs), an economy allocates resources to investment (the new factories and machinery that produce tomorrow's goods and services). Resources diverted to war cannot be used to create new productive capacity for future consumption, and this reduces the living standards of the population below what they otherwise would have been in the future.

In summary, the total costs of war include the cost of the foregone use of the economic resources used up in the conflict. These include the cost of the foregone lifetime earnings of those killed in the war, the cost of lifetime medical care for those permanently incapacitated by the war, the cost of replacing the physical capital destroyed or damaged by the war, the cost of supplying the armed forces with the weapons of war, the cost of sustaining the armed forces and those in support functions (including their pay and pensions), and the losses to the economy caused by the diversion of resources from peaceful investment in future economic capacity.

COMPARISON BURDENS

International comparisons of how governments arrange their defence spending are fraught with conceptual discrepancies. The defence burden of a country is measured by the d/GDP ratio, which indicates how much of the nation's resources are being allocated to defence each year, but different estimates of both d and GDP are possible, each giving a different d/GDP ratio. Capitalist economies, which use the GDP, measure economic activity differently from communist economies, which use a net material product (NMP) system.

The NMP excludes many expenditures, including state administration and defence, normally included under GDP. This complicates comparisons between these systems. Defence expenditures themselves are subject to controversy.

The North Atlantic Treaty Organization (NATO) has agreed on a measure of defence activity to which it adheres when making comparisons of its members' defence burdens, but other countries follow different conventions. Some, largely low-income countries, exclude internal security expenditures, which can be relatively high, thus lowering their official d/GDP ratio. Others, such as the Soviet Union, exclude defence-related research and development, frontier guards, and paramilitary reserves, thereby reducing the nominal defence expenditure by up to 30 percent.

Even if agreement could be reached on what constitutes defence expenditure, this would still leave countries with a measure denominated in their domestic currencies. For meaningful comparisons of the absolute amounts spent on defence, every country's defence expenditures would have to be reduced to a common currency. But the act of converting each currency into, for example, U.S. dollars could lead to distortions, because official exchange rates reflect official policies and not existing realities. Thus, two countries with similar amounts in dollars spent on defence, and therefore in balance in their defence capabilities, could face a growing imbalance in their dollar-based defence expenditures purely because one of their currencies has changed its exchange rate with the U.S. dollar.

Comparisons of the absolute amounts each country spends on defence are prone to error and must always be used with caution. Nevertheless, because each country measures its defence spending and its GDP in its own currency, the d/GDP ratio is an acceptable measure of a country's defence burden. Ratios can be compared across countries and in different time periods. The d/GDP ratio rises rapidly during a major war—in Britain in 1944 the d/GDP ratio reached 60 percent—and it falls in periods of prolonged peace. A country raising its d/GDP ratio signals that it is concerned with security, in turn causing concern among countries likely to be affected.

Defence Burdens Universal

Security expenditures for both external defence and internal law and order account for major shares of government expenditures. In many low-income countries, these expenditures often exceed 20–30 percent of the state budget and more than 10 percent of the country's GDP. The higher-income countries, while spending higher absolute amounts on defence, tend to spend smaller proportions of state expenditure (under 15 percent) and smaller proportions of GDP (under 5 percent). Given the perilous security situation in the lower-income regions of the world, these discrepancies are understandable (if also regrettable in view of their other pressing needs).

By looking at the actual defence burden of an individual country and comparing it with the norm for similar economies, analysts can infer localized circumstances that may be influencing the government's perceptions of security. For instance, a poor country with a very low d/GDP, or a rich country with a very high d/GDP, is behaving differently from the norm for similar economies. An economist would seek explanations for this in the perception of a threat indicated by the public statements of the government concerned. In the absence of such statements, or where public statements are contrary to the behaviour of the government (for example, if it is raising its d/GDP but publicly proclaiming its peaceful intentions and denying that it is threatened by, or is threatening, any other country), the economist would rely on the d/GDP as an indicator of true intentions. It is likely that the intelligence services of neighbouring countries would draw similar conclusions from the economic data. Within the higher-income countries there are notable differences in the amounts spent on defence. The United States and Britain have spent relatively high proportions (5 to 10 percent) of their GDP on defence since 1955, compared with Japan, which has spent less than 1 percent of GDP over the same period. Germany and France also have tended to spend a smaller proportion of their GDPs than Britain on defence.

The Japanese case is interesting because of the differences in economic achievement between Japan and the big defence spenders. Many economists believe that there is a connection between the amount of GDP spent on defence and a country's economic growth, investment, and living standards. Japan's limit of d/GDP to under 1 percent was a result of its defeat in World War II. There is no doubt that it benefited enormously from limited defence spending (particularly while it could free ride under the military protection of the United States), since resources not allocated to defence went into economic investment, to the direct benefit of civilian employment and output. However, at the same time Japan also spent much less (about half as much) of its GDP on general government expenditure (g) than the United States and western Europe. Whether it was the low d/GDP (1 percent) or the low g/GDP (9 percent) that allowed the resources for Japanese economic successes to be mobilized is arguable. A low g/GDP ratio implies a lower level of taxation than a high g/GDP. This releases a higher flow of savings into the economy, enabling higher investment ratios to be maintained. High rates of investment, which are associated with higher growth rates of GDP, characterized the Japanese post-war economy and are a more likely explanation for the Japanese economic success than its low d/GDP.

The Soviet Union has long spent a high proportion of its national resources on defence. Estimates vary, but the consensus among Western economists is that Soviet d/GDP for much of the postwar period was around 14 percent. (The official Soviet d/GDP was 6 percent.) If defence spending competes with economic growth in the capitalist economies, contributing to inflation, low investment, and lower living standards, then it must have a devastating impact on poorer economies such as the Soviet Union. The need to compete with the United States at all technological levels across the weapons spectrum has been met at the cost of heavy distortions in the rest of the Soviet economy. This has compelled the

Soviet Union to review its priorities and to consider whether its security is best assured by continually raising the military ante with the West or by living at some lower level of military tension with a reduced offensive military capability.

MANAGEMENT: INFORMATION

The Army is developing its Managing Information Long-Range Plan (MILRP) to provide for the future direction of the Information Mission Area (IMA). It supports the Army Information Architecture (AIA) and the IMA cycle. While helping to focus on capabilities for the objective configuration of the AIA, it also has short and mid-range importance. MILRP influences the acquisition process by providing guidance to the Information Management Plan, the Long-Range Research and Development Acquisition Plan, The Army Plan, the Army Command and Control Master Plan, and the Information Management Master Plan. MILRP's longer range focus seeks to anticipate the impact of change and to design an effective transition of Army programs and resources to form the IMA into the 21st century. Because of rapid technological change, MILRP will identify those technological advances that have high potential for IMA use. It also will investigate the usefulness of consolidating the five IMA disciplines (automation, communications, printing and publications, records management, and visual information) into a common technological base, combining similar information programs, and adapting command and control systems for deep battle doctrine, which foresees reliance on autonomous small unit operations. The Office of the Director of Information Systems for Command, Control, Communications, and Computers (ODISC4) released an MILRP draft for staffing in FY 88.

In June 1986 the Army announced its standards for procuring Army information systems equipment and indicated that any limitation on competition from vendors would comply with existing laws. Several federal agencies and many vendors complained that the Army had restricted competition, and the General Accounting Office (GAO) conducted an investigation of the allegations. With the emergence of approved Defence Department, federal, national, and international standards, the DISC4 rescinded the Army's original standards on 14 December 1987 and confirmed the Army's support for the Defence Department standardization program. These Defence Department standards include the government Open Systems Interconnection (OSI) Profile, Standard Query Language, and Portable Operating System Interface for Computing Environments, which are rapidly becoming federal, national, and international standards. OSI standards, for example, allow computers made by different nations or manufacturers to interoperate. A NATO standardization agreement ratified OSI standards and served as the basis for the SIGMA/HEROS command and control interoperability demonstration between the U.S. and West Germany in 1984. Acceptance of OSI standards by the federal government will provide the Army the capability to interoperate in garrison the same way it can interoperate with NATO and other allies.

Progress continued during FY 88 in procuring improved information systems for Army functional area operations. Project 80X is acquiring integrated hardware and communications to replace outdated, leased automatic data processing equipment (ADPE) that supports the TAPA. The new system will support Headquarters, Department of the Army, processing for officer, enlisted, and civilian personnel records to include such applications as officer and enlisted assignments. Contractors installed the initial large-scale ADPE at the Army Personnel Center in St. Louis, Missouri, in January and another one at the Information Systems Command, Alexandria, Virginia, in May 1988. Networked minicomputers installed at the Enlisted Records Evaluation Center, Fort Benjamin Harrison, Indiana, and the Central Clearance Facility, Fort Meade, Maryland, facilitate integration of the system expected to become fully operational in early FY 89.

The Acquisition Information Management (AIM) program will help implement the 1986 reorganization, which centralized

Headquarters, Department of the Army research, development, and acquisition management in the Secretariat and established the program executive officer (PEO) concept. By using existing information systems, it will integrate the classified and unclassified acquisition data exchange requirements of the Army Acquisition Executive, the Army Staff, PEOs, the Army Materiel Command, the Training and Doctrine Command, the Information Systems Command, and other acquisition managers. The Assistant Secretary of the Army (Research, Development, and Acquisition) (ASA [RDA]) acts as the functional proponent for the AIM program, which he regards as the top priority Information Mission Area project in the RDA community. The Major Army Information Systems Review Committee approved the AIM program in September 1988. Progress in the implementation of AIM, expected to continue into the mid-1990s, depended upon available funding at the close of FY 88.

The Reserve Component Automation System (RCAS), authorized in August 1986 and assigned to Forces Command, sought to consolidate essential data to facilitate Army mobilization requirements. In January 1988 Congress moved RCAS from Forces Command to the reserve component and placed responsibility for the program upon the Chief, National Guard Bureau. In February a new project manager took charge of RCAS with the intent of using office automation, telecommunications, distributed data bases, and distributed processing capability to provide timely and accurate information for mobilization planning and execution. RCAS will incorporate two major subsystems-Mobilization Command and Control (MOBC2), the primary RCAS element, and Unit Administration. In FY 88 the National Guard Bureau did not foresee significant immediate progress in the development of RCAS but anticipated fielding of critical elements of the program by FY 92. The Army made additional improvements in its visual information programs during FY 88.

On 25 March the Vice Chief of Staff dedicated the Video Teleconferencing Facility located in the Army Operations Center Conference Room in the Pentagon. It and several other Army organizations-the Training and Doctrine Command, Forces Command, Army Materiel Command, Information Systems Command, Health Services Command, and the Army War College-now comprise the Headquarters, Department of the Army, Video Teleconferencing Network.

The network allows secure conferencing on data classified through secret between two facilities and unsecure conferencing between multiple facilities for unclassified matters. It also permits conferencing with subscribers in other networks such as the major subordinate commands of the Army Materiel Command. Officials anticipate expansion to the Command and General Staff College and Western Command by the end of 1988 and video teleconferencing between Army and other Defence Department organizations to follow in the near future. Headquarters, Department of the Army, and the Army Materiel Command are decentralizing authority for managing visual information resources.

For example, the Army Materiel Command now allows its 56 visual information activities to buy equipment directly, which costs no more than $5,000, and to report such purchases only once a year. Another change affected Headquarters, Department of the Army, and other Defence Department authorities' approval of videotapes. Now, Army major television facilities can produce and distribute technical/safety reports immediately to commanders.

Headquarters, Department of the Army, granted authority to the Army Materiel Command to allow installations to control their local television and motion picture productions. Installations can make category one productions for official use, acquire some commercial productions for internal consumption, and maintain pertinent records locally. Release of visual information materials or productions to the public still requires clearance by Army public affairs.

Management: Resources

The Army leadership established Task Force ROBUST (Redistribution of BASOPS (Base Operating Information System)/Unit Structure within TDA) on 1 May 1988. They charged ROBUST to analyse all active and reserve component TDA organizations to assure that each one has the proper configuration and manning to support the warfighting CINCs and to accomplish critical mobilization missions. ROBUST requested each TDA unit to develop its Mission Essential Task List (METL) and to focus it on the organization's contribution to the Army's warfighting capability. The results determined unit requirements and the subsequent allocation of manpower to meet those requirements. ROBUST evaluation teams performed human intelligence collection on selected unit identification codes; three used an area approach-CONUS, Europe, and the Far East/Panama-and one used a functional approach. Army officials intended the work of Task Force ROBUST to complement the Army of Excellence concept. The ROBUST staff expected to submit a final report to the Secretary of the Army and the Army Chief of Staff in November 1988.

An allied topic, The Army Authorization Documents System-Redesign (TAADS-R) project begun in 1986, is updating the automation employed by TAADS. TAADS serves as an automated system and a management process that records approved unit structures, Modification Table of Organization and Equipment (MTOE) and TDA. Army agencies use it to requisition people and equipment. TAADS-R is combining current automated systems-TAADS, VTAADS (Vertical-TAADS), ITAADS (Installation-TAADS)-into a single system, consolidating official authorizations' data into one data base, supporting either centralized or decentralized management by allowing the building of MTOEs and TDAs at all authorized Army echelons and providing worldwide electronic linkage of unclassified information. The Decision Resource Data Base located at the Army Information Systems Command-Pentagon will maintain centralized documentation. Processing will take place on the mainframe and personal computers at user sites, but review and approval prerogatives remain unchanged. Full deployment, projected for two to three years, will include Headquarters, Department of the Army, the major Army commands, and 68 installations worldwide. The Army Civilian Personnel System (ACPERS)-Field Level, begun in July 1987, will upgrade and standardize automated data processing support for Army civilian personnel administration.

It will replace existing systems and interface with other automated systems, meet expanded peacetime requirements, and support mobilization. ACPERS will assist local commanders and civilian personnel offices by supporting position management, personnel program planning, recruitment and placement, training and development, and sustainment of the work force. The Army decided to adopt the Air Force Personnel Data System-Civilian as the baseline for ACPERS. Programmers are modeling Army requirements into the system that will operate at a data service center in San Antonio, Texas. The Air Force Manpower and Personnel Center will maintain the software as it already does for the Navy Department. The major Army commands and installations will participate in the installation of the system. The schedule calls for the ACPERS systems acceptance test in early FY 89 with deployment to commence shortly thereafter.

The Army has adopted the standard general ledger (SGL) for financial accounting now required for all federal agencies. In the early 1980s the Grace Commission, the General Accounting Office, Army Inspectors General, and other investigative groups emphasized that federal agencies used hundreds of inconsistent accounting systems. In 1984 the Office of Management and Budget formed an interagency group to develop an SGL chart of accounts for all federal agencies that would control all financial transactions and resource balances, satisfy basic OMB and Treasury Department reporting requirements, and integrate proprietary and budgetary accounting. In FY 87 OMB published the new SGL chart of accounts. Treasury Department Bulletin 87-08, dated 30 September 1987, required all federal financial systems to adopt the SGL for preparing external reports by 1 October 1988. Responding immediately, the Army issued its SGL accounting policy and procedures statement also on

30 September 1987. The SGL integrates appropriation, property, revenue, and expense accounting to facilitate control of all resources from receipt to consumption or disposal.

Following successful development and testing of Standard Financial Systems (STANFINS)-Redesign Subsystem 1 (SRD1) by the program executive officer for Financial Management Information Systems, the Army installed SRD1 at Forts Hood and Sam Houston, Texas; Benjamin Harrison, Indiana; Huachuca, Arizona; and McCoy, Wisconsin, in FY 88. SRD1 automates the finance office disbursing and collection operations for travel pay and commercial vendor payments. It provides substantial manpower savings by automating manual operations and system-to-system interfaces. The Army's largest interactive data base management system, SRD1 uses 149 interactive data base files and 670 COBOL programs, which contain more than 1,077,000 lines of code. Still in progress at the end of FY 88, an Army cost benefit/economic analysis was evaluating whether SRD1 should run on microcomputers and installation processors or in the Army Standard Information Management System network. The Army Finance and Accounting Center hoped to deploy SRD1 to 28 additional CONUS installations during FY 89.

Training ammunition management has undergone re-evaluation in the 1980s. In the past, projected requirements based on unit forecasts routinely exceeded actual expenditure of selected items by more than 300 percent. The Standards in Training Commission (STRAC) developed Department of the Army Pamphlet 350-38, *Standards in Weapons Training,* in FY 86 that, for the first time, provided models for training ammunition planners. STRAC models, however, coupled with idealized training plans by managers, resulted in authorizations exceeding expenditures by 65 percent in FY 86. Planners revised their models in FY 87 and utilized historical expenditure data to predict training ammunition requirements. They computed tank, Bradley fighting vehicle, and mortar ammunition at STRAC levels and all other systems at 110 percent of units' historical expenditure levels. A revised methodology approved in January 1988 established Program

Objective Memorandum (POM) and budget requirements at 110 percent of historical expenditures for tank, Bradley, artillery, and mortar systems and 105 percent for other systems while also adjusting for known changes in the training environment. Other ongoing efforts to improve training ammunition management include examining ways to procure less costly ammunition and increasing the use of training devices and simulators.

Several developments in Army logistics management took place in FY 88. The ODCSLOG published Volume I, *Logistics Vision,* of the Army Long-Range Logistics Plan (ALRLP). It assists logistics planners, materiel developers, Army and private sector schools, and industry to visualize the Army's future logistics needs. The other two volumes of the ALRLP consist of internal implementation and control instructions for the ODCSLOG, which include an automated data base that resides on the Headquarters, Department of the Army, Decision Support System. To improve logistics support during training exercises in Central and South America, ODCSLOG implemented a system of routing requisitions directly from a supply support activity to the national inventory control point. It reduced order and shipping time from more than fifty days to less than twenty. The system operates on tactical Army combat service support computer system hardware, uses standard Army retail supply system software, and requires no training or increased resources. Officials expected to test the system with a heavy division for possible application to all Army units. Logistics Applications of Automated Marking and Reading Symbols (LOGMARS) employs bar codes and scanners to expedite processing materiel throughout the Army. By the end of FY 88, LOGMARS was helping to process more than 40 percent of Army retail receipts.

The Military Traffic Management Command (MTMC) is fielding two new ocean terminal automation systems that improve deployment management. The Terminal Support Module (TSM) incorporates LOGMARS and interconnects with the Standard Port System overseas and the Terminal Management System in CONUS to move cargo quickly through ports. Fielded to all MTMC CONUS outports and reserve component Transportation Terminal Units (TTU) and being fielded to MTMC OCONUS ports, TSM successfully supported REFORGER and TEAM SPIRIT training exercises in the mid-1980s. The other ocean terminal automation system, Computerized Deployment System (CODES), provides an automated ship-loading planning tool to MTMC. Being fielded to all CONUS terminals and reserve TTUs, CODES uses the same basic hardware as the TSM and also performed successfully during testing with REFORGER and TEAL SPIRIT exercises. CODES allows loading planners great flexibility with its rapid ability to consolidate, process, and display a wide variety of cargo data and ship characteristics. It lets CINCs make extensive changes in deploying units, and loading planners still can make optimum use of available stowage space.

For the last several years the Army has experienced continual underfunding for its nontactical vehicles (NTVs). The Army's NTV fleet consists of commercially designed vehicles used for recruiting, training, security, medical care, sanitation, facilities maintenance, and other like needs worldwide. In FY 86 Congress directed the Army to investigate cost reduction measures for its NTVs. The Army made an agreement with the General Services Administration (GSA) to convert its CONUS NTVs, about two thirds of its total NTV fleet of 60,000 vehicles, to GSA ownership by FY 91. In effect, the Army would lease its CONUS NTVs from GSA for less cost than direct procurement by the Army from commercial suppliers. Recently, the Army has disposed of more NTVs than it replaced. With only $28.7 million for NTV procurement in FY 87, the Army purchased 1,728 vehicles and disposed of 2,731. The Army received $39.8 million and $18.0 million in the FY 88/89 budgets but estimated that it needs $100 million annually to replace its NTV fleet. By the end of FY 88 the Army was leasing 17,000 NTVs from GSA and redoubling its efforts to obtain increased NTV funding from Congress. The FY 86 Defence Authorization Act directed the Army, as the Defence Department executive agent for chemical demilitarization, to destroy the entire unitary chemical stockpile by 30 September 1994. The FY 89 Defence Authorization Act extended the program completion deadline to 1997. Congress has directed the Defence Department to replace unitary weapons with a modern binary chemical stockpile. In 1986 the Army established the program manager for chemical demilitarization located at Aberdeen Proving Ground, Maryland, to manage the estimated $3.2 billion chemical demilitarization program. Assisted by the EPA, the Federal Emergency Management Agency (FEMA), and the Department of Health and Human Services, the Army developed a programmatic environmental impact statement (PEIS) for destroying the unitary stockpile stored in CONUS. This affected eight CONUS installations-Aberdeen Proving Ground, Maryland; Anniston Army Depot, Alabama; Lexington-Blue Grass Army Depot, Kentucky; Newport Army Ammunition Plant, Indiana; Pine Bluff Arsenal, Arkansas; Pueblo Army Depot Activity, Colorado; Tooele Army Depot, Utah; and Umatilla Army Depot Activity, Oregon.

The PEIS considered destruction of the stockpile both on-site and at central locations. The Army decided in February 1988 that it would involve less risk to destroy the chemical stockpiles at their current storage sites rather than move them off post. As directed, on 16 March 1988 the Defence Department forwarded to Congress a revised Army plan for chemical demilitarization. It included the PEIS Record of Decision of on-site incineration at all eight CONUS facilities. The Johnston Atoll Chemical Agent Disposal System has been constructed and will undergo testing soon. It is the first full-scale chemical disposal facility that employs the reverse assembly/incineration process, which mechanically separates the different components of the chemical munition (agent, explosives, and metal parts) before burning them in separate furnaces. Sixteen months of verification testing at Johnston Atoll will precede its use at any other site. Another disposal method being tested, cyrofracture/incineration, freezes the whole munition in liquid nitrogen, fractures the munition in a press, and then incinerates everything in one furnace.

Budget

Aware of congressional insistence upon tighter military spending, the Army Chief of Staff announced his priorities for the FY 88 budget. The Army must maintain essential force readiness and give priority to forward-deployed and quickly deploying units. It must protect essential sustainability by addressing the highest requirements of the warfighting CINCs. The Chief of Staff sought to minimize the impact of tight money upon force structure and to reduce spending by slowing the pace of modernization and eliminating marginal programs. The Army began FY 88 with about $76 billion rather than fine $79 billion it had requested and then encountered a series of additional money problems. The Army budget based the foreign currency exchange rate with West Germany at 2.06 Deutsche Marks, but the rate fell much lower and created a deficit in excess of $500 million. Congress authorized a pay raise for Army civilian employees but did not appropriate the $101 million necessary to cover it. Congress underfunded the Army's portion of the Civilian Health and Medical Program of the Uniformed Services by $169 million, while the Army faced unexpected increases in civilian health benefit payments by $45 million and GSA price increases of $40 million. Congress further restricted Army budget operations by prohibiting the transfer of monies in long-term procurement accounts to pay current year operations and maintenance expenses.

In May 1988 the Deputy Secretary of Defence issued a plan for reduced spending to all Defence Department offices. His initiatives included a restriction on routine maintenance, a freeze on civilian hiring, a halt to civilian overtime pay for hourly workers, and deferral of some supply and equipment purchases. Late in FY 88 Congress relented in its prohibition of transferring monies between accounts, which allowed the Army to sustain its operations and maintenance expenses. The Army's FY 89 budget request of $78 billion reflected a 1.3 percent reduction in FY 88 purchasing power. Nevertheless, the Army leadership expected to continue essential improvements in readiness and sustainability. Favourable aspects of the proposed FY 89 budget included adequate support for the most essential requirements of the warfighting CINCs; active component ground OPTEMPO of 850 miles and air OPTEMPO of 15.8 hours; continuance of the conversion of heavy forces to modern designs, the Forward Area Air Defence Program, the development of improved armor/antiarmor weapons, and most quality of life programs. Funding would remain inadequate, however, to maintain sufficient equipment modernization and war reserve stocks. It also would provide for only 50 percent of required depot maintenance for major end items and would allow the backlog of maintenance and repair of facilities and housing to worsen.

MILITARY MODERNIZATION

The military modernization begun in the late 1970s had three major focuses. First, under the political leadership of Deng Xiaoping, the military became disengaged from civilian politics and, for the most part, resumed the political quiescence that characterized its pre-Cultural Revolution role. Deng reestablished civilian control over the military by appointing his supporters to key military leadership positions, by reducing the scope of the PLA's domestic nonmilitary role, and by revitalizing the party political structure and ideological control system within the PLA.

Second, modernization required the reform of military organization, doctrine, education and training, and personnel policies to improve combat effectiveness in combined-arms warfare. Among the organizational reforms that were undertaken were the creation of the state Central Military Commission, the streamlining and reduction of superfluous PLA forces, civilianization of many PLA units, reorganization of military regions, formation of group armies, and enactment of the new Military Service Law in 1984. Doctrine, strategy, and tactics were revised under the rubric of "people's war under modern conditions," which envisaged a forward defence at selected locations near China's borders, to prevent attack on Chinese cities and industrial sites, and emphasized operations using combined-arms tactics. Reforms in education and training emphasized improving the military skills and raising the education levels of officers and troops and conducting combinedarms operations. New personnel policies required upgrading the quality of PLA recruits and officer candidates, improving conditions of service, changing promotion practices to stress professional competence, and providing new uniforms and insignia.

The third focus of military modernization was the transformation of the defence establishment into a system capable of independently maintaining a modern military force. As military expenditures remained relatively constant, reforms concentrated on reorganizing the defence research-and-development and industrial base to integrate civilian and military science and industry more closely. Foreign technology was used selectively to upgrade weapons. Defence industry reforms also resulted in China's entry into the international arms market and the increased production of civilian goods by defence industries. The scope of PLA economic activities was reduced, but the military continued to participate in infrastructure development projects and initiated a program to provide demobilized soldiers with skills useful in the civilian economy.

Civil-Military Relations

Lines between civilian and military leadership and institutions in China are indistinct. All high-ranking military leaders have high-level party positions, and many high-ranking party officials have some military experience. When military leaders participate in national policy making, therefore, it is not clear whether their positions reflect PLA corporate interests or the interests of groups that cut across institutional lines. In general, in times where there was national leadership consensus on national policy, such as in the 1950s, the PLA was politically quiescent. Once the PLA was drawn into civilian politics during the Cultural Revolution, the military became divided along the lines of civilian factions. As long as the national leadership remained divided on a number of policy issues, the PLA, fearing factional struggles and political instability, was reluctant to leave the political scene. When Deng Xiaoping was rehabilitated in 1977, however, the stage was set for the withdrawal of the military from politics and a partial return to the PLA's previous political passivity.

Political Role of the People's Liberation Army

Deng Xiaoping's efforts in the 1980s to reduce the political role of the military stemmed from his desire to reassert civilian control over the military and to promote military modernization. To accomplish his objectives, Deng revitalized the civilian party apparatus and leadership and built a consensus on the direction of national policy. He also established personal control over the military through personnel changes, and he reduced the scope of the PLA's domestic political, economic, and social roles. Finally, he strengthened party control over the military through institutional reforms and political and ideological education. The revitalization of the party and the establishment of a consensus on national policy assured top military leaders of political stability and a vigorous party capable of handling national and regional affairs without extensive military participation.

Deng's personal political control was established over the military through his assumption of the position of chairman of the party Central Military Commission in June 1981 and through his appointment of his supporters to key positions in the party Central Military Commission, Ministry of National Defence, and the PLA's General Staff Department, General Political Department, and General Logistics Department. Occasional replacement of military region and military district commanders also strengthened Deng's hand. Military leaders who objected to Deng's policies were replaced with more amenable personnel.

The creation of the state Central Military Commission in 1982 aimed to further strengthen civilian control over the military by stressing the PLA's role as defender of the state and by establishing another layer of supervision parallel to party supervision. The civilianization of several PLA corps and internal security units reduced the size of the PLA and the scope of its involvement in civilian affairs. The placement of defence industries under civilian control and the transfer or opening up of military facilities, such as airports and ports, to civilian authorities also limited the PLA's influence in economic and political matters. Propaganda using the PLA as a model for society also diminished, and emphasis was placed on the PLA's military rather than political role.

Party Control

In addition to making personnel changes, Deng revitalized party control over the PLA and diffused the military's political power by designating provincial-level, municipal, district, and county party committee secretaries to serve concurrently as the first political commissars of their equivalent-level units in the regional PLA. The percentage of PLA personnel permitted to join the party was limited by restricting party membership to military academy graduates. Political and ideological training stressed the military rather than the social, ideological, or economic role of the PLA. Special effort was made to discredit the PLA's role in the Cultural Revolution; the PLA's support for the left was described as incorrect because it caused factionalism within the military. While emphasizing the necessity and appropriateness of reforms to modernize the military, political education also sought to guarantee military support for Deng's reform agenda. Beginning in 1983 a rectification campaign (part of the party-wide rectification campaign aimed primarily at leftists) reinforced this kind of political and ideological training.

Beginning in the late 1970s, Deng Xiaoping succeeded in decreasing military participation in national-level political bodies. Military representation on the Political Bureau fell from 52 percent in 1978 to 30 percent in 1982, and military membership in the party Central Committee declined from 30 percent in 1978 to 22 percent in 1982. Most professional military officers shared common views with the Deng leadership over military modernization and the fundamental direction of national policy, and they willingly limited their concerns to military matters. Nonetheless, some elements in the PLA continued to voice their opinions on nondefense matters and criticized the Deng reform program. Dissent centered on prestigious military leaders, notably Ye Jianying, who feared that ideological de-Modification, cultural liberalization, and certain agricultural and industrial reforms deviated from Marxist values and ideals. The Deng leadership contained these criticisms with the help of the personnel changes, political education, and the rectification campaign just mentioned. In this way it was able to keep military dissent within bounds that did not adversely affect civil-military relations.

Popular Attitudes Toward the People's Liberation Army

Starting in the late 1970s, popular attitudes toward the PLA also underwent considerable changes. In the 1950s and 1960s, the military's prestige was very high because of its wartime exploits, because it was held up as a role model for society, and because of its participation in civilian construction projects. But the power gained by the PLA during the Cultural Revolution reawakened civilian resentment of military privileges and abuses of power. By the early 1980s, with the circumscription of the PLA's domestic role and the implementation of agricultural reforms offering greater opportunities for rural youth, the PLA's reputation as a prestigious, elite, Marxist-model organization and a promising channel for social mobility was severely tarnished. Society's perception of the military appeared to be returning to the traditional viewpoint that "one doesn't make nails out of good iron; one doesn't make soldiers out of good men." To restore this damaged image in the late 1980s, the media extolled the PLA's martial virtues and the great strides made in military modernization in recent years.

ORGANIZATION, MANAGEMENT AND BUDGET

The Army Long-Range Planning System is supplanting the Army Staff Long-Range Planning System. It allows the warfighting CINCs through the Army component commands, the major Army commands, and the major subordinate commands to participate in the Army Staff's long-range planning process. Spokesmen for the nine Army Staff functional areas (manning, sustaining, equipping, managing information, facilities, structuring, training, mobilizing/deploying, and managing), planners in the three Army Staff special interest areas (space, intelligence, and health services), the Army component commands, the major Army commands, and the major subordinate commands now will develop their individual long-range plans that will combine to create the next biennial iteration of the Army Long-Range Planning Guidance. A draft AR 11-32 on the new Army Long-Range Planning System circulated among the participants during FY 88 with publication expected in early 1989.

Organization

The 1986 Defence Department Reorganization Act imposed reductions in Army headquarters personnel. Title V prescribed a maximum combined strength of military and civilian personnel permanently assigned to Headquarters, Department of the Army, during peacetime at 3,105, or a 15 percent cut that also applied to general officers, effective 1 October 1988. Title VI called for other personnel strength changes. Section 601 (a) levied a 10 percent cut by 1 October 1988 on the Army's permanent military and civilian employees who performed management headquarters and management headquarters support duties, and also those assigned to combatant commands, based on their September 1986 strength. Section 601 (a) excluded the Secretariat, Army Staff, and the immediate headquarters staff of combatant commands. Section 601 (b) specified a 15 percent cut by 1 October 1989 for Army personnel of the same description as 601 (a) and 10 percent for those in nonmanagement headquarters who worked for Defence Department agencies and field activities. The law prohibited compliance with these headquarters personnel strength limits by redefining duties, functions, or agency organization. Congress expected the Army to relocate functions and jobs from headquarters to field activities rather than abolish them. Army compliance with these required changes proceeded on schedule during FY 88.

The TAPA became a reality as a provisional organization on 1 October 1987. The leadership of the Army's personnel systems had studied the need for TAPA for several years prior to passage of the 1986 Defence Department Reorganization Act. The Secretary of the Army and the Chief of Staff authorized creation of TAPA as a part of the Army's implementation of that legislation. Intended by its creators to integrate the execution of personnel management policy for military and civilian personnel from enlistment through separation, TAPA failed to attain fully centralized personnel management operations. The Army leadership decided that the Recruiting Command, the Community and Family Support Center, and the Safety Center, which some personnel managers hoped to integrate within TAPA, would remain separate entities. TAPA acquired five directorates-enlisted, officer, civilian, personnel service support, and mobilization and contingency operations-and four field operating agencies-Military Police Operations Agency, Military Academy Prep School, Physical Disability Agency, and the Drug and Alcohol Operations Agency. Commanded by a major general, TAPA maintains advisory relationships with the Army Reserve and National Guard personnel centers.

The Army redesignated the Army Space Agency as the Army Space Command on 7 April 1988. Located in Colorado Springs, Colorado, the Army Space Command has attained equal status with the Air Force and Navy Space Commands as components of the Space Command. The U.S. Space Command has three missions-space operations, surveillance and warning, and ballistic missile defence planning. The Army Space Command, with about 100 people including those previously assigned to the Army Space Agency and the Defence Satellite Communications System Ground Mobile Force managers from the Army Information Systems Command, remains a field operating agency of ODCSOPS. Activation of the Army Space Command marks the first step of a plan to consolidate all Defence Satellite Communications System command and control ground functions under the Army during the next several years. The Army Space Command also has responsibility for oversight of deep space surveillance conducted at Kwajalein Atoll in support of the Space Command's worldwide space surveillance net and a detachment at Johnson Space Center.

ODCSOPS made organizational and functional changes during FY 88. In June 1984 the Chiefs of Staff of the Army and the Air Force established joint Assessment and Initiatives Offices (JAIO) to facilitate the joint Force Development Process. It increased the number of joint warfighting initiatives from 31 to 38, resolved 44 candidate initiatives, and prompted 21 interservice agreements. In September 1988 the Army disbanded its JAIO as a functioning element within the Office of the Assistant Deputy Chief of Staff for Operations and Plans for Joint Affairs. In another area, the Strategy, Plans, and Policy Directorate created a new division, the Conventional Arms Negotiations Division. Effective 1 July 1988, it became the Army action office for all conventional arms control matters. These include acting as the Army Staff point of contact for all conventional arms control negotiations such as Mutual and Balanced Force Reductions, Conventional Stability Talks, the Conference on Security and Cooperation in Europe, and the Conference on Disarmament in Europe.

The number of federal and state environmental laws has increased dramatically in recent years. As a consequence, the Army has witnessed increased environmental violations, litigation, and curtailment of missions because of environmental considerations. The Army received 129 Notices of Violation during FY 88 from regulatory agencies. Actually, this number represented a significant reduction from FY 87, but wastewater and drinking water violations increased. The Army's installation restoration program grew significantly as seventy-three additional installations entered the program. The Army completed a fivefold increase in preliminary assessments/site investigations, which brought the total to 3,054 sites. It also completed 55 remedial investigations/feasibility studies, which brought this total to 300, along with

99 remedial design/remedial actions. Notable among these cleanups were Cornhusker Army Ammunition Plant (incineration of explosive contaminated soil), Alabama Army Ammunition Plant (Area A Cleanup), West Virginia Ordnance Works (remediation of explosives contamination), Twin Cities Army Ammunition Plant (installation of a ground water recovery system), and Rocky Mountain Arsenal (Basin F cleanup).

In order to streamline Army environmental management, effective 1 October 1988, the Army Environmental Office became a Headquarters, Department of the Army, staff support agency under the Assistant Chief of Engineers who serves as the Army's Program Manager for the Environment. The U.S. Army Toxic and Hazardous Materials Agency (USATHAMA), located at Aberdeen Proving Ground, Maryland, transferred from the Army Materiel Command to the Corps of Engineers as a field operating agency that also reports to the Assistant Chief of Engineers. USATHAMA has performed hazardous waste cleanup on Army properties since the mid-1970s. Its primary responsibilities have included the Installation Restoration Program, the Army equivalent to the Superfund program, and development of new technologies to abate or permanently treat hazardous waste. With its transfer to the Corps of Engineers USATHAMA assumed two new duties-providing oversight on environmental compliance at Army installations, ultimately the responsibility of installation commanders, and developing and implementing an environmental training program for the entire Army:

The issue of closing or realigning military installations received considerable attention within and without the Defence Department during FY 88. A matter of ongoing concern to the Army, it received recent investigation by the Army Long-Range Stationing Study (LRSS) established by the Chief of Staff in November 1986. He tasked the LRSS group to examine the Army's long-range stationing needs through the year 2020. It has produced a computer model for making stationing decisions and will develop a plan to transfer the model to Army Staff operational proponency. In May 1988 the Secretary of Defence chartered the Commission on Base Realignment and Closure to investigate workable methods for the Defence Department to eliminate installations and property excess to American defence needs. Composed of twelve persons-former members of Congress, retired Pentagon officials, and military and environmental specialists-commission members deliberated eight months.

Prompted by the deliberations of the Commission on Base Realignment and Closure, Congress passed PL 100-526, which President Ronald Reagan signed on 24 October 1988. The law endorsed the work of the commission and cited particulars to implement its findings. It required the Secretary of Defence to approve or disapprove the entire list of the commission for closing or realignment of American military installations. If he approved, he must forward it to Congress no later than 16 January 1989 or the action would automatically terminate. Congress could not modify the list and had forty-five working days, beginning 1 March 1989, to disapprove the complete list by a majority in both houses or the measure would become law. The commission released its findings on 29 December 1988 and recommended that the Pentagon close 86 bases (13 of them major ones), partially close 5 others, and realign another 54, which would result in either adding or losing personnel. Recommended action on Army installations included closing Fort Sheridan, Illinois, and the Presidio of San Francisco, realigning Fort Dix, New Jersey, to semiactive status, but significantly increasing personnel at Fort Belvoir, Virginia, and Fort Devens, Massachusetts. Public Law 100-526 stipulated that closings and realignments would begin 1 January 1990 and end by 30 September 1995.

2

Military Budgeting

A military budget (or military expenditure), also known as a defense budget, is the amount of financial resources dedicated by an entity (most often a nation or a state), to raising and maintaining an armed forces.

Military budgets often reflect how much an entity perceives the likelihood of threats against it, or the amount of aggression it wishes to employ. It also provides an idea of how much finances could be provided for the upcoming year. The size of a budget also reflects the entity's ability to fund military activities, with factors including the size of that entity's economy, other financial demands on that entity, and the willingness of that entity's government or people to fund such military activity. Generally excluded from military expenditures is spending oninternal law enforcement and disabled veteran rehabilitation.

According to the Stockholm International Peace Research Institute, in 2011, world military expenditure for the world amounted to 1.735 trillion US$.

SIPRI Yearbook 2012-World's top 15 military spenders

Currently, the world's five largest military spenders (the United States, China, Russia, the United Kingdom and France) are recognized to be world powers with each being a veto-wielding permanent member of the United Nations Security Council. This was established after the end of WW2.

Historic expenditure

1897

In the *Saturday Review* magazine in February 1898, indicates that the percentage of tax revenue spent on military budgets as follows:

- United States: 17%
- Russian Empire: 21%
- France: 27%
- British Empire: 39% (40 million pounds or 2.5% of GNP)
- German Empire: 43%
- Empire of Japan: 55% (132 million yen).

2003

In 2004, the yearly report by the Stockholm International Peace Research Institute showed that the purchase of military products by NATO member nations during the year 2003 rose 11 percent relative to 2002 (6.5 percent in volume). In some countries, this budget had been increased to the level maintained during the Cold War. The military budget of the United States lead this increase; U.S. purchases accounted for 47% of world military expenditure in 2003. A total of about US$415 billion. Additional funding for the War in Iraq and the supplementary expense of US$83 billion accounted for much of the increase; other spending only accounted for 3.5 percent of the increase. The military budgets of the United Kingdom, France and Italy represented about 15% of world military spending. France and the United Kingdom increased their equipment expenses, so as not only to act in US military operations with the same technological level of their ally, but equally to be able to act independently in smaller military campaigns. (Such as was seen in the Libya). Among non-NATO nations, Japan spent US$46.9 billion in 2003, The People's Republic of China, US$32.8 billion, and Russia, US$13 billion. As a percentage share of world military spending this represented 5%, 4%, and 1%, respectively.

MILITARY BUDGETING AND FISCAL MANAGEMENT

Sound fiscal management of the entire security sector is essential if a country is to have effective, efficient and professional security forces that are capable of protecting the state and its population against internal and external threats. Highly autonomous security forces that are able to act with impunity in the economic and political spheres are invariably professionally weak and highly cost-*in*effective. Because the armed forces generally absorb the majority of resources allocated to the security sector and tend to have a high degree of political autonomy, this project focuses on the process by which military budgets are developed, implemented and monitored.

A central premise of this paper is that, from a public policy and process perspective, the military sector shares many of the characteristics of other sectors and that the citizens of any country will benefit from a military sector that is subject to the same broad set of rules and procedures of other sectors. As such, gives high priority to principles such as transparency, accountability to elected civil authorities, and comprehensiveness of budget coverage. The differences between the need for confidentiality in the defense sector, on the one hand, and a lack of public scrutiny of the military sector, on the other hand. The relevance of good practice. The process of integrating the military sector into the planning, policy-making, and budgeting systems and procedures of a country in a manner consistent with democratic, civil control of the defense forces.

FINANCIAL MANAGEMENT PROCEDURES

Failure to follow sound financial management procedures in the military sector is often justified by the need for secrecy to protect national security. It is clear that some degree of confidentiality is necessary in the area of national security. However, there appears to be a tendency to conflate the concepts of "sensitivity" and "confidentiality" and to use the need for confidentiality in some areas of the military sector to reduce opportunities for scrutiny by appropriate management and oversight bodies in government and by civil society. Military-related issues – in particular, those relating to military intelligence-are sensitive in all societies. Even long-established democracies retain varying degrees of confidentiality in the realm of national security. It is important to be clear, however, about the distinction between confidentiality and the lack of public scrutiny. It is possible to retain a high degree of confidentiality in highly sensitive areas without compromising the principle of public accountability. It is also important to be clear about what is being held in confidence and why it is considered sensitive. War plans should be held in confidence. That the armed forces are regularly exceeding their budget allocations, are purchasing expensive military equipment with scant attention to need or ability to maintain this equipment, or are engaged in illegal, off-budget activities are clearly sensitive matters, but should not be held in confidence.

A highly non-transparent military sector provides the perfect cover for off-budget transactions. [It also provides the perfect cover for the diversion of resources into private hands (or pockets).] The issue of off-budget military spending is addressed in more detail in a companion article ("Off-Budget Military Expenditure and Revenue"). The point to be made here is that when a significant portion of a country's military expenditure occurs off-budget and is fed by off-budget revenues, not only are core principals of fiscal responsibility in the public sector violated. It is also highly likely that the operational capacity of the armed forces will suffer and that the military will not receive value for money. Therefore, an important component of the Sipri/ASDR project on military budgeting will be to determine the extent and nature of off-budget financing and expenditure.

FOCUS ON RELEVANCE OF GOOD PRACTICE

This paper focuses on good practice and identifies key principles of democratic governance in the security sector and of sound budgeting and financial management. One might well question the relevance of dwelling on good practice when dealing with an issue like military spending where actual practice diverges significantly from good practice.

Governance in the military sector (indeed any portion of the security sector) should be approached as a three-level process. The first level consists of relevant international law, norms and principles. The second level consists of national legislation and policies. It is desirable for these to reflect international law, norms and principles to the greatest degree possible. In developing national laws and policies, however, it is important to recognize that there is a wide range of ways to structure national law and policies and that there is no one-size-fits-all approach.

The third level is that of national practice. National practice may or may not reflect the two preceding levels. Some of the deviations may constitute illegal practice but much will not. Every country develops methods of addressing issues that reflect the spirit of the laws and policies of that country but which may not follow exactly the procedures specified in those laws and policies. That is true for OECD countries as well as for non-OECD countries. This is what makes it challenging to decide exactly how to affect policy in a given area and why a contextual approach is so important.

The point about starting with good practice is that it provides a clear vision of the objectives of policy reform – in this case, a democratically governed military sector under civilian leadership. Without such a vision, it is impossible to develop either a strategy for reaching the ultimate objective or benchmarks to measure progress along the way. It is also impossible to determine where the problems lie with existing policy and practice. Accordingly describes an ideal-type process for managing and overseeing the military budgeting process by democratic, civilian governments in order to provide a point of reference against which actual practice can be measured.

MILITARY BUDGET

The Finance Division of the Ministry of Defence is headed by the Secretary (Defence Finance)/Financial Adviser (Defence

Services). The SDF/FADS is tasked with the exercising of financial control over the proposals involving expenditure from the Defence Budget and the Ministry of Defence (Civil) estimates, and with the responsibility for internal audit and accounting of the Defense Expenditure and expenditure from the Civil Estimates. In the task of internal audit and accounting, the Controller General of Defence Accounts (CGDA) assists the SDF/FADS.

Defense planners face the task of reviewing programmes in the light of changes, which have taken place at the global level, as well as in the context of specific threats in the region. The endeavour of the defence planners is to balance the minimum requirements of Defence Forces and the need to modernize them, without unduly straining the national economy. The rules provide that no expenditure which has not been provided for in the Budget or which having been provided, has not been sanctioned shall be authorized without the concurrence of the Finance Division. The strict observance of this rule is automatically ensured as the Controllers of Defence Accounts will not make any disbursement in respect of charges not covered by regulations or Government orders.

Until 1962 defense spending was deliberately limited. In the wake of the war with China, defense spending rose from 2.1 percent of the gross national product in fiscal year 1962 to 4.5 percent in FY 1964. In FY 1994, defense spending was slightly less than 5 percent of gross domestic product. In terms of dollars, FY 1994 total defense services expenditures were projected at US$7.2 billion (but are likely to have been close to US$7.8 billion). Proportionately, based on figures provided by the government, 48.4 percent of expenditures were for the army, 15.7 percent for the air force, 5.9 percent for the navy, and 30 percent for capital outlays for defense services and defense ordnance factories. The latter provide matériel to the armed forces through some thirty-nine ordnance factories and eight public-sector enterprises that build ships, aircraft, and major defense items. The defense budget for FY 1994 was 6.5 percent higher than the revised estimate for FY 1993. The allocation increased to 14.9 percent of the total central government budget, up from 13 percent in the previous two fiscal years. Nuclear energy and space research are not fully accounted for in the defense budget, but most paramilitary forces fall within the purview of the Ministry of Defence.

After the Kargil war in 1999, the defence forces were spending less than the allocation. During 1999-2000, the defence forces spent Rs 48,504 crore-nearly Rs 3,000 crore more than the allotted sum of Rs 45, 694 crore. In 2000-01, they spent Rs 54,461 crore as against the allocation of Rs 58,587 crore – less than Rs 4,000 crore. In 2001-02, the defence forces are estimated to have spent Rs 57, 000 crore as against the revised allocation of Rs 65, 000 crore – a big gap of Rs 8,000 crore.

The increase in defence allocation for 2002-03 over 2001-02 was modest. The Finance Minister, Mr Yashwant Sinha, proposed a defence budget of Rs 65,000 crore against Rs 62, 000 crore allocated in the fiscal which is coming to an end. A significant development in the current fiscal is that the Defence Ministry will be spending only Rs 57,000 crore out of the allotted Rs 62,000 crore, leaving a shortfall of Rs 5000 crore. Thus, compared with the actual expenditure during the current fiscal, the budget proposes an increase of Rs 8,000 crore. The allocation for the Army has been fixed at Rs 35,368.72 crore, marking an increase of 6.69 per cent. It, in fact, gets reduced to 2.59 per cent while making allowance for inflation. The increase covers a number of sectors ranging from other equipment like tanks, artillery and electronic hardware such as weapon-locating radars, welfare and housing and stores (upgradation of existing assets). The increase on account of other equipment is a huge Rs 1,400 crore, revealing the government's plan to provide the Army with the modern tools of war. The Air Force gets Rs 15, 589 crore, an increase of 30 per cent over the revised estimates. The allocation is expected to take care of the upgrading of the fighter aircraft (MiG-21 BiS), licence payment for manufacturing of SU-30 fighter aircraft and purchase of Jaguars from Hindustan Aeronautics Limited.

In July 2004, in order to catch up with the backlog of expenditure that had not been provided for, the Government increased the allocation for Defence to Rs.77,000 crore. After a gap, defence expenditure in 2004-05 has matched the Budget Estimates. It was proposed to increase the allocation for Defence in 2005-06 to Rs.83,000 crore, which included an allocation of Rs.34,375 crore for capital expenditure.

The Defence and Defence related Expenditure is about Rs.95,922 crores (2004-05), including the Civil Estimates of around Rs.16,000 crores comprising about Rs.11,000 crores towards Defense Pensions. The outlay for defence services in the Budget 2004-05 is Rs 77000 Cr. This consists of Rs 43,517.15 Cr for revenue expenditure and Rs 33.482.85 Cr for capital expenditure. The allocation is 17.92 per cent more compared to 2003-04 Budget. The increased outlay, particularly for capital expenditure, is a reflection of the Government's keenness to ensure speedy modernisation of the Armed Forces.

The budget estimates 2004-05 cater to increased allocation for each of the services and research and development activities. An attempt is made to provide funds to meet the Service commitments both for meeting their maintenance requirements and modernisation. In addition to the above, one new feature in this year's Budget is exempting from income tax the family pension received by widows, children and nominated heirs of members of the Armed Forces and the para military forces killed in the course of operational duties.

The Union Budget for 2005-06 was presented to the parliament by the Finance Minister, Mr. P. Chidambaram on the 28th of February, 2005. In this, the allocation for Defence has been increased by about eight per cent over that of the last year from Rs.77,000 crore to Rs. 83,000 crore, or about $18.5 billion at current exchange rates. Purchasing Power Parity [PPP] is an indicator of the real conversion factor that should be used when comparing dollar and rupee costs. Prior to the the switchover to a flexible exchange rate arrangement in India in 1993, by one estimate the PPP ratio was about three. In the period after the float, by this analysis the market rate was close to the PPP value. [SOURCE] Another observer suggested that by 2003 the PPP was around six, that is, a salary of Rs 6 lakh in India is equivalent to a salary of one lakh dollars in the US. By 2004 the PPP was estimated at about five, or perhaps somewhere between six and eight. The precise PPP would depend on the basket of good — that is, in principle there is a PPP that is specific to military spending, which would be different from that for the economy in general. Factoring in PPP, India's military budget might thus be estimated as the equivalent of about $100 billion.

The allocation for defence for the year 2005-06 is well in tune with the policy of the government to give this core sector its due. The defence expenditure pegged at Rs 83,000 crore for the year amounts to an increase of Rs 6,000 crore or 7.79 per cent over the current year (2004-05). The revised estimate for the new fiscal has been kept at the level of Rs 77,000 crore, the same as in the budgetary estimate (BE) of the current one. The provision for revenue expenditure in the forthcoming fiscal is Rs 48,624.86 crore. The allocation for capital is Rs 34,375.14 crore which includes Rs 2,541.86 crore for research and development and Rs 1,364 crore for married accommodation project.

The proposed increase in defence expenditure should take care of the normal growth in pay and allowances, inflation and other specific requirements. The bulk of the capital outlay goes to meet the requirements for the ongoing acquisition projects. The allocation for capital will be providing over Rs 7,000 crore for new projects for modernisation of the forces.

India has to make up for what has been known as the lost decade of defence modernisation. In 2002-03 alone, it surrendered Rs 9,000 crore (Rs 90 billion). In view of this, last year the Budget had Rs 33,483 crore earmarked for capital purchases. But that was hardly sufficient for the whole purpose. The government decided to buy Mirage jets as well as Hawk trainer fighters. For the Navy, India had decided to go in for the aircraft carrier Admiral Gorshkov along with its MiG-29 fighters. Payments had to be made to honour contracts for airborne warning and control system (AWACS). The previous Government had signed these contracts but made no allocation for the same. Besides, New Delhi has had plans to purchase submarines, more multi-role fighter aircraft, multiple-rocket launchers, plane-based radar systems, light helicopters and artillery guns and many other sophisticated equipment for the three Services. The multi-role fighters and submarines alone are estimated to cost over Rs 20,000 crore. In other words, the last year's capital outlay left little for any fresh defence acquisition. No wonder, immediately after the Budget was presented last year, Defence Minister indicated that the amount earmarked for capital purchases might not be enough for other necessary fresh contracts and he might have to seek additional funds from the Union Finance Ministry. The proposed capital expenditure has to be assessed in this context.

It is, however, expected that the new allocation would enable the Services to move forward in the direction of their fresh acquisitions. Pertinently, in the new budget the revised estimate (RE) of the defence expenditure (DE) is the same as the budgeted estimate (BE). It means that the amount allocated at the beginning of the current fiscal has been fully spent. One can hope the trend to use the capital outlay would continue. The capital outlay for research and development has been increased from Rs 1,657.78 crore in the current fiscal to Rs 2,541.86 crore in the new one. This should help the DRDO in giving a momentum to some of its ongoing programmes. India has already started deploying its short range 700 kms Agni-I and intermediate range 2,000 kms plus Agni II surface-to-surface missiles. The DRDO is all set to carry forward the process of missile research and development programme so crucial for the country's doctrine of 'credible nuclear deterrence' and triad. There has,of late, been an increasing interface between the designer engineers and user agencies so as to determine what exactly is needed by the Services.

The DRDO is developing a contemporary weapon locating radar for the Army. It is speeding up the manufacture of the main battle tank (MBT) Arjun to ensure its supply to the Army by due date. It has also been working on several naval projects. There are some analysts who argue that there is no fair increase in capital allocation this year. According to them, the provision for Defence Services Estimates in the Budget Estimates-2004-05 was Rs 77,000 crore. This had Rs 43,517.15 crore for Revenue Expenditure and Rs 33,482.85 crore for Capital Expenditure. The allocation of Rs 77,000 crore was an increase of 17.92 per cent over the provision of Rs 65,300 crore made in Budget Estimates of 2003-04. The capital outlay of the DE in 2004-05 increased by an almost 100 per cent from Rs 16,863 crore to Rs 33,483 crore. In contrast, in the fiscal year 2005-06, the capital outlay has increased marginally by 2.66 per cent from Rs 33,483 crore to Rs 34,375 crore.

In the Interim Budget 2009-10, the allocation for Defence was increased to Rs.1,41,703 crore (US $29 billion), about 35 percent increase in current prices from the previous year's revised estimates. The total revised expenditure for 2008-09 was Rs.1,14,600 crore. The Plan expenditure will be to the tune of Rs.86,879 crore against Rs.73,600 crore and will include Rs. 54,824 crore for capital expenditure as against Rs.41,000 crore in the RE for 2008-09. The raise has been made "to strengthen the security in view of the recent terror attacks." The Interim Budget 2009-2010 was presented to the Parliament on Feb 16, 2009 by Shri. Pranab Mukherjee, Hon. Min. of Finance and External Affairs, Govt. of India.

SYSTEM OF BUDGET THE TASK FORCE ON MANAGEMENT OF DEFENCE

To overcome some of the shortcomings in the system of budget the Task Force on Management of Defence recommended certain steps to improve matters. A Study Group on Budgetary Reforms (set up under the Task Force on Management of Defence) was constituted in August 2001, with the following terms of reference:

- To reveal the form and content of DSE;
- Examine the expansion of budgetary classification to promote programme-based budgeting;
- Reveal the classification of expenditure between revenue and capital in respect of defence services/ departments.

The Study Group on Budgetary Reforms, in its Report submitted in January 2002, suggested that the existing DSE may include additional inputs under certain heads of accounts in the various detailed demands for grants. The estimates for the defence research and development organisation were also segregated from the army and a separate major head opened. Thus the demands for grants were expanded from five to six. Based on the Study Group's recommendations, an additional volume, called DSE Volume II, has been introduced for better budget management. With the additional details provided, internal management control by the services/departments/ MoD/MoD (Finance) has improved. It is important that the existing scope and content of the budget documents are enhanced before taking up more complex tasks. The significance of opening budget centre heads and additional classification categories needs no emphasis. The Group, consisting of representatives of all the services and departments, recognised that the first step in implementation would be an evolution of a comprehensive financial information system in respect of all the three services and the departments and the real time availability of budget centre data pertaining to budgetary allocations, progress of expenditure and committed liabilities. Meanwhile, to make the existing classification between 'revenue' and 'capital' more meaningful, it was recommended that guidelines be drawn up for identifying items which are appropriately capital but are being placed under revenue. The Study Group also recommended the expansion of budgetary classification in the DSE to provide better budgetary control, which will facilitate the future formulation of a programme budget. For purposes of expenditure monitoring and feedback controls, the group also recommended a more detailed classification with a separate volume covering all categories of expenditure, right down to the services and departments with budget centre-wise allocations. These are now available in Volume II of the DSE, which is an internal document. The gap in the existing document is sought to be bridged to some extent by the DSE Volume II.

The introduction of DSE Volume II has enabled the stakeholders to get a feedback on activities related to various budget centres. Put in simple language, this volume is a document that shows where the money is allocated, on what it is to be spent and by whom. This format is applicable to all the three services, ordnance factories, DRDO, etc., and has made monitoring, control and evaluation of the results of budgetary allocations more meaningful. This is an important step towards better management. It would also be a step towards planned allocation down to the various cost centres, based on a plan of expenditure, linked to the performance of activities.

Deficiencies

The content of the existing budget still falls short of a document oriented towards outcome. The recent reforms, additions and modifications would, no doubt, help all those who are deeply involved in the Ministry of Defence and service headquarters in managing expenditure and evaluating the results of the existing budget, with the additional facility of detailed accounts, papers and supporting documents. But to the rest of those involved/interested in not so intense a manner, some gaps in understanding the intended results of the outlay, outputs and outcomes remain. So it would appear the system of budget calls for a change.

The question arises: for whom the budget is made? It is principally for the services/defence departments, MoD and all the players who receive allocation of funds as per objectives and norms that get translated into policy and allocations when the budget is prepared. It is also for all those who have a stake in knowing whether the value for money has been realised. However, the problem is that the feedback mechanism is inappropriate for fully meeting the need for information and even the reports of various parliamentary committees are received too late for incorporation in the Budget. Even though the appropriation accounts are available on time, the performance evaluation is confined to only two areas of activities: military engineering services and the military farms. The system does not provide for concurrent/annual review of all expenditure. So, the budget as a whole gets neglected in terms of evaluation of the outcome. This is the position, in respect to the budgeting system for the defence though certain improvements have been built into the system over time, these are not adequate for a full scale evaluation of a large part of the budget.

At this stage, it would be appropriate to comment on the meaning of the terms 'performance budget', 'programme budget' and 'outcome budget'. Performance budget primarily indicates the physical progress of various schemes and programmes in relation to budget estimates. This was introduced by the Government in a number of Ministries, especially those handling development programmes, based on the recommendations of the Administrative Reforms Commission in 1969. Programme budgeting was first introduced in the US Defence Department as a system contrary to conventional budgeting. It describes and gives details of costs of all activities or programmes in a budget. Objectives, outputs and expected results are described fully as are the necessary input costs, such as of raw materials, equipment and staff. The sum of all activities or programmes constitutes the programme budget. The major task is to consolidate all activities that could be classified as a programme mission, such as training, coastal defence, etc.

Programme based budgeting requires linkage between plan and programmes, and input and output. As A. K. Ghosh has stated in his book India's Defence Budget and Expenditure Management in a Wider Context, the terms "performance budgeting and programme budgeting has been used interchangeably as both concepts are based on functions and activities and the emphasis is on results." He further states,

"The time dimension is of immense importance for expenditure management in defence, which is emphasised by programme budgeting. Programmes are inherently forward-looking. Performance, on the other hand, is based on past activity and evaluation of the past performance becomes a focal point of attention."

However, as Ghosh himself states that confusion has somewhat been removed in the UN manual, which has viewed performance budget as an all inclusive concept, embodying programme formulation as well as measurement of the performance of work in accomplishing programme objectives. The outcome budget, as the Ministry of Finance in its memorandum dated 30th December 20053, stated, is a pre-expenditure instrument. It helps to realise the ministries' vision through clearly defined outcome/output as a supplement to the current system built around postexpenditure scrutiny. The need for this has been felt as there is a lack of clear cut one-to-one relationship between the final budget and the performance budget as it was evolved earlier and inadequate setting of physical targets for the ensuing year. Development of outcome budget is not as complex as of a programme budget and can be built around the existing systems with some modification and expansion.

Concept of Budget Centres

Alongside budgetary reforms, another committee was constituted to further expand the concept of accountability and responsibility, budget centres, and delegation of financial powers. The concept of budget centre allocation was recommended to be further expanded. This concept involves planning, programming, accounting, reporting and evaluation systems. The report of the Committee on Delegation of Financial Powers for the army, navy and air force emphasised that the following facts need to be taken into account:

- Responsibilities centre with clear objectives;
- Decentralised authority-cum-responsibility centres;
- Physical targets, linked to input and output in financial terms;

- Set of financially feasible and clearly defined objectives;
- A network of accounting and effective reporting systems.

The committee had the advantage of the framework already created by the first new management strategy concept was tried out in the naval dockyard, when B.V. Adavi was the Financial Adviser Defence Services (FADS). The concept of budget centres, along with integrated finance sector, was established in the services headquarters when A. K. Ghosh was the FADS. The budget centres, in concept and operation, facilitate generation of necessary inputs and outputs, which, in turn, enables evaluation of performance from field level and upwards. The measures implemented during the last decade and a half have gone a long way in enhancing the value of budget and supporting documents towards achieving better monitoring and control, and better insight of the results.

OUTCOME BUDGET

The Department of Expenditure, Ministry of Finance on 30th December 2005, has given guidelines for preparation of an outcome budget which was introduced by the finance minister in Para 100 of his budget speech (budget 2005-06). The need for an outcome budget has arisen owing to weaknesses that have crept into the performance budget, given the absence of a clear one-to-one relationship between the financial budget and the performance budget. Though the MOD and a few other ministries/departments have been exempted from the preparation of the outcome budget, they have been asked to carry out this exercise for internal reviews and to voluntarily decide to place it in the public domain, fully or partially. The memorandum called for a tabular format which could be visualized as "vertical compression and horizontal expansion" of the budget estimates (BE) as given in Volume II. The components in the format for the outcome budget comprise financial outlays, projected physical outlooks, and projected/budgeted outcomes (intermediate/partial and final). The system of budget, as evolved by the Ministry of Finance, thus includes the outcome budget for the ensuing year and performance budget for the previous financial year. It implies that the performance budget format now includes linkage with not only the financial budget but also the outcome budget. The implication for the Ministry of Defence is that an outcome budget can be evolved for the ensuing year even within the existing structure and format of the budget without waiting for the development of a programme budget in a number of areas of activities in defence.

The key terms 'outlays', 'outputs' and 'outcome' in the budget have been defined by the Ministry of Finance as follows:

Outlays imply total financial resources deployed for achieving certain outcomes. Outputs are a measure of a physical quantity of the goods or services produced under a scheme or a programme. They are usually an intermediate stage between outlays and outcomes. Outcomes are the end products/results of various initiatives and interventions, including those in partnership with public sector undertakings, autonomous bodies, etc. They involve much more than mere output since they cover the quality of the goods or services.

The Finance Minister in his foreword to the outcome budget document on 25 August 2005, aptly stated: "I must caution that outlays do not necessarily mean outcome. People of the country are concerned with the outcomes." The Ministry of Finance has recognised that, in respect of certain ministries, the conversion of outlays into outcomes is a complex process. The Ministry of Defence and certain other departments have been exempted from preparation of outcome budget. But it is evident that the principles enunciated in regard to the outcome budget in the civil ministries such as benchmarking standards/quality of outcome in services, standardising unit cost of delivery, capacity building for requisite efficiency at all levels in terms of equipment, technology, knowledge and skills, and to further ensure flow of appropriate funds at the right time to the right level, with neither delay nor "parking" of funds, effective monitoring, evaluation and feedback system are equally applicable to the defence setup. The introduction of outcome budget in defence will further enhance and ensure accountability at all levels. Outcome will be readily transparent to all those involved in the management of budget as well to the parliament and the tax payers.

The outcome budget, linked with performance budget, should not merely reflect results of a year but also indicate the progress in achieving certain long-term objectives, such as cumulative performance and final outcome. As an example, hypothetically if an outcome budget has been finalised reflecting the goal and vision of the self reliance plan, formulated in 1993, which aimed at 70 per cent self-reliance in certain areas of defence production over a 10-year period, it would have known by now what has been achieved and where the government has fallen short. This would have helped in taking corrective measures for the next decade to reduce imports and achieve greater self-reliance. The eleventh report on the demand for grants of the Standing Committee on Defence (April, 2006) has emphasised the need to enhance indigenisation and reduce imports. It is felt that the formulation of an outcome budget would help to monitor the results with respect to the plan. There are a number of areas in the defence sector which are amenable for introduction of outcome budget. Areas where these could be considered with definite yardsticks for measurement are:

- Maintenance and production workshops in the three services
- Ordnance factories
- Training
- Repairs and refit of certain ships under the navy
- Certain components of research and development establishments
- Capital works other than those connected with any weapon system.
- Ordnance depots (at least other than arms and ammunition), etc.
- Married accommodation project
- Ex-servicemen's health scheme.

There could also be a number of other items. A rough conservative estimate of those that are non-sensitive in nature, show that at least Rs. 15,000 crore of the defence budget could be brought under the outcome budget and placed in the public domain. This could form part I of Volume I of the outcome budget. In these areas, the public has as much right to information as in the civil sector. Many more categories, especially of equipment, can also be brought under outcome budget for purposes of internal controls. This second segment could be Volume II of the outcome budget and can be the internal document of the government, which has the right to keep information to itself in case it is of a sensitive nature. Preparation of an outcome budget would automatically imply preparation of performance budget vis-à-vis the outcomes planned. The formats of the documents are given in the Ministry of Finance office memorandum cited earlier.

Evaluation of performance indicators has a major role in providing credible information to decision-makers. Such an evaluation is not easy in intangible areas. Premchand in his book, Public Expenditure Management, 4 has identified this issue as follows: "Performance indicators should follow the objective set for the organisation. These objectives should be specific, disaggregated, and measurable in one form or the other. Indicators in such a context seek to serve as a bridge between the objectives, resources allocated and the organisation's outputs. They could indicate the following aspects:

- Throughput or volume;
- Productivity and cost; Time target;
- Demand for services;
- Availability of services; and
- Outcome".

Programme Budget

The development of programme budget is a complex task. As a first step, the Integrated Defence Staff needs to formulate elements of the programme budget after defining various programmes. Some steps have already been undertaken by them. A multi-disciplinary group, which will also comprise a cost committee, would need to complete this task.

There are several questions that could arise while considering the introduction of a programme budget. As per the knowledge and experience of the author, the issue has been under consideration at least for the past two decades. It is not clear whether all concerned in the defence set-up are keen about a programme budget. The question also arises whether the programme budget is feasible within the existing structures and systems. It is also common knowledge that in the last decade much more information was available in the media about defence matters than before. This has also motivated many defence departments to rush to the press for publicity about success of a mission, weapons system, etc. While this may be good from the point of view of morale of the citizens, quite a few achievements are being publicised though the projects may be far from achieving their ultimate outcome. Another complexity in evolving a programme budget arises when the definition of the programme cuts across the services. Even within a service, especially a large service like the Army, there could be complexities in reflecting the estimates and expenditure of different arms especially in a situation where not all transactions are cashbased and many are on the basis of documents. Jointness in the field among the three services, if achieved, could facilitate evolution of a programme budget. The IDS are in the process of experimenting and evolving some concepts in this regard. The identification of various programmes should be the starting point for spelling out the elements of a programme budget.

Development of a programme based budgeting would require a huge amount of cost accounting. Work needs to be done for each type of transaction in various units, formations, workshops, headquarters, etc., within a service and across the services. A highly automated system, with networking cutting across the boundaries of services and departments, would facilitate the task. The methodology and structure for programme based budgeting in a time-bound manner would require systematic planning and implementation in a phased manner.

In the interim, the best approach would be to enhance the financial information system and networking, and operate an outcome budget as spelt out in the preceding paragraphs, which will enable better-decision making. A danger is that even a system once created or established tends to get into disuse with poor maintenance. For instance, the initial enthusiasm for creation of websites in various institutions, especially in the government sector, was not sustained thereafter due to poor maintenance in terms of updated information. The financial system without regular and online update and with thousands of inputs coming from different units would make any budget and reporting systems incomplete and may even be misleading.

The defence budget is already of a very large magnitude. In a period of 15 years, it has grown five and a half times-from an outlay of Rs. 16,347 crore in 1991–1992 to Rs. 89,000 crore in 2006-2007. As a component of the central government budget, it continues to be the largest among all departments, some 15.78 per cent. It has very large components of expenditure that are totally non-sensitive in nature and on which information is available through various documents. But what is lacking is information on results of the large outlays and sometimes even the output. The defence budget has not had the benefit of having a performance budget component. Though the performance budget in many of the civil ministries does not always help in assessing the value of money realised out of the outlays, these aspects can be rectified through the outcome budget. Allocation of funds to the defence would soon touch Rs 1,00,000 crore and would continue to grow from year to year, especially in view of the huge costs involved in certain modern systems. Therefore, the financial information systems need to be improved and enhanced. The budget system should ensure transparency and accountability and responsibility at all levels and display that value for money has been realised. The information technology available today will facilitate tasks which were not possible earlier. A document such as an outcome budget will enable a single point reference for all concerned in place of a multiplicity of papers that need to be consulted. An outcome budget, along with a performance budget, would be a first step in this direction. These would be supplements to the existing volumes of DSE. There is also a need to make a beginning in preparing programme budget in select areas, given the manpower resources constraints and the gaps in total connectivity and network.

Financial Information System

A crucial aspect for achieving success in evolving any improved budgetary systems for evaluation of results in the defence set-up, would be the development of a total and comprehensive financial information system with a wide area network covering all the three services, the concerned defence department, the defence accounts department and the Ministry of Defence. A report in this regard was submitted in August 2002 to the Ministry of Defence by the author who after his retirement as Secretary Defence (Finance) in February 2002 had been appointed as Adviser to the Ministry of Defence. In the Report, a number of recommendations were made to improve the existing system and to make available more information to the MoD officials.

The need to build an information system on liabilities has been felt for more than a decade and half and some progress has been achieved, especially in regard to items under 'capital'. But building an institutionalized reporting system on commitments made in contracts, supply orders and liabilities incurred thereon is a necessary adjunct to any budgetary exercise. Once this reporting system is institutionalised and relevant information becomes part of supporting budget documents, the seriousness would be bestowed to the preparation of liabilities figuring in the report. The review of contracts, supply orders and updating of the figures would then become a continuing exercise from the point of view of ensuring outcomes as well as taking corrective action when required. There is also a need to have convergence between various services/departments on aspects like unit code and contract code to facilitate the creation of a better information system.

Uniformity in redesigned source documents needs to be enforced by the MoD in all services/departments. This has implications for the right kind of information-control the MoD would like to exercise. Network needs to be established between various services, departments, and especially between the CGDA and the Service Headquarters and other defence departments. Computerisation without a total communication network for exchange of data/information would produce less than optimum results. Adequate networking would facilitate better output in terms of content, details and availability of information on time. Quality of information would be crucial in any system and modern technology facilitates it. To evolve an improved budgetary control system, this would be a necessary prerequisite since, in the manually dominated or partially computerised system, and the manual process itself adds to the difficulties.

3

Indian Defence Budgeting

INDIA'S DEFENCE BUDGET 2012-13

The Union Budget 2012-13, presented to the Parliament on March 16, 2012 hiked the defence outlays to Rs. 1,93,407.29 crore (US$ 40.44 billion1). This represents a growth of 17.63 per cent over the previous year's outlays – one of the highest increases in recent years excluding that for 2009-10 when the budget was increased by over 34 per cent, mostly to accommodate the pay hikes caused by the implementation of the recommendations of the Sixth Central Pay Commission.

The increase in the latest defence budget was made possible by the expansionary fiscal policy adopted by the government in general. Further, although the increase looks impressive at first glance, it is not however driven by the modernisation needs as much as by manpower needs.

DEFENCE BUDGET ESCAPES ECONOMIC SLOWDOWN

The new defence budget comes at a time when the performance of the Indian economy is under stress and the prospect of recovery is tenuous. As the *Economic Survey 2011-12,*presented to the Parliament a day before the Union Budget, puts it, GDP growth is projected at 6.9 per cent in the present fiscal year and at 7.6 per cent in 2012-13. These growth rates, which are significantly lower especially in comparison to the nearly 10 per cent growth registered in

2006-07, has however not forced the government to tighten its purse. Instead, it has resorted to what can be termed as fiscal profligacy, by increasing the overall central government expenditure by a hefty 18.54 per cent, with little regard for the fiscal situation.

Consequently, the fiscal deficit, which the Finance Minister had promised in his previous budget speech to reduce to 4.1 per cent of GDP in 2012-13, is now projected to increase to 5.1 per cent. This expansionary fiscal policy has been the prime mover for the large increase in the budget of the defence ministry, which would otherwise have come under severe budgetary pressure if the Finance Minister had chosen a tight budget.

Key Aspects of the Defence Budget 2012-13

Although the latest defence budget has witnessed an increase of 18 per cent, the growth rate is only 13.15 per cent over the revised estimate of the now concluding fiscal year. In other words, the defence budget for 2011-12 has been revised upward by Rs 6,521.32 crore to Rs. 1,70,936.81 crore. However, unlike the revised estimate for 2010-11, in which both the Revenue Expenditure and Capital Expenditure were higher than their respective budget estimates, the revised estimate for 2011-12 shows an increase in Revenue Expenditure (by Rs. 9,576.32 or 10.06 per cent) and decline in Capital Expenditure by Rs. 3,055 (or 4.41 per cent).

The large increase in the defence budget notwithstanding, its impact on various components has been different. From the perspective of resource allocation, while the share of the defence budget in the GDP has marginally increased, its share in central government expenditure has fallen.

One noticeable aspect of the new budget is that in comparison to Capital Expenditure, the Revenue Expenditure has increased faster. This growth has however been driven primarily because of the increase in pay and allowance of the armed forces, which has increased by 27 per cent to Rs. 63,182.46 crore, accounting for around 46 per cent growth of the total defence budget.

Table: Comparative Statistics of Defence Budgets, 2011-12 & 2012-13

	2011-12	***2012-13***
Defence Budget (Rs. in Crore)	164415.49	193407.29
Growth of Defence Budget (%)	11.59	17.63
Revenue Expenditure (Rs. in Crore)	95216.68	113828.66
Growth of Revenue Expenditure (%)	9.01	19.55
Share of Revenue Expenditure in Defence Budget (%)	57.91	58.85
Capital Expenditure (Rs. in Crore)	69198.81	79578.63
Growth of Capital Expenditure (%)	15.33	15.00
Share of Capital Expenditure in Defence Budget (%)	42.09	41.15
Share of Defence Budget in GDP (%)	1.83	1.90
Share of Defence Budget in Central Government Expenditure (%)	13.07	12.97

Note: Rs. 1.0 crore = Rs. 10 million = US$ 209,105.39

Shares in Defence Budget

The Army with an approximate budget of Rs. 97,302.54 accounts for 50 per cent of the latest defence budget, followed by the Air Force (Rs. 48,191.16; 25 per cent), Navy (Rs. 37,314.44; 19 per cent), Defence Research and Development Organisation (Rs. 10,635.56 crore; six per cent) and Ordnance Factories (Rs. 135.13 crore). It is noteworthy that compared to the previous year's budget, Navy is the only service which has increased its share in total defence allocation (from 15 to 19 per cent). The Air Force's share has decreased the most (by four percentage points), whereas the Army's share has declined by one percentage point.

The 15 per cent increase in the Capital Expenditure has resulted in an additional amount of Rs. 10,379.82 crore. Given that most of the Capital Expenditure is incurred on modernisation of the armed forces, it is vital to see how the increase would affect each of the services. It is however to be noted that the three services (Army, Navy and Air Force) account for 94 per cent (Rs. 74,439.95 crore) of total Capital

Expenditure in 2012-13, with the Air Force at the top with a share of 38 per cent (Rs. 30,485.35 crore), followed by the Navy (31 per cent or Rs. 24,766.42 crore) and the Army (24 per cent or Rs. 19,188.18 crore). Of the total Capital Expenditure of the three services, around 89 per cent (Rs 66,459.43 crore) is earmarked for capital acquisition or modernisation.2 These impressive figures do not however reveal the complete story. A closer look at the growth of the modernisation budget of 2012-13 would reveal that the focus is entirely driven by the Navy, which has got a 72 per cent hike (to Rs. 24,151.51 crore) in its modernisation budget. The Air Force's modernisation budget has increased marginally (by 0.5 per cent) to Rs. 28,503.9 crore, while the Army's has declined by three per cent to Rs. 13,804.02 crore.

The marginal increase in the Air Force's modernisation budget and the decrease in the Army's do not seem to be in sync with their modernisation requirements. This is more so given the pending signing of some of the big-ticket contracts (including the multi-billion dollar Rafael), and the sharp devaluation of the Indian rupee against the US dollar. As regards the latter, although the rupee has appreciated from its lowest point in mid-December 2011, the present exchange rate, which is around fifty rupees to a dollar, is still high and, if it remains at the same level could further erode the import capacity of the acquisition budget.

Return to Under-spending

When the defence budget 2011-12 was presented in February 2011, it gave an impression that the years of effort put in by the defence ministry to fine-tune its procurement process has finally yielded dividend. This impression now seems to be premature, as the defence ministry has once again come back to under-spending its capital budget. As the new budget reveals, of the total Capital Expenditure earmarked for 2011-12, Rs. 3,055 crore (4.41 per cent) has been surrendered at the time of revised estimate. The unspent amount could have been much higher if the Navy had not been allowed to overspend its allotted capital budget by Rs.

2801.25 crore (the Air Force and the Army together have surrendered Rs. 5,727.15 crore).

While the surrender in the Air Force's modernisation budget is mostly from the head of 'aircraft and aero-engine', in the case of the Army the surrender is from a number of heads, including 'aircraft & aero-engine', and 'other equipments'. The surrender of funds under such critical heads and of such magnitude not only reflects poorly upon budgetary management and the procurement system, but is also a cause of concern given the huge gap in national military capability and the rapid modernisation in neighbouring countries, particularly China which is pursuing an unprecedented level of military modernisation with a double-digit annual increase in defence expenditure for two decades. Given this scenario, the least that needs to be avoided by the services is the surrender of allotted funds. The defence establishment including the service headquarters therefore need to introspect and arrive at solutions that expedite procurement in a time-bound manner.

DEFENCE BUDGETING OF INDIA

The Union Budget 2010-11 has raised the defence outlays to Rs. 1,47,344 crore (US $31.9 billion). This represents a growth rate of a mere 3.98 per cent, in nominal terms (or 0.3 per cent in real terms) over the previous years' allocation of Rs. 1,41,703 crore, and far below the 34 per cent nominal increase witnessed in the budget for 2009-10. The sudden dip in the defence budget's growth rate follows two related steps taken by the government. While the first one is related to the government's resolve about fiscal consolidation, the second is on account of the acceptance by the government of the recommendation of the Thirteenth Finance Commission (TFC). This commentary analyses the latest defence budget as well as the likely impact of TFC's recommendation on India's future defence spending.

DEFENCE BUDGET 2010-11

Although the defence budget for 2010-11 has been

increased by less than four per cent over the previous year's allocation, it has nonetheless been increased by a modest 8.13 per cent over the revised estimate for 2009-10. In other words, the Ministry of Defence (MoD) has surrendered (at the time of revised estimate) Rs. 5,439 crore from the original allocations made in 2009-10. The surrendered amount could have been more if the Revenue Expenditure-which accounts for running expenses of the defence services-had not been revised upwards by Rs 1,561 crore over the original estimates. On the other hand, the Capital Expenditure-most of which is accounted for acquisition of defence hardware-has been revised downward by Rs. 7,000 crore.

The marginal increase in the defence budget has a negative impact on almost all key components. On the positive side, however, the ratio between Revenue Expenditure and Capital Expenditure has been improved towards the latter. The improvement is largely due to the marginal increase in Revenue Expenditure, which itself was inflated in last year's budget by salary increases and one-time arrears due to implementation of Sixth Central Pay Commission recommendations. Among the defence services, the Army with a budget of approximately Rs. 74,582 crore in 2010-11 has the largest share, distantly followed by the Air Force (Rs. 40,462 crore), Navy (Rs. 21,467 crore), DRDO (Rs. 9,809 crore), and Ordnance Factories (Rs. 1,015 crore). However, in terms of Capital Expenditure, the Air Force with a budget of Rs. 25,251 crore holds the largest share (42 per cent) among the three services, followed by the Army (Rs. 17,255 crore; 29 per cent) and the Navy (Rs. 12,138; 20 per cent).

From the modernization point of view, out of Rs. 60,000 crore, nearly 78 per cent (Rs. 46,521) crore will be available to the three services for procurement of Aircraft and Aero-Engine, Heavy and Medium Vehicles, Naval Ships, and Other Equipments (Armaments, Electronics, Ammunition, Missiles, etc.) among others. Within each service's acquisition budget, the Air Force will have Rs. 15,206 crore for procurement of Air Craft and Aero-Engine; while Rs. 10,464 crore have been provisioned for procurement of Other Equipments for the

Army. The Navy will get Rs. 6,950 crore for procurement of Naval Fleet.

Why Meagre Growth in Defence Budget?

While presenting the Union Budget, the Finance Minister (FM) emphasised that "Secure border and security of life and prosperity fosters development." The 3.8 per cent increase in the defence budget (in comparison to the 8.6 per cent increase in total central government expenditure) does not however seem to be fully in sync with the above emphasis. This is more so when India's more troubling neighbours have increased their defence spending at a sharp pace. Of particular interest is China, whose double digit increase in defence spending over the past twenty years and resultant military modernisation in both qualitative and quantitative terms has been taken 'note' of by the Ministry of Defence. (China's 2009 official defence budget of $70.37 billion is 2.2 times that of India's 2010 budget.) However the above 'note' does not seem to be backed by adequate growth in India's defence budget. In fact, in the last 10 years, India's defence budget has grown by 10 per cent and more only in three years.

Notwithstanding the seemingly 'direction-less' growth in India's defence budget, the reasons for the small increase in the latest defence budget is not so difficult to fathom. There are in fact two clear reasons for it. The first is related to the government's resolve to "come back to the path of fiscal consolidation at the earliest." It is noteworthy that the central government had announced several stimulus packages to fight the economic crisis which was harsher in 2008-09. As a result the fiscal deficit had increased to an unsustainable level.

Now with the crisis less severe, the government has made an attempt to bring down the fiscal deficit for 2010-11 to 5.5 per cent of GDP, as against 6 per cent in 2008-09 and 6.7 per cent in 2009-10 (revised estimate). The fiscal tightening means limited the scope for accommodating more resource demands from the MoD which accounts for over 13 per cent of total central government expenditure. The scope has been further limited by the government's focus on 'inclusive growth', by way of increased agricultural, social and infrastructural spending. For instance, in the Union Budget, the Finance Minister has increased the Central Plan Outlay on Agriculture, Rural Development, Transport and Social Sector by 14 per cent to Rs. 2,97,065 crore.

If the imperatives of fiscal consolidation and 'inclusive growth' have limited government spending capacity, the MoD's inability to spend the resources allocated in the previous year's budget has also not helped its cause. As mentioned earlier, the MoD has so far surrendered. Rs. 5,439 crore from its 2009-10 budget. This inability to spend has no doubt strengthened the Finance Ministry's justification for a smaller increase with the customary promise that "any additional requirement for the security of the nation will be provided for." The Finance Ministry is fully aware that the MoD has difficulties in spending the allocated resources, especially the amount given in the capital account.

INDIA'S DEFENCE BUDGET 2010-11

As per the Budget Estimates (BE) proposed for the year 2010-11, the total expenditure of Central government will be Rs. 11,08,749 crore, which is an increase of 8.6 per cent over total expenditure in BE of 2009-10. The Plan and Non Plan expenditure in BE 2010-11 are estimated at Rs. 3,73,092 crore and Rs. 7, 35,651 crore, respectively. While there is a 15 per cent increase in Plan expenditure, the increase in Non Plan expenditure is only 6 per cent over BE of 2009-10. The fiscal deficit has been projected as 5.5 percent of GDP in 2010-11 against 6.9 per cent during the preceding year.

The fiscal year 2009-10 was a challenging year for the Indian economy. The significant deceleration in the second half of 2008-09 brought the real GDP growth down to 6.7 per cent, from an average of over 9 per cent in the preceding three years. However, due to implementation of broad based counter cyclic policy package, the negative fallout of the global slowdown has been arrested. Although due to fiscal expansion and liberal monetary policy, the Indian economy is showing some signs of stabilization, unless there is consolidation of gains achieved during the last fiscal year the economy may take longer to revert to the high GDP growth path.

The Thirteenth Finance Commission has recommended a calibrated exit strategy from the expansionary fiscal stance of the last two years. As a part of the fiscal consolidation process, the Finance Minister in his Budget speech on February 26, 2010 proposed to reduce the domestic public debt-GDP Ratio. In the Medium Term Fiscal Policy Statement, the Government has proposed a rolling target for fiscal deficit in the next two fiscal years. It is proposed to bring down the fiscal deficit from 5.5 per cent of GDP in 2010-11 to 4.8 per cent in 2011-12 and to 4.1 per cent in 2012-13.

The expenditure on Defence comes under Non Plan expenditure. As per the Budget Estimates for the year 2010-11, Defence has been allocated Rs. 1,47,344 crore, i.e. a marginal increase of 3.98 percent over the BE of 2009-10. The outlay for Defence comprises of Rs. 87,344 for Revenue expenditure and Rs. 60,000 crore for Capital expenditure. Keeping in view the requirement of Defence for modernization of forces, the Capital budget has been given an increase of 9.44 per cent over the BE of 2008-09. The revenue allocation has increased only by 0.5 percent. However, there is a net reduction in allocation of Rs. 1096 crore in Revenue budget in comparison to the Revised Estimates of 2009-10. Last year, the Revenue budget was increased by 50.85 per cent over the BE of 2008-09 due to implementation of the Sixth Pay Commission's recommendation. Since part of that was a one time expenditure, thus no additional funds were required under the Pay and Allowances head this year. However, considering the fact that a substantial part of Revenue expenditure is incurred on Stores & Equipment, Transportation, Revenue Works, Maintenance of Buildings, Installation, etc. and there is a danger of double digit inflation, thus the proposed allocation under these heads of expenditure will require extra effort on the part of defence functionaries to prioritise expenditure without compromising the operational readiness of the forces. Due to rising social and political tensions in different parts of the country, there is far greater need for inclusive growth. To achieve this goal the government has to allocate more resources for infrastructure development, health and education, etc. Thus Plan expenditure is bound to rise in the coming years and consequently the Government will have to take steps to reduce Non Plan expenditure to achieve reduction in the fiscal deficit. Considering the security environment in and around India, the government will have to provide more funds under the Capital budget required for modernization of forces. Thus, Defence authorities will have to work out how to function with a minimal increase in the Revenue budget. The Thirteenth Finance Commission has observed that there exists considerable scope to improve the quality and efficiency of defence expenditure through increased private sector engagement, import substitution and indigenization, improvements in procedures and practices and better project management, within the parameters of Government of India's policy. Efforts in this direction will further expand the fiscal space available for defence spending.

The Standing Committee on Defence in its report on Demand for Grants (2009-10), placed in the Lok Sabha on December 16, 2009, also recommended that there is an urgent need to curb wasteful expenditure. The Committee has consistently been raising this issue in its earlier reports as well. In pursuance thereof, the Ministry had constituted a Defence Expenditure Review Committee (DERC) to comprehensively review all aspects of defence expenditure. The committee has already submitted its report. However, the action taken report on DERC recommendations indicating the areas where expenditure can be curbed is awaited. Since tax payer's money is spent on such committees it is essential that the outcomes of their recommendations be placed in the public domain.

The Ministry of Finance had projected a growth rate of 7 per cent per annum for defence revenue expenditure. Capital expenditure is projected to grow at 10 per cent per annum. The resultant projection for overall annual growth rate of defence expenditure works out to 8.33 per cent. However, due to the economic slowdown and the compulsion of providing more funds for inclusive growth, the allocation for Defence is less (particularly for revenue expenditure) than what was projected by the Ministry of Finance. This situation is likely to continue into the near future.

Thus, Defence Mangers need to initiate immediate measures to control the rising revenue expenditure. The Revenue expenditure of Defence has grown from Rs. 10,194 cores in 1989-90 to Rs. 87,344 crore in 2010-11, i.e. an increase of almost nine times during the last two decades. A look at the graph below shows that Revenue expenditure is growing at a much faster pace in comparison to Capital expenditure.

The revenue expenditure trend for the last three years shows that about 46 per cent of expenditure is incurred on pay and allowances, 35 percent on stores and equipment, 10 per cent on revenue works, 4 per cent on transportation, and 5 per cent on Miscellaneous Charges. To check the rising revenue expenditure, the following measures could be considered:

1. Since more than half of revenue expenditure is spent on pay and allowances, to reduce expenditure on this account in the short term is not possible. However, considering the fact that the nature of war has changed, there is a need to develop force structures that are capability based and not threat based. Defence transformation through technological improvements is the need of the hour. Further, the three Services need to be integrated through reorganisation of higher formations and through joint training and joint procedures, which will ensure coherence and synergy. All this will facilitate the downsizing of the armed forces and result in a reduction in revenue expenditure.
2. A substantial portion of expenditure is incurred on stores and equipment. It also comprises of expenditure on maintenance of equipments. It is a well established fact that the cost of arms acquisition is only a small fraction of the life cycle cost and logistics and

maintenance management is a far more important activity. Consequently, countries like the United States and United Kingdom have adopted a performance based logistics (PBL) strategy for system support as a result of which the availability and reliability of systems have improved. Under this strategy, the original manufacturer or its nominated contractor maintains the weapon system at the specified level of operational readiness and usage, and is paid a graded incentive for exceeding the specified levels of system maintenance. The PBL has been found to be a far more cost effective solution than in-house logistics and maintenance management. The requirement of existing service logistics and maintenance infrastructure could be reduced by adopting this strategy. Further, modern supply chain management techniques need to be employed to reduce storage echelons and inventory holding, by making more use of ICT.

3. The process of implementation of outcome budgeting in Defence needs to be expedited. It will bring accountability into the system and authorities will be required to define and identify the objects for which funds are required and then intimate what outcome(s) have been achieved. It will reduce ad-hoc decision making and thus reduce wasteful expenditure. Some of the service-specific organizations and establishments, such as workshops, repair organizations, naval dockyards and depots, should immediately be brought under the regimen of outcome budgeting.
4. In the case of transportation, expenditure could be reduced by making more use of railways facilities instead of road transport. There are some coordination problems with the Railways which need to sorted out since it is in the interest of both the departments. Now large numbers of Defence Personnel are entitled to fly by air. There is a tendency to go for full fare ticket

(even in normal circumstances) when cheap air tickets are also available. The total expenditure on this account may be negligible but the issue is not that of amount. In fact, it reflects the fact that while spending Government money the canons of financial propriety are not being adhered to in letter and spirit.

5. The revenue expenditure is regulated by the principles and procedures contained in the Defence Procurement Manual (DPM)-2009. With a view to improving the quality of expenditure, the Ministry of Defence has delegated substantial powers to Services Headquarters and lower formations. This delegation has certainly helped in improving the speed of the expenditure but the same cannot be said about the quality of expenditure. There are instances of procurement of items without adequate justification and in excess quantity. To reduce wasteful expenditure the system of allocation of some grants every year without ascertaining the actual requirement needs to be reviewed. For example, every year funds under Hot Weather Grants are allotted which is not required since many units do not need Matkas (earthen wares) as they have made provision for water coolers.
6. Moreover, the units get a number of grants and in many cases the amount is a few thousand Rupees only. These grants are received by units through different directorates of Service Headquarters. Since processing and intimation of these grants involves a lot of manpower, it needs to be considered whether units should be given a lump sum amount for Miscellaneous expenditure and be authorised to use the same as they deem fit for the defined purpose. It will improve quality of fund utilisation and reduce manpower requirement of Headquarters, thereby resulting in savings in expenditure.
7. While delegating financial power to lower formations it was assumed that Local Purchases would be more economical. However, it is difficult to say that the

desired purpose has been achieved. To bring economy in local purchases it is essential that Central Authorities ensure that as far as possible Rate Contracts for the items required by field units are concluded.

8. Presently Units/Formations prepare procurement plan (except for ACSFP & TAG Grant) after funds are received. Presently, the endeavour is to ensure that all allotted funds are utilised and in the process many items are procured which are not required or purchased in excess of requirement. To overcome this situation it should be made mandatory for units/formations to prepare Priority Procurement Plan for all types of purchases in advance and no new items shall be included unless unavoidable. The present system compels officers to spend the allotment even though it may not be essential or urgent.
9. Defence should adopt Project Management approach for inducting complete systems or setting up facilities to enhance operational readiness on a life cycle basis. By adopting new methodologies along with Information Technology, optimal control of the projects at each phase of the project life cycle is feasible. Effective Project Management will facilitate achievement of desired outcome and time and cost over-runs could be minimised, resulting in substantial savings in expenditure.

INDIA'S DEFENCE BUDGET 2009-10: AN ASSESSMENT

In its interim budget for 2009-10 the Union Government has allocated Rs. 1,41,703 crores for the country' Defence Services that include three Armed Forces (i.e., the Army, the Navy and the Air Force), and other Departments, primarily Defence Research and Development Organisation (DRDO) and Defence Ordnance Factories. This is apart from Rs. 24,960 crores which have been earmarked to defray civil expenditures of Ministry of Defence (MoD) and its affiliated organisations, including, the Coast Guard, and for defence pension (Rs. 21,790 crores). In other words, the total resource available for the MoD and its various establishments is Rs. 1,66,663 crores. By convention, only budgetary provisions for the Defence Services constitute India's defence budget.

Though the allocations made in the interim budget are not binding for the next government to follow, it is unlikely that the new government will make any major changes in the allocation, given the mandatory increases in certain components of the defence budget, the worsening security situation in the country's neighbourhood and the gap in the country's defence preparedness. This commentary examines the various components of the defence budget, analyses the impact of the budget on the modernisation requirements of the Armed Forces, and the problem of under-utilisation of resources under the capital head.

Vital Components

The defence budget for 2009-10 has increased by 34.19 per cent over the previous year's budget estimate (BE) of Rs. 1,05,600 crores. However, BE of 2008-09 has been scaled upward by 8.52 per cent (Rs. 9,000 crores) to Rs. 1,14,600 crores at the revised estimate (RE) stage.

This means, this year's allocations has increased by 23.65 per cent over the RE of 2008-09. Of the total defence budget, revenue expenditure, which caters to the 'running' or 'operating' expenditure of the three Services and other departments, is pegged at Rs. 86,879 crores. Capital expenditure, which mostly caters for modernisation requirements, accounts for Rs. 54,824 crores. Of these two, revenue expenditure has been increased-in comparison to its last year's growth of less than 7 per cent-at a much faster rate of 50.85 per cent (Rs. 29, 286 crores). The growth of capital expenditure has however declined, over the previous year's growth, to 14.20 per cent (Rs. 6,817 crores). The sharp rise in revenue expenditure has taken its share in the defence budget to 61.31 per cent, from 54.54 per cent a year before. In other words, the share of capital expenditure has gone down by nearly 7 percentage points in these two years.

The faster growth of revenue expenditure is primarily due to the hefty increase in pay and allowances flowing from the implementation of Sixth Central Pay Commission (CPC).

To put the figure in perspective, total budgeted pay and allowances debited from the Services' budgets has more than doubled from 21,891.67 crores in 2008-09 to Rs. 44,500.69 crores in 2009-10.

Service-wise, the Army accounts for the largest share of the 2009-10 budget with an approximate allocation of Rs. 76,680 crores, followed by the Air Force (Rs. 34,432 crores) and the Navy (Rs. 20,604 crores). While the Ordnance Factories (OF) have a budget of Rs.1,505.45 crores, the DRDO's budget is Rs. 8,481.54 crores.

Impact on Modernisation

The Indian Armed Forces are on a modernisation drive. The shopping list of the Services includes virtually all types of weapons and systems, including big-guns, fighter aircrafts, armoured vehicles, radars, missiles, naval vessels, among others. The most pertinent question is whether the latest budget makes necessary provisions to meet these requirements. Given the fact that the modernisation programme of the armed forces largely depends on capital acquisitions, it boils down to how capital budget is allocated.

Assuming that nearly 80 per cent of the capital budget is meant for capital acquisitions, the latter consisting of 60 per cent of committed liabilities and 40 per cent of new schemes, the main sub-divisions of the capital budget are as below:

- Total Capital Budget: Rs. 54,824 crores
- Capital Acquisition: Rs. 43,859 crores
- Committed Liabilities: Rs.26,316 crores
- New Schemes: Rs.17,544 crores.

Moreover, over Rs. 17,500 crores (nearly 30 per cent of the capital budget) will be available for new weapons and systems that the Armed Forces have planned for induction. While this augurs well from the modernisation point of view, much depends on how much and how the resources are spent in the coming fiscal.

Higher Allocation and Under-utilisation of Resources

The growth of over 34 per cent in India's defence budget is one of the highest in the country's history of defence spending (the last time the defence budget was increased by over 30 per cent was in 1987-88 when allocation was increased by 43.4 per cent to Rs. 12,512 cores). In the recent past, the defence budget, despite registering modest growth rates, has been subjected to criticism in view of its declining shares in total central government expenditure and gross domestic product. In fact, the defence budget had decreased to below two per cent of GDP in the last fiscal year.

The new budget, defying all criticism, has made a substantial increase in allocations. From the perspective of resources allocation, the defence budget for 2009-10 represents 14.87 per cent of total central government expenditure, and 2.35 per cent of gross domestic product (GDP). However, accompanying the growth in defence budget is the problem of utilisation of resources under the capital head. As the latest budget reveals, the budgeted capital expenditure for 2008-09 has decreased by Rs. 7,007 crores (15 per cent) from Rs. 48, 007 crores to Rs. 41,000 crores at the RE stage. Its implication is also seen in the wide variation in the growth of the capital budget. If the defence establishments had fully spent the entire 2008-09 capital budget, the 2009-10 capital expenditure would have seen only 14.2 per cent growth instead of 33.72 per cent rise (Rs. 13,824 crores) that has been registered over the previous year's RE.

It is ironical that while capital expenditure has been increased substantially over the years, not sufficient attention has been devoted to spending those resources in a time-bound manner. As a result, under-utilisation of resources has increased with the growth in each year's capital expenditure. In absolute number, under-utilisation has increased by over four-and-a-half times between 2004-05 and 2008-09. In percentage terms, it has increased from 4 per cent to 15 per cent in the same period. As the defence preparedness of the country largely depends on the firepower it possess, which in turn depends on capital expenditure, the latter's timely and efficient utilisation deserves due consideration. Though MoD in recent years has tried to improve acquisition procedure, it appears inadequate to expedite the process. The recurring underutilisation of resources is a case in point to seriously examine the weakness in the system. If necessary a complete overhaul of the acquisition system may be considered to ensure that funds are utilised in a proper time frame and for the purpose it is envisaged for. India's defence budget 2009-10 has no doubt registered an impressive growth of over 34 per cent. However, much of the growth is accounted for by the increase in revenue expenditure, which, in turn, has been inflated by the surge in pay and allowances necessitated by the implementation of the recommendations of the Sixth Pay Commission. The impact of the increased provision for pay and allowances is such that the revenue budget's share in the defence budget has increased to more than 61 per cent, compared to its previous year's share of less than 55 per cent. The consequent decrease in the share of capital expenditure has resulted in its modest 14.2 per cent growth amounting to an additional provision of Rs. 6,817 crores over last year's allocations. Nonetheless, the allocation of Rs. 54,824 crores under the capital head is still substantial in absolute terms.

Considering that around 80 per cent of the capital budget would be available for procurement of weapons and systems, including some new ones, the defence establishment would be under pressure to spend the resources in a time-bound manner. Experience in the recent past shows that under-utilisation of capital budget has increased with each year's allocations. This necessitates a critical examination of the acquisition system to ensure that the Armed Forces are equipped with the right equipment at the right time.

INDIAN SERVICES ARE THE NET LOSERS

As per the figures released by Defence Offset Facilitation Agency (DOFA), offset agreements worth Rs 8125 crores had been signed by the end of 2009. The share of aero systems is 94 percent at Rs 7645 crores and that of naval systems 6 percent at Rs 480 crores. While bulk of the export orders have gone to the public sector (mostly HAL Ltd), some orders have been placed on the private sector companies for the supply of goods and services. To generate offset contracts worth Rs 8125 crores, the value of main contracts would be close to Rs 17000 crores (assuming offset percentage to be mere 30 percent). Again, considering the standard cost penalty of 10 percent, the Indian defence budget has already suffered an extra outflow of close to Rs 1550 crores on account of offsets-only to facilitate export orders of sundry items for some select Indian companies.

It will not be incorrect to state that the Indian offset policy is designed to obtain export orders for the public sector at the cost of the defence budget. Take the case of 126 fighter aircraft that India proposes to buy at an indicative cost of 11 billion dollars. The proposal carries an offset liability of 50 percent, resulting in a likely cost penalty of 10 percent. It implies that India could save one billion dollars if no offset obligations are imposed or buy up to 15 additional aircraft with the same budget. It is certain that extra outflow of one billion dollars will finance export orders for HAL. Worse, HAL would manufacture and supply low-tech items like doors and windows of aircraft and not systems/sub-systems that may boost its technological prowess. On the whole, offsets are not contributing to the upgradation of indigenous technological base but adding to the woes of the services and taxing the defence budget. Indian policy makers have failed to appreciate the full potential of offsets and trivialised a powerful instrument of industrial growth for transitory gains for DPSU and other entities.

The Way Forward

The offsets cost a country considerable extra expenditure. The question therefore arises whether they are desirable. It is universally accepted that offsets make sound business sense only if the trade-off results in extraordinary economic or technological gains. Technologies that industrially-advanced countries are reluctant to sell can only be obtained through the leverage of offsets. Over 130 nations are demanding offsets in defence purchases today. Despite knowing that the seller is bound to amortise the offset expenditure by suitably factoring it in his price quote, the countries find the proposition appealing.

India has an unusual knack of inserting provisions in a policy that are totally contrary to the stated objectives of the policy itself. Self reliance is a stated aim of DPP-2008. Yet, India does not accept technology under offsets. It is a dichotomy that the services fail to understand. The common reason given by the Government functionaries is that they are unable to price technology. It is a totally specious and hollow excuse. India purchases technology as a part of 'Buy and Make' deals-either contracted as a part of the main deal itself or negotiated separately at a later stage. Apparently, no ToT contract can be entered into without pricing the technology involved.

There is no standard price of technology in the world market. It is purely need-based and determined by the degree of desperation of the technology seeker. DRDO can be asked to identify technologies that it needs. Normally, DRDO should seek technologies in which it has made considerable headway but not mastered-commonly referred to as lacking 'last mile connectivity'. Thereafter, DRDO can work out the anticipated expenditure on indigenous effort to master the said technology as also urgency of its application. These two factors help decide fair, reasonable and acceptable price of technology.

Many knowledgeable observers are of the opinion that MoD has been pressurised by the public sector to disallow ToT against offsets as the public sector wants to perpetuate its monopoly on receipted technology through the current system of 'Buy and Make' deals. The public sector fears that acceptance of ToT against offsets would make the private sector preferred partner of foreign vendors. Therefore, opposition of the public sector is purely to safeguard its exclusive turf. It is time MoD rises above extraneous considerations to ensure that the benefits accruing from offsets do not get outweighed by the cost penalty. Transfer of technology should be made the preferred form of offsets. Through a well-evolved system of application of multipliers, irresistible incentives should be provided to foreign vendors to offer technologies that India needs the most.

BUDGETING PROCESS AND SOME ISSUES

This budget as usual was prepared under limited space available to Finance Minister and his team the current political equation with Left-parties sharing the policy platform with congress. In some way it has kept check on runaway liberalization euphoria, which has till date proved to be anti-poor, if we go by various indices of socioeconomic welfare and growth. The same old beaten practice of cut and paste technique and lowering taxes on a few things and then increase on some other things has been adopted. Nowhere concept of zero-base budgeting, setting growth targets and addressing distortion in economic and social administration systems is evident. This way you can always favour 2-3 industries by turn every year and collect moneybags for party funds and favours to politicians and their cronies.

Taking past budget as a base and then trying to mobilize more taxes is an idiotic approach. It is not 'budgeting' as a policy instrument. It is merely routine accounting of {Munims}. There is hardly anything radically different in 2006 budget. I don't understand what government wants to achieve by varying taxes on umbrella and lipsticks? Is this the job of Union government? How it affects economy and productivity of country? Does it really matter if excise duty is 4% or8% on lipsticks or writing chalks? What government should do is have simple three slabs 4 % 8% and 10% in all kinds of indirect taxes and duties and straight two slabs of 10% and 20% in Income tax with dividing income line of Rs 1 million per annum. All incentives and rebates should be withdrawn except for Provident funds and pension plans for social security and interest paid on housing purchase. We are not addressing viability of a product industry by building its fundamental strengths and removing structural weaknesses, but merely through tax regulation of government by giving tax relief and grants. This is old and outdated model of economics management and has no relevance left. Politicians are still functioning in 1956 mode. In fact all tax manuals should be 4-5 page booklets with simple procedures and automated formats so that corrupt tax officials are taken out from scene and put on monitoring and recovery process in cases of tax evaders. They should be given tough targets and thrown out if not successful.

Middle class is again under attack this time through different route. Service taxes have been hiked which is bad decision.12% is too high a rate. You can't tax everything. Tomorrow you will tax housemaids and tutorial services and public toilets. It is absurd and stupid. It will result in now more tax evasion. It is unjustified too.{now 95 services will be under service tax-existing 81+15 new proposed including ATM withdrawal}. The argument to tax ATM use is bizarre and reflects old mindset of bureaucrats to try to regulate systems through taxation route. It is odd that you have to pay for taking out your own cash put in banks at virtual no returns on savings bank. Banks can charge overheads but how government can tax this? An average Indian pays out almost 60% of his expenditure amount on account of various taxes only. So he gets merely 40% component as real value i.e. labour, material, design and benefits of products required in his average life routine. India is one of the most unproductive, mismanaged and highly taxed country. Still the funds collected by government annually in range of just Rs 4 lac-crores {INR 4000 Billions or US $ 82 Billion} is just peanuts.

This works out to only INR 3800/-per year per citizen. What any Government can do by this meager amount and plan for citizens? And imagine almost 50% out of this being siphoned off or spent on government officials and clerks themselves, their salaries, perquisites and pensions etc. All welfare schemes are meant for public servants only and not for people whom they are to serve.

Average Per capita income of a government (public servant in India currently) is 10 times that of per capita income of India. This is ridiculous. Is this country working to feed corrupt, unproductive public servants? 98% of Indian people are feeding a package of luxury to just 2% civil servants at cost of their two time meals. There is need to contain the rot of corruption, slim down government machinery and freeze their salaries and perks which are umpteen numbers. The productivity of public servants is very poor and they are generally corrupt and misbehaved because of job security and lack of accountability. This is anti thesis in model of democracy.

Why government has so small collection? Reason is simple-Mass scale rampant tax evasion and parallel economy running in country. Actually India's GDP is at least double of official figures {may be close to three times}. This has direct impact on inflation, hidden currency circulation, *havala* transactions and pressure on resources. People who consume most services actually pay least as percent of their real income. Widespread theft of basic services and energy is causing havoc in economic and social welfare planning. Only middle class is squeezed out every year more and more.

Politicians are party to this game. Income gap is increasing between rich and poor. Prostitution, illegal affairs and now organized crimes are increasing in bigger cities and also small too, just because cost of living has gone up tremendously and there are virtually no jobs. Police force is totally criminalized and ineffective reduced to brokerage centres. Over last 15 years of so-called reforms and competition being encouraged, the prices of general use household items and even simple OTC medicines have gone up by in at least 3-5 times range excepting for auto and electronic goods, meaning average 20% annual escalation in Consumer prices. And every year government data lie about actual inflation rate.

Against this double-digit inflation rate we have fixed 6% FDR rate and are reducing Provident fund interest thereby impoverishing old citizens who will die of deprivation and penury. There is no social security net in India. Government is virtually forcing people to divert to stock markets whose operations are highly shady at the moment and illogically elevated prices are ruling in stock markets. These prices defy all theories and concepts. Greed and manipulation is behind this. Mutual Funds are dumping common men's money there. Who is going to loose? Warning signals are clear.

The budget is not at all a long term or even mid-term planning document. It is based on very poor intellectual and expertise inputs. Problems like employment generation, increasing of productivity in economy, investment in long overdue judicial reforms and expansion, social security schemes like old age homes, effective logistics for commodities and goods distribution and storage facilities and a good infrastructure have not been addressed. India badly needs large number of decentralized new townships that are self contained with housing, hospitals, utilities, business centres and industries to release pressure on real estate and bring down soaring prices of land. Where black money is dumped too. Housing loans should be provided at low interest rates of 7-8% to encourage people to invest in housing and bring down prices of houses and commercial property. Stamp duties are too high in States forcing people to convert property into black assets. But knowingly politicians continue this.

Higher education is unnecessarily under control of State governments whereas most universities should now be privatized with well-defined UGC aid criteria, tighter quality control by setting up autonomous college councils and fixing of fair fees by an empowered panel in Ministry of HRD for private sector to meet expenses of quality education and seriously enter here. Same way allocation of funds in absolute terms for the schooling sector is peanuts despite charging of education *cess*. The biggest drain is government salaries and perquisites on unproductive, corrupt and unfit employees recruited by bribes, political connections and caste and reservations basis. This is of immense concern. Coupled with corruption in bureaucracy and siphoning off of almost 50% of public expenditures to the coffers of politicians, bureaucrats, engineers and contractors, hardly anything is left for actual public investment and welfare. Some new approach to public administration system coupled with fast automation and slimming down of civil services with moderate salaries to them should be implemented. There is need to tame corruption in civil services and defense services too. Defense outlay should be reduced by India and Pakistan sitting together and resolving issues. Education, healthcare, social security and basic services are lacking seriously in the country. We are moving towards chaos and crisis after about a decade's time. India is going to be largest polluting nation including local colony level pollution. There is going to be acute shortage of housing, land, water and electricity.

Selling cheap cars is not priority of this nation, nor to sell mobile phones and boast about highest growth rate of this sector in world. This is idiotic. These sectors are a liability and expenditure of resources with shortage of petroleum. In a country Where 1.5 crores people are added every year and you go and fight in WTO for Agriculture Market Access for exports of agro-goods, you should be talking about agriculture growth rate and not auto-sector and electronic equipment growth rate. Condition of agriculture in India is pathetic. The growth rate is too low. Farm productivity is poor. Basic commodities are not available to poor citizens and not at all affordable. What you will export?

India has no petroleum. So expansion of auto sector is foolish. Instead we should focus on mass rapid transport and decentralization of self-contained townships in massive drive to reduce land scarcity, which is causing meteoric, rises in property.

Basic and radical reforms are required to make country a healthy society to live where people feel safe, get two times square meals, have opportunities for employment and where honest can work productively Nothing of this sort has been addressed in the mere accounting jugglery of figures called Union budget. This certainly is not budgeting. I fail to understand why so many rebates and clauses are there in all tax manuals. Why can't they have simply a 4-5-page manual with simple procedures and all types of taxes pegged below 10% cap? No one wants to pay taxes in two digit rates? It is psychological barrier and there is no need for high taxes. But then how black money will be generated, how politicians and corrupt bureaucrats will thrive. From 1991 to 2005,economic planning and public administration in India are more or less failure. Current budget is on beaten track and will lead to more misery to people in coming times. It is mediocre exercise without application of brain and not with good intents and future focus.

Conclusions: The budget document should first list budgeting premises, the indicators used and the targets of growth and reforms set for next 5 and 10 years period, shortcomings identified in economy and the methods of budgeting adopted so people can critically evaluate proposals after approving the budgeting premises of government. Economic survey is not adequate document for this purpose and why it is put only one day in advance? It should come out at least 30 days in advance for people and experts to digest and comment and send budgetary proposals. Finance minister and his team should not think that they have got a unilateral license to impose whatever they think good or right just because they have been elected and empowered to do this. They are answerable to people and should consult in major issues before bringing out laws and budgets. This is how democracy should function. Indian politicians and bureaucrats are still living in British colonial era just mentally replacing British and acting like them instead.

That is how an IPS or IAS behaves when you visit him or her. Arrogant, superior, elite and unaccountable with little indications of humility and realization that s/he is public servants and paid by visitors to work for their welfare and for general service of humanity. Their only qualification is that they have slogged and passed one UPSC examination with little proven background. It is imperative to reduce Government establishment expenses of union and state governments to less than 10% of their annual budget or 2% of India's GDP. It is much more directly and indirectly. In fact corrupt nexus of Businessmen-politicians and bureaucrats drains off 50% of India's official GDP.

Citizens' satisfaction and feedback survey on an ongoing basis through Internet portals: In the end I would suggest FM to come out next year with Draft budget after economic survey of India and circulate it. Ministry of Finance or Planning Commission should setup a portal where public suggestions and opinion about draft budget should be invited. These information and objections should be compiled and then incorporated in Final Budget document.

Citizen's satisfaction survey should be started in India for all major government services including police and judiciary as is done in several countries like US, Canada, Australia, Singapore to get broad public feedback about required reforms rather than from only a handful of psuedo-experts and opinion makers in power corridors.

OFFSETS IN ARMS TRADE: NEED FOR A NATIONAL POLICY

As India has no national offset policy, Ministry of Defence (MoD) took the initiative to evolve its own defence offset policy. Initially announced in early 2005, the policy was made a part of Defence Procurement Procedure-2005. As the primary aim of the policy was to boost exports from the public sector, it allowed discharge of offsets either through FDI in Indian public sector undertaking for defence industrial infrastructure or direct purchase of products/components/services from DPSU/OFB/other industry identified by MoD. Interestingly, the task of monitoring implementation of every offset contract was to be assigned to a DPSU or OFB.

The private sector protested strongly against the unfair treatment meted out to it, forcing MoD to revise the policy in 2006. Scope for direct purchase of defence goods and services was enlarged to include the whole Indian defence industry. It also allowed FDI in Indian defence industry and defence R&D. Further, it defined Indian defence industry to include DPSU, OFB and any private defence industry manufacturing defence products under an industrial licence granted for such manufacture. As no major manufacturing activity was taking place in private sector under licence, the policy continued to favour the public sector.

As was expected, industry associations were not satisfied and appealed to MoD for a level playing field. Bowing to pressure, MoD removed the mandatory requirement of an industrial licence for private companies in 2008. Now, the only stipulation to being an offset partner is that the Indian company should not have more than 26 percent foreign holding. Before examining the effect of offsets on the services, it is essential to understand three aspects that have a profound bearing on the modernisation plans of the armed forces, i.e. objective of seeking offsets, receipt of technology against offsets and cost of demanding offsets.

OBJECTIVE OF SEEKING OFFSETS

Offsets are universally accepted as a powerful leverage to obtain compensatory benefits by asking the seller to undertake well-designated activities to satisfy vital economic necessity or fill critical technological void. Therefore, before embarking on offsets every country identifies and spells out objectives that are proposed to be achieved through offsets. Thus, the objectives are always nation-specific and in consonance with national aspirations and long-term vision. In the absence of well evolved objectives, offsets lose focus and prove highly wasteful. An aimless offset policy can neither contribute to the growth of indigenous industry nor provide long term economic benefits.

India may be the only country whose defence offset policy has no stated objectives. MoD has not considered it necessary to explain as to what it intends to achieve through offsets and the roadmap for the same. However, as offset policy is a part of Defence Procurement Procedure-2008 (DPP-2008), it can be reasonably inferred that its objective would be in line with the objective spelt out in DPP-2008, i.e. achieving self-reliance in defence equipment. Additionally, India has been reiterating its resolve to reduce the current proportion of imports from 70 percent to 30 percent. If that be so, primary thrust of the Indian policy should be to seek infusion of technology to strengthen its indigenous defence industrial base. However, contrary to all rationale, the Indian offset policy has been formulated to continue dependence on imports. India has not considered it necessary to direct offsets to pre-designated areas of its choice. It has abrogated the right to select methodology, areas and offset programmes in favour of the vendors, thereby rendering India's needs inconsequential. It is natural for every foreign vendor to opt for programmes that cost the least and are easy to fulfil-Indian needs do not count at all.

INFUSION OF TECHNOLOGY AGAINST OFFSETS

Every country that strives to develop indigenous industry seeks technology through offsets to bridge the gap and use acquired technology as a take off platform for indigenous development of more advanced technologies. More than 35 percent of all offsets worldwide relate to technology transfer. Transfer of Technology (ToT) is rightly called as the engine that drives offsets.

For technology transfer, all countries adopt a two-step approach, as given below:-

Identification of Critical Technologies. These are technologies that are considered essential for stimulating and expediting the growth of indigenous industrial competence. For economies of scale, sought technologies should not be product-specific but have much wider application across a large range of systems. Ability to absorb identified technology and monitor its transfer is another major consideration.

Persuasion of Vendors to Offer Required Technology. To persuade vendors to part with the technology sought, a system of assigning different multiplier values to various offset programmes is put in place. Multiplier value is a factor applied to the actual value of an offset transaction to calculate the credit value earned. For example, by undertaking an offset programme worth Rs 100 crores with a multiplier value of 3.5, a foreign vendor would earn offset credits equal to Rs 350 crores. By assigning differential weightage to offset programmes, buyer nations provide sellers with incentives to offer offsets in targeted area of buyer's choice. Despite repeated assertions of wanting to make India self-reliant in defence production, India does not accept technology against offsets. This aspect will be dealt with subsequently.

Offsets and Cost Penalty

One of the major misconceptions is that offsets are free add-ons. Nothing can be farther from the truth. Offsets certainly do not come for free as foreign vendors have to incur additional expenditure to fulfil them. There are a number of factors that affect offset overhead costs and it is not feasible to fix an exact yard-stick. Value of an offset is always expressed in terms of percentage of the value of the main contract. It is generally seen that offsets up to 50 per cent inflate the cost of the main contract by close to 10 per cent. Similarly, 100 and 200 per cent offsets may result in cost escalation by 15 and 20 percent respectively.

The graph on the following page shows:-

- Cost penalty is not directly proportional to offset percentage. Cost penalty varies with the type of programmes undertaken.
- Initial cost of establishing infrastructure and initiating offset programmes is considerable. Once the process becomes functional and gets streamlined, rate of increase in cost penalty drops.
- Cost penalty tends to plateau after offset percentage reaches 200 percent. It implies that beyond this stage, both the offset provider and the receiver remain engaged in programmes which make commercial sense to both.

It may come as a surprise to many that the US allows its defence producers to charge offset costs even for government to government Foreign Military Sales (FMS). Although the US Government considers offsets to be detrimental to free and fair trade, it appreciates the need for companies to recover offset costs as they are considerable. The Defence Federal Acquisition Regulation Supplement (DFARS) of May 1995, allowed US companies to recover full cost necessary to 'implement an offset agreement' in connection with FMS purchases. Subsequently, the scope was widened by using the term 'offset costs', thereby facilitating recovery of full expenditure incurred in fulfilling offset obligations. It proves the point that fulfilment of offset obligations costs a company considerable expenditure which it can not absorb and has to recover by factoring it in the sale price.

Offsets and the Indian Services

When the idea of demanding offsets was initially floated in official circles, most service officers thought it to be a harmless appendage to the procurement procedure. Very few were fully aware of its implications. Many welcomed it in the hope that offsets would result in giving an impetus to the Indian defence industry. Being terribly uncomfortable with the continued dependence on foreign vendors and the resultant uncertainties, the services did not grudge encumbrance of offsets in order to make India self-reliant. However, the services were in for a shock. The Indian offset policy is anything but self-reliance centric.

India allows three routes for the fulfilment of offset obligations and they are:-

- Direct purchase of or executing export orders for defence products or services provided by Indian defence industries. For the purpose of defence offsets, services mean maintenance, overhaul, upgradation, life extension, engineering, design, testing of defence products, defence related software or quality assurance services.
- FDI in Indian defence industries for industrial infrastructure for services, co-development, joint ventures and co-production of defence products and components.
- FDI in Indian organisations engaged in research in defence R & D.

An examination of the viability of the above three routes is very revealing. At the face of it FDI route appears highly viable but when considered in the light of upper cap of 26 percent, the dissuasiveness of the policy becomes apparent. A foreign investor is expected to invest his resources in a venture where he has no significant control, strict capacity/ product constraints, no purchase guarantee and no open access to other markets including exports. The FDI policy was announced in May 2001 and has elicited no response. Therefore, options (b) and (c) above mean little.

Export of defence goods and services is thus the only possible method to fulfil offset obligations under the Indian policy. It amounts to compensation trading which is considered to be the least beneficial form of offsets.

Export of goods and services provide temporary and illusory gains, as has been the experience the world over. New markets dry up soon after the offsets are fulfilled, leaving created infrastructure idle and bereft of orders. Therefore, such trading does nothing to either strengthen the defence industrial base or promote technology upgradation. In other words, a potent tool like offsets is wasted on one-time exports.

Undoubtedly, the services have been taken for a ride. Offsets have added to their disquiet and anxieties without any boost to indigenous defence industry. A look at the following major concerns of the services will reveal the intensity and magnitude of the dilemma faced by them:-

- Offsets impose a cost penalty on all procurements that carry offset obligation clauses. This implies that the outflow from the defence budget gets proportionately increased. For example, for a deal that mandates 50 percent offsets, the defence budget will have to pay up to 10 percent extra in costs.
- Simultaneous signing of offset contract can result in a loss of focus, away from the main contract. DPP-2008 lays down that at every stage of evaluation, offset proposals would be examined along with the main technical and commercial proposals to confirm compliance. A competent vendor may get eliminated by default if his offset proposal is found unsatisfactory.

- Offset obligations have to be fulfilled co-terminus with the main contract. The policy allows imposition of penalty and its recovery by way of deduction from the bank guarantee of the main contract or the amount payable to the vendor under the main contract. Further, failure to implement full offset obligations during the period of the main contract makes the vendor liable to be disqualified for participation in future defence contracts. With such punitive provisions in place, any default in offset programmes can delay the main contract and even jeopardise it.
- Offsets are notorious for corruption as they are often formulated in broad and imprecise terms, leaving enough leeway for multiple interpretations and manipulations. Furthermore, offset contracts are never monitored as closely as the main contract. Allegations of malpractice in offsets can put a foreign vendor under cloud and affect his commitment to timely completion of the main contract. Additionally, MoD may be forced to debar the vendor to exhibit its zero tolerance for dishonest activities, thereby endangering the main contract as well.

INDIA'S DEFENCE BUDGET 2008-09

Union Budget 2008-09 has allocated Rs. 105,600 crores for India's Defence. Crossing the one lakh barrier for the first time, and accounting for nearly 14.1 per cent of total central government expenditure, the Defence Budget looks quite impressive. But when seen in the context of India's expanding interests, this allocation remains as moderate as ever. Moreover, an in-depth analysis reveals problems in defence and budgetary management, none of which show signs of abating. For fiscal year 2008-09, India's defence allocation has increased by 10 per cent over the previous year's allocation of Rs. 96, 000 crores, and by little over 14 per cent compared to last year's revised allocation of Rs. 92,500 cores. In the last five years, the defence budget has increased by nearly 37 per cent from Rs. 77,000 crores in 2004-05, which represents over

8 per cent growth per annum. Notwithstanding the current allocation and growth of the defence budget over the years, the question remains whether India's defence spending is compatible with its economic and security interests.

A brief survey of the Indian economy reveals its great potential and global reach. The economy registered an average growth of nearly 8 per cent a year during the 10th Plan, and seems set to continue the growth momentum in the 11th Plan period. What is more important is that much of this growth is driven by the external sector, mainly growing trade with the rest of world. India' total trade (exports plus imports) has increased by more than five times in the last decade and now accounts for over 35 per cent of its gross domestic product (GDP). This testifies to the fact that the economy is much more globalized than, say, 10 years ago when trade accounted for less than 20 per cent of GDP. The growth of the Indian economy and its global character has also infused confidence among international investors who see India as an attractive place for investment. The growing inflow of foreign direct investment is testimony to this fact. This process of greater integration with, and concomitant acquisition of greater stakes in, the international economic system is likely to continue in the coming decades. Military capability is necessary, for instance, to protect the country's sea lines of communication – 90 per cent India's trade by volume and 70 per cent in value moves by sea.

A survey of the regional military balance shows India's unfavourable position vis-à-vis its neighbours. China's relentless military modernisation, backed by double-digit growth in military expenditure for more than a decade, is a case in point. Its military modernisation, exemplified by the recent demonstration of IT-and space-based capability, has expanded its military reach from the traditional battlefield into the 'space and cyber-space domains'. This is besides the other 'anti-access/area denial capabilities' developed through a range of modern weapons systems that, according to a 2008 Pentagon Report, have left even the United States worried. Given the long-standing India-China border dispute, China's war preparations for winning "local wars under conditions of informationalization" together with its massive infrastructure development along the border, have certainly given it a definite military advantage.

At the same time, the sharpening of Pakistan's armoury, especially with the help of US military aid, is no less worrying. Since 9/11, Pakistan has received more than US $10 billion worth of military assistance from the United States. Such assistance, which includes F-16 fighter aircraft, air-to-air missiles, cluster bombs, air defence radars and surveillance technologies, has direct security implications for India, since it narrows the advantage in conventional warfare that has been in India's favour.

The moderate nature of India's defence spending, the question arises as to how much India should spend on defence. Though an answer lies in a complex set of issues ranging from the nature of threats, the fiscal health of the government and the kind of diplomacy it chooses to pursue, yet some statistical references can be drawn from other countries that are devoted to building or have attained world-class military capability.

While the United States, with a military budget (for Fiscal Year 2009) of more than $700 billion and a share of nearly 50 per cent of global military expenditure, remains the largest military spender in modern times, India's defence budget estimated roughly at $26.5 billion for 2008-09 constitutes a mere two per cent of the global total.

In terms of proportion of economic resources devoted to defence, India's latest defence budget, which accounts for 1.99 per cent of expected GDP in the coming Fiscal Year, is less than the global average of around 2.5 per cent, and lags behind America's 4.1 per cent and Pakistan's 3.5 per cent. In absolute terms, India's defence spending, ranked 10th in the list of major spenders in the world, constitutes a fraction of the American military budget and less than half of China's 'under-reported' but official defence budget of $57.22 billion for 2008.

Given the higher proportion of economic resources being devoted to defence in these countries, should India raise its defence allocation, say, to 3 per cent of GDP? The answer lies in the adequacy of the present budget to meet the country's security requirements. As the evidence shows, the proportion of financial allocations made available to the defence establishment vis-à-vis its demand has increased to nearly 95 per cent in recent years, even though its share in GDP has decreased significantly in the same period.

This indicates that there is hardly any shortage of funds to meet the defence establishment's financial requirements irrespective of its share in GDP. In any case, the fixing of defence allocation to a certain portion of GDP is not theoretically a sound proposition, given the volatilities in economic growth rates and threat perceptions in the long run. What is more important is that the security requirements, which ultimately get translated into the annual defence budget, need to be adequately financed.

A close look at the formulation of the Indian defence budget, however, reveals little evidence of the country's security concerns being properly addressed or financed. The annual defence budget, which follows from the Defence Capability Plan, 15-year Long Term Integrated Perspective Plan, 5-year Services Capital Acquisition Plan and Annual Acquisition Plan, is handicapped in terms of catering to the true security needs of the country because of the poor formulation and execution of, and inordinate delays in, planning. In other words, the security needs of the country are poorly reflected in the budget, and the capability requirements of the Armed Forces either get delayed or come to possess a short shelf-life. As a result, the Armed Forces are under-prepared to meet any worsening in the security scenario as well as technological upgrades by adversaries.

Another major problem in defence management, as reflected time and again in successive budgets, is the inability of the defence establishment to fully utilise the allocated funds, especially those meant for the modernisation of the country's security infrastructure. Though the modernisation expenditure, credited under the 'capital expenditure' of the budget, has increased considerably from nearly 25 per cent in 2000-01 to over 45 per cent in 2008-09, the problem of timely utilisation of allotted resources continues to haunt the defence Services. As the latest budget reveals, out of Rs. 41,922 crores earmarked for 'capital expenditure' for 2007-08, Rs. 4412 crores, or over 10 per cent, remained unutilised. These unutilised funds, which mean opportunities lost or delayed in acquiring needed capability, have become a regular feature despite reforms in the acquisition structures/ procedures.

An examination of the capital acquisition structure/ procedure reveals several weaknesses in the system: poor planning; deficiency in formulation of qualitative requirements; lack of motivation for indigenisation efforts; single-vendor approach towards selection of weapon systems; poor human resource and information management; 'large number of submission and approval points'; and 'multiple agencies with dispersed centres of accountability'. The cumulative effect of all this is a gap in the capabilities sought by the Armed Forces; under-optimisation of the huge resources spent over the years; and a poor self-reliance index.

The Indian acquisition system defies the best international practices prevalent in counties such as France, the UK and Australia. In contrast to the Indian system, the acquisition process in these countries is undertaken by an integrated body encompassing all the stakeholders – Armed Forces, Industry, R&D organisation, quality assurance organisation, civilian bureaucrats and other skilled workforce.

This integrated body is responsible for all acquisition functions, right from the planning level to the disposal of equipment, and thus owns the responsibility of the whole life-cycle process of any equipment or system. The advantage of this integrated body lies in its single-point accountability to provide timely solutions to the Armed Forces' requirements and, in the process, it provides the best value for money and also a thrust towards self-reliance. Keeping the above merits of the integrated acquisition organisation in mind, India could possibly adopt a similar institutional arrangement for expediting its acquisition process.

As regards self-reliance in critical military technology and production of advanced weapons systems, India, despite decades of effort, has remained import-dependent. The poor self-reliance index of 30 to 35 per cent against the target of 70 per cent by the end of 10th Plan testifies to this fact. Inadequate budgetary provision for defence research and development (R&D) is the major reason behind India's poor defence industrial production and heavy outflow of financial resources to foreign suppliers. Overdependence on foreign suppliers not only has its costs and industrial disadvantages but also provides opportunities for corruption and delays in procurement.

The present allocation of Rs. 6,486.35 crores for defence R&D constitutes a mere 6.1 per cent of the defence budget. In contrast, major military powers spend a much higher proportion of their budgets on military R&D. For instance, the United States spends around 16 per cent of its defence budget on R&D. American dominance in military technology and production of sophisticated weapons systems is the result of higher allocation, concerted efforts in the right direction and involvement of industries in research activities.

In India, almost the entire defence R&D activity is undertaken by the DRDO (Defence Research and Development Organisation), with little budgetary or technological support from the defence industry, which largely comprises of state-owned Ordnance Factories and Defence Public Sector Undertakings (DPSUs). The private sector, which is a key contributor to civilian technology and a key driver of economic growth since liberalisation began in the early nineties, is still kept out from contributing to military technological advancement.

The absence of R&D efforts by the defence industry has forced the DRDO to concentrate on every aspect of military technology, many of which could be undertaken by the industry itself. As a result, a very small proportion – 8 to 10 per cent of R&D budget – is percolated down for fundamental research. If India wants to be self-reliant in critical military technology and defence production, it needs to enhance its R&D spending. At the same time, increased allocations need to be channelled in the proper direction, and industry, including in the private sector, needs to be engaged in R&D activities so as to make DRDO focus on key and critical technologies.

Considering its economic and security imperatives, India's defence spending is not only moderate but also fails to capture the true security needs of the nation. The defence budget, because of the problems in the acquisition system, is constrained to translate budgetary resources into required military capability in the given time and at optimal cost. To augment defence spending, what India needs is an efficient defence planning mechanism, backed by an integrated acquisition organisation. Also, given its poor self-reliance index, India needs to enhance R&D spending. Enhanced budgetary allocations should be channelled in the right direction, with the industry (including private sector) taking a lead in technology development.

DEFENCE FINANCE AND MANAGEMENT

The contents of the general, as well as, the defence budget of the Government of India have normally been widely discussed and debated. However, the focus mostly has been on the magnitude of the budget rather than the system of budgeting. Yet it is the system that needs to be the focus of discussions and requires reforms. Over a period of time, the budget documents had become quite static in terms of structure, content and communication of results. With the demands of those needing information from the budget changing with time, reforms in the structure and content of the defence budget had become overdue.

A budget is an instrument of policy. Through the annual financial statements it can translate a long term or medium term plan into action. The questions that arise are: what do we expect out of the budgeting system? And does it facilitate a meaningful translation of the intended objectives as reflected in the budget estimates? The perception about what the Defence Budget: Towards an Outcome and Programme Based System 709 defence budget should contain also depends on various categories of users. The institutions/persons looking into the budget can be divided into the following three main categories:

- Parliament, which votes the budgetary appropriations and also reviews the performance through the appropriation accounts and audit reports. Preceding the vote on the budget, Parliament has the report of the Standing Committee on Defence, which examines the demands for grants in detail.
- The administrative ministry, the executive arm and supporting institutions working with it. The administrative ministry formulates the budget and, after necessary backing of the Finance Ministry, gets the approval of Parliament to enable it to operate.
- A mix of users such as experts in the field, institutions, beneficiaries, academics and the common citizens who are interested in the information, especially the value for money derived from the actual expenditure.

To meet the changing needs of the diverse sets of users, the defence budger needs to change both its format and contents with time. Yet systemic changes in structure, form and content of the budget have been slow to come about in India. Changes have been made from time to time but essentially in amplification of contents or deletion of certain items, or addition of new service relating to expenditure. We, therefore, need to know how far and why it has not been feasible to introduce new concepts.

The Defence Services Estimates (DSE) have an amalgam of outlays that can be converted in terms of outcomes into tangibles and some intangibles. As far as the defence budget is concerned, it is clear that the Parliament, the executive, defence analysts and the tax payers would be interested to know the outcomes. They would be keen to know the quantum of funds provided for air defence, the cumulative total of such allocations in the budget over a period of time and the results achieved in providing protection against potential air attacks. While evolving any modifications in systems, it is necessary to know what is needed in the Indian context by various users.

Having recognized the inherent advantage of a budget that can reveal what it has achieved in terms of intended objectives, the question arises as to whether the existing structure and content need a total substitution, partial modification or supplements in order to serve as a conclusive document for evaluation of the outcomes. The past legacy also needs to be tackled in any overhaul or change in the existing system. The legacies are located in the content of the basic administrative and accounting data generated from the source levels, the mode of transmission, the organisational entities involved in the processing of the data, the relationships between these entities, the command and control, the technology used and, most important, the manpower resources, both in terms of skills and the numbers at the appropriate levels. Other relevant factors are: reluctance to exchange information in an institutionalised manner and an exaggerated sense of secrecy in publishing and disseminating information.

This article attempts to delineate feasible reforms to make the budget speak for itself in terms of intended objectives and the outcome or value for money realised out of the expenditure incurred.

The Existing System

The Defence Services Estimates (DSE), as a document, has evolved over a period of time to its current structure. Though its structure has largely remained the same in form and contents, it has had modifications. It is believed by many that, as a public document, its existing format is adequate to convey the objectives of the government. The comments/ reactions to a budget presentation are made in terms of judgement on magnitude of allocations for army, navy, air force, DRDO and for new services, etc. However, a growing number of people, especially in the ministry and service headquarters, well-informed defence experts and academics have persuasively argued for a change. Many Members of Parliament have often sought more information, than what is available in the existing document.

The criticism of the present system is that it is largely input oriented. Specifically this means that it focuses on expenditure in generic terms, i.e., in terms of pay and allowances, stores, transportation, etc., and not in terms of targets and its actuals. The budget is also devoid of details in a number of major components of expenditure. The figures of expenditure on certain categories such as 'stores', 'works', etc., are such that it is not clear as to why and for what the funds are provided.

The budget is divided in terms of 'revenue' and 'capital'. Even in this regard, the classification was until recently carrying legacies of the past and did not reflect the basic nature of certain items. In several areas, assets of a capital nature were being classified under revenue. Consequently, capital assets were underpitched, especially in respect to the army. The omnibus nature of items under capital expenditure indicated as 'other equipment', 'aircraft', etc., do not reveal adequate information on specific items of expenditure, even where these are of large magnitude. The word 'maintenance' nowhere figures under Revenue Budget but is covered under 'pay and allowances', 'stores', etc.

With substantial increase in funding for defence, the need for adequate information has become of great importance for interpretation of the budget. At present, information on the budget is available to the executive/parliament through the following three main reports:

- The Appropriations Account

- The audit report of Comptroller and Auditor General
- Reports of Parliamentary Committees – especially those of the Standing Committee on Defence and, in certain cases, the reports of the Public Accounts Committee, based on the audit reports.

The Appropriation Accounts signed by the Controller General Defence Accounts (CGDA)/Secretary Defence (Finance) and by the Defence Secretary gives the actual expenditure against allocations under various minor and sub heads. The reasons for variations of actuals against allocations are also indicated. However, it does not throw adequate light on physical achievements (outputs) in respect to a bulk of the items since the document is not intended to be an account on performance. However, there are exceptions. For two organisations-military farms and military engineering services-assessment of performance is given in separate sections.

Under the present system, getting an overall picture of budget in financial/physical terms and the actual performance is not easy and requires a lot of derivation, collation of data/ information and enormous effort on the part of the ministry/ services/departments. A document reflecting outcomes of at least major items provided in the budget would make the whole task easier apart from serving the basic and very important task of effective management of schemes and achievement of objectives.

By and large, the existing structure of the DSE with classification and sub-heads such as 'stores', 'works', etc., cannot facilitate the understanding of what is the outcome intended from the money spent on various items of expenditure related to defence. Even in an important area of maintenance of aircraft, it is difficult to derive from the budget that if Rupees "X" have been allocated for maintenance of an aircraft type "A", whether the required level of maintenance has been achieved. This information becomes available much later when an Audit Para is raised and even becomes an item in the report of the Public Accounts Committee (for example MiG-29). The existing budgetary system has another deficiency. For instance, allocations made for a gun are spent and the expenditure reports also reflects this position but the guns may still not be inducted for the purpose for which they were procured.

The existing system may show good financial progress with almost entire payments having been made in respect of an item, but the crucial phase of testing, which is vital towards achieving the final outcome, could drag on. Successful tests of many systems do not necessarily lead to a successful outcome or their timely induction into the armed forces. The DSE reveals very little about allocations even of a non sensitive nature. There are only one line entries in the budget documents for amounts running up to a few thousand crore of Rupees.

There are a number of other weaknesses in the system. The time taken for transactions does not get reflected in the financial information reports pertaining to a budget, and a continuous update of information on liabilities incurred by various sanctioning/spending authorities is not available An equally serious shortcoming is the inability to fully disseminate information to the concerned authorities and the absence of a synergised effort among various wings under the MOD for creating a comprehensive integrated report that would reflect the financial-cum-physical programmes.

Steps have been taken from time to time to make the existing DSE and the annual compilation of accounts more meaningful.

In 1987, a reform was initiated in segregating pension from the DSE and ordinance factories from the army budget, with the objective of making this production organisation into a separate cost centre. Further reforms took place in 1992, based on the report of the task force (under A. K. Ghosh) which added over 150 categories in the classification of accounts, revealing more on the content of the expenditure, so that certain specific activities could be made transparent. It is clear that a well evolved coding section, in vogue since the 1930s and subsequently enhanced by computerisation in 1971, has enabled further expansion of codes, meeting the growing need for giving information on expenditure related to an item.

FUTURE DEFENCE SPENDING UP TO 2014-15

If the Finance Ministry's emphasis on fiscal prudence and inclusive growth has resulted in a smaller increase in the latest defence budget, the Report of the Thirteenth Finance Commission, tabled in Parliament on February 25, 2010, also does not paint a very optimistic scenario for India's future defence spending.

The Constitutional Commission, which has recommended on specific aspects of Centre-State fiscal relations, has also proposed a roadmap for defence spending for the period 2010/11-2014/15. As per the roadmap, defence spending is to grow by an annual average of 8.33 per cent during this period, with the revenue and capital components slated to increase by an annual average of seven per cent and ten per cent, respectively. As a percentage of GDP, defence spending is to be progressively decreased to 1.76 per cent in 2014-15.

The fiscal consolidation part outlined by the Commission. More importantly, the Finance Ministry, which is in charge of implementing the Commission's recommendations, is not only in agreement with the path but also tries to better the fiscal roadmap suggested by the Commission. This means that MoD's future spending as outlined in the TFC could come under further stress in coming years.

The Road Ahead

While projecting the MoD's budget through 2014-15, the TFC took into account the projections made by both the Finance Ministry and the MoD. The final projection by the TFC however turned out to be the same as made by the Finance Ministry-possibly to the dissatisfaction of the MoD, which argued for "the need to provide adequately for enhanced force multipliers." The TFC however stuck to its guns, saying "the Finance Ministry's projections address these needs [of the MoD]" and further added that:

"we [the Thirteenth Finance Commission] are of the view that there exists considerable scope to improve the quality and efficiency of defence expenditure through increased private sector engagement, import substitution and indigenisation; improvements in procedures and practices and better project management, within the parameters of Government of India's policy. Efforts in this direction will further expand the fiscal space available for defence spending."

The Finance Commission needs careful consideration, given the indication that India's future defence budget may not grow as desired by the MoD. In this regard, the Defence Ministry needs to carve out a plan as to where it can bring efficiency in its spending.

At present, the defence budget is broadly divided into Revenue and Capital expenditures, with the former accounting for nearly 60 per cent of total budget. However, given the cost-intensive nature of capital acquisition, the MoD, as argued rightly before the Finance Commission, needs more resources for 'enhanced force multipliers'.

This makes a case for rationalisation of revenue expenditure, if the overall budget is to grow by a fixed 10 per cent annually. The MoD has therefore to revisit its spending on major revenue components such as Pay and Allowance; Stores and Equipment; and Transportation, among others. Of particular focus should be Pay and Allowances, which has increased significantly from Rs. 24,690 crore in 2007-08 (budget estimate) to approximately Rs. 46,767 crore in 2010-11.

The way defence Capital budget is spent has been major a source of major concern, expressed by various authorities, particularly the Comptroller and Auditor General of India (C&AG). Besides, the repeated surrender of capital funds and India's heavy import dependency have probably attracted the maximum attention for remedial measures.

Although the MoD has taken a keen interest in alleviating the problems by way of revising the Defence (Capital) Procurement Procedure (DPP), some lacunae still persist. The biggest problem perhaps is the lack of an integrated acquisition structure, as brought out by the Reports of Group of Ministers (2001) and C&AG (2007). In the absence of accountability at one place, various acquisition functions, carried out by different agencies, lack a mission-oriented approach, often at the cost of optimum time-cost trade offs and indigenisation/self-reliance. This not only raises the acquisition cost but also delays or hampers defence preparedness. It is high time the MoD looks deep into this issue.

4

China's Defence Budgeting

China's Defence Budget 2012 announced in the first week of March 2012 significantly draws global and regional attention in that China has shot through its defence expenditure over the $ 100 billion mark, making China's military expenditure at the global level, second only to that of the United States, even though there exists a wide differential between the two.

In terms of global concerns, China's hikes in defence expenditures in 2012 military budget come under sharper scrutiny when China's defence hikes are placed in the context of a sharp drop in United States defence budget by about $ 380 billion necessitated by US Congressional mandates. Though President Obama has reiterated that the Asia Pacific regional military posture of the United States would not be in the purview of budgetary cuts because of the new US strategic pivot to Asia Pacific, what cannot be ruled out is that in case of a sudden Middle East contingency, the United States would be forced to redirect US Forces from its strengthened posture against a fast militarily rising China.

Regionally in Asia, steep hikes in Chinese military expenditure cause multiple strategic and military concerns for China's neighbours. Contextually, China's recent aggressiveness and military assertion (facilitated by China's military rise, fuelled by expanding economic resources) on territorial disputes foisted by China on virtually all its neighbours, multiply these concerns.

China's military hikes would have been understandable had China's peripheries on land and sea would have been threatening to China's security. Such is not the case because the military balance is overwhelmingly in favour of China. China could convert this military balance in its favour for the last two decades because of United States earlier permissiveness to tolerate China's military build-up as it suited United States and in the last decade because of the military and strategic distractions in Iraq and Afghanistan.

China's expanded military budget comes immediately after President Obama's announcement of the policy of a strategic pivot to Asia Pacific. China denies that the two are connected. In this connection it needs to be pointed out that China would continue to increase its military expenditure irrespective of any strategic steps of the United States. China's strategic aims are to emerge as the undisputed military power in Asia and a rival power centre on the global strategic calculus.

In this connexion, it needs to be pointed out that scientific projections have been made which state that China's military budget hikes are expected to total $ 238.2 billion by 2015 which when translated amounts to more than doubling China's military expenditure in just another three years. China's existing military profile a before the announcement of Budget 2012 is considerably powerful and would become more powerful with $106 billion planned for this year. Doubling of the budget by 2015 would facilitate China's military profile to emerge so powerful that no Asian country, not even India, can ever hope to militarily catch up with China.

India's defence budget in the year ending was about $36 billion—a fraction of China's military budget. Shockingly, a former Defence Secretary was quoted in the media that every year the Finance Ministry would demand in March that the Defence Ministry surrender Rs 5,000 crores or so to balance the deficit in the Union Budget. He further added that for the last ten years the Defence Ministry was being made to surrender such amounts. This would total to Rs 50,000 crores cut from announced Defence budgets. This year the news has come that the Defence Ministry has been ordered not to sign existing defence purchases agreements till after 31 March 2012 including the order to purchase the 126 fighter planes badly needed by the Indian Air Force. It is distressing that to balance the Finance Ministry books and Union budget deficits arising from exorbitantly wasteful schemes, the Government plays around with India's war preparedness in an extremely hostile environment.

India should be more than seriously concerned about China's hiked defence expenditures considering that 'The China Threat' to India is more real than to other nations, simply because China perceives that India is its sizeable and comparable strategic and military Asian rival and could impede China's rise and emergence as the undisputed military power in Asia. Strategically, it is ironic that despite the credibility and potency of 'The China Threat', India's political leadership and apex national security establishment traditionally disconnected from its Armed Forces who manage 'The China Threat', continue to de-emphasize this threat and get tricked into China's protestations that China's rise is a 'peaceful rise'.

Against such a backdrop it becomes incumbent on India's strategic community to highlight and reiterate the implications arising for India's national security of China's rising military expenditures. This Paper intends to do so under the following heads:

- China Defence Budget 2012: Salient Features and Thrust Areas for Military Up-gradation
- India's National Security: Implications of China Defence Budget 2012
- Can India Ever Militarily Check-mate China?

CHINA DEFENCE BUDGET 2012: SALIENT FEATURES AND THRUST AREAS FOR MILITARY UP-GRADATION

Statistical data and comparative analyses of China Defence Budget abound in the international media and are not going to be repeated here. The aim in this Paper is to provide a macro-level overview the Chinese defence budget for 2012 and the issues arising from the salient features that will be examined. This part of the Paper intends to examine it under the following heads; (1) Chinese Defence Budget 2012 –salient details of increased military expenditure (2) Chinese official explanations for the increased military spending (3) Analytical explanations for China's increased military spending, and (4) Main thrust areas for Chinese military up-gradation.

Very briefly, Chinese military spending in 2012 is planned to increase by 11.2% to $106.4billion from $ 95.6 billion last year. China has on the average registered an annual increase of 12% in its defence spending. Between 2006 and 2011 China doubled its defence spending and by 2015 it will again be doubled. That indicates the colossal military expenditures that China has indulged in and what is going to be spent by China in the next three years. The strategic and political implications for the United States, China's Asian neighbours and particularly India are serious, deep-rooted and long-range.

China's official explanations are the traditional choreographed ones of defending national sovereignty, internal security and the requirement of protecting China's long borders with fourteen countries and China's long coastline. However, some official explanations forthcoming need to be quoted verbatim, and these are as follows:

- Chinese Prime Minister Wen Jiao Bao: *"We will enhance the armed forces capacity to accomplish a wide range of tasks, the most important of which is to win local wars under information age conditions".*
- China NPC Official spokesperson and Former Foreign Minister Xao Zhing: *"China's limited military power is for the sake of national sovereignty, security and territorial integrity. Fundamentally, it constitutes no threat to other countries".*
- Professor Su Hao, Chinese Foreign Ministry University, Beijing: *"There are new issues (that need*

funding) like the protection of citizens and investments overseas"

The stress on winning local wars needs to be noted as this is reference to China's peripheries where territorial disputes abound and which notably includes India. The 'new issues' are significant as it is a pointer to China's expansion of force-projection capabilities without which protection of Chinese citizens and Chinese investments abroad cannot be undertaken. Is China signalling its future intentions of military interventions being undertaken much beyond China's peripheries?

Analytically, one can advance a number of explanations for China's increased military expenditures, the chief of which being are: (1) China's present increase in military expenditure and doubling of that figure by 2015 is predictable in light of the United States strategic pivot to Asia Pacific which China perceives as US fencing-in of China (2) Chinese increased defence expenditures are aimed at upgrading of China's military capabilities to deter any possible US military intervention against China or making it prohibitive (3) China's quest for equal strategic weight with the United States would involve China's military up-gradation to reduce the differential in the US-China military power.

China's main thrusts in military up-gradation of its capabilities is obviously US-Centric in that China is aiming to dilute US military superiorities which can come in play militarily against China. However, Chinese enhancement in relation to the United States has more than disproportionate strategic impact on India. Contextually, in light of the preceding analysis China's main thrust areas for sizeable military investments will be concentrated on the following:

- Second Artillery Corps which is entrusted with the management and operational use of China's nuclear weapons arsenal and ballistic missiles arsenal. New generation of ICBMs and other missiles with greater emphasis on range and increased accuracy are in the pipeline.

- China Navy: China's first aircraft carrier will be operational by the end of this year. China is planning to induct at least four aircraft carriers in the next few years. In terms of force projection, China is inducting amphibious warfare ships and logistics tenders. In terms of Chinese "anti-access and area denial" strategies against any United States possible military intervention, the Chinese Navy is planning introduction of land-based long range anti-ship missiles against US aircraft carriers, greater number of nuclear attack submarines, increased maritime reconnaissance and patrolling, and an overall increase in number of naval combat ships.
- China Air Force: China has planned a complete turn-over of its fighter aircraft fleet. Introduction of the J-20 Stealth Fighter planes is being speeded up. China has also expressed interest in the acquisition of the Russian SU-35 latest combat aircraft which competed for the Indian Air Force competition also. Up gradation of the bomber fleet and heavy lift strategic transport aircraft akin to the US C-17.-are in the pipeline to augment Chinese force-projection capabilities.

China is investing significantly in space warfare capabilities. China is working on anti-satellite weapons designed to neutralize US spy, targeting, navigation and communication satellites. China's cyber warfare increasing capabilities have become a strategic headache for the United States military.

Not to be forgotten in terms of China's military up-gradation is an increase of Chinese nuclear weapons arsenal. So far Chinese nuclear weapons arsenal has not been subjected to any strategic arms limitation treaty or any other scrutiny. The United States while raising hype on Chinese military up-gradations has steadfastly been muted on the subject of the increasing nuclear weapons stockpile of China.

Also to be noted is that China's arms imports have shown a decrease indicating an increase in greater sophistication of its own R&D technological expertise and expanding defence production capabilities.

INDIA'S NATIONAL SECURITY: IMPLICATIONS OF CHINA DEFENCE BUDGET 2012 ANALYSED

India's national security has consistently stood compromised by the persistent annual double digit increases in Chinese defence expenditure, and China Defence Budget 2012 is no exception. China crossing the $ 100 billion mark in defence expenditure in military plans for 2012 further accentuates and highlights India's military unpreparedness to meet any possible Chinese military adventurism against India. In military budget comparisons itself, the Indian defence budget at about $36 billion pales into insignificance against China's earmarked figure of $ 106.4 billion for 2012. The comparison gets more sombre when in comparison China faces no credible military threat from any global power or Asian power whereas India has pronounced military threats from an ever-military rising China and its strategic ally Pakistan, with comparable long and sea frontiers to protect against them—both of them having a record of military adventurism and an expanding nuclear weapons arsenal.

Dispelling notions that one is advocating an arms race with China, it however needs to be noted and commonly understood within India and by Indians is that India's defence postures against China are grossly inadequate both in terms of conventional military power and nuclear weapons and ballistic missiles. Suffice it to say that India today lacks both nuclear deterrence and conventional military deterrence against China. There is no such thing as minimum credible deterrence. Credible deterrence is relative to the adversaries strike capabilities to be effective.

In this Paper, I have no intention to draw a detailed comparative military balance between a military powerful China and an India where military up-gradations and effective war preparedness are at best given notional attention by the political leadership and apex national security establishment at best, and at worst a strategic obliviousness by both these entities arising from their strategic naivety in benign reading of Chinas military intentions underlying its recurrent and relentless military build-up. The aim is to educate the India that exists outside the sphere of India's apex national security decision-makers and the Indian Armed Forces hierarchy which gets disconnected from its political masters by Nehru's archaic interposing of a strategic culture-deficit civilian bureaucracy of India's Ministry of Defence.

India in relation to war preparedness to effectively meet 'The China Threat' can be said to be in the same repeat Nehruvian strategic mind-set of de-emphasis and underplaying of 'The China Threat' as that existed in the run-up to India's 1962 military debacle foisted on the gallant Indian Army by its political leadership and its civilian bureaucracy. This assertion can be substantiated by Indian TV channels, particularly which stands reported having been pressurised to downplay Chinese intrusions into Indian Territory and not give them prominence.

The Chinese Prime Minister has reiterated this month and is quoted above, that China's strategic aim is to win local wars under information age conditions and that is significant in relation to India for obvious reasons. Recently a high-powered committee in its report has been quoted in the media as having expressed that China is likely to make a military grab for portions of Ladakh and Arunachal Pradesh. This belated recognition of 'The China Threat' against India provides the setting for the succeeding brief examination of our 'Defensive Postures" against China across the entire military spectrum. It is intended to do so under the following heads (1) India's Nuclear weapons and missiles arsenal (2) Military postures in Ladakh and Arunachal Pradesh reviewed (3) Indian Air Force-the major voids (4) Indian Navy-Need for wholesale expansion (5) Strategic infrastructure along Himalayan Borders sadly neglected.

India's nuclear deterrence against China is woefully inadequate both in terms of numbers and reach. International reports indicate that even Pakistan is outstripping India in this sphere. China accorded delayed grudging strategic respect to India only after the 1998 nuclear weaponization of India. The crying need is to make India's ICBM operational which so far has been held back by India's strategic timidity against US pressures. That materialization would greatly offset India's current lack of dissuasive conventional military deterrence.

Military postures in Ladakh and Arunachal Pradesh have been analysed in fair detail in my earlier Papers. Briefly to be highlighted is that both the Ladakh and Arunachal Pradesh Sectors require force accretions in addition to those planned by an additional mountain division each and integral limited offensive capability. Protecting India's national sovereignty involves boots-on-the-ground along the Himalayan borders which cannot be replicated by high technology. To that extent the argument of those who advocate a 'leaner meaner military machine' does not hold ground.

India's skies stand naked against Indian military adversaries today with voids of nearly 150 combat fighter aircraft. It took the Indian decision-makers ten years to clear the choice of the next MRCA and even now the agreement is on hold due to Finance Ministry's budget-deficit balancing. India's transport aircraft fleet has out-lived its normal operational life and no replacements are in view. The switch to US inventories would carry its own problems. The Indian Air Force both in wartime and in peacetime too needs to be maintained at optimum levels in terms of its authorised aircraft holdings. Case exists for increasing the Indian Air Force combat squadrons to 45 squadrons—a figure that was recommended immediately in the wake of 1962 military debacle.

China has made no secret of its naval ambitions on a strong Chinese naval presence in the Indian Ocean and is working in a focused manner towards that ambition. China's acquisition of four to six aircraft carriers, nuclear attack submarines and amphibious warfare capabilities, makes a strategic call on Indian decision-makers to embark on a wholesale fast-track expansion of the Indian Navy assets.

India cannot afford to await 10-12 years lead times for materialization of naval orders to Indian shipyards. The biggest worry is the slippage allowed in replacement of the current fleet of submarines.

India's' strategic infrastructure along the Himalayan borders is sadly neglected The Prime Minister should have made a personal push in this direction as critical lifelines are 3-5 years behind schedule due to inter-ministerial wrangling. After the 1962 War with China some notable projects which needed speedy implementation were a double road artery to Tawang and Bumla in Arunachal Pradesh, a road tunnel under the Rohtang Pass for the alternative road to Ladakh, widening of the Rangli road axis to Jelep La in Sikkim and a major bypass of Gangtok with a highway to Nathu La. Space does not permit greater elaboration. Lastly India's decision making elite should answer as to why the Indian aeronautical industry which goes back to around 1943 has not been encouraged to become capable of fast-track development of Indian Air Force requirements of fighter aircraft and transport aircraft within the country.

Can India Ever Militarily Checkmate China?

Strategic analysis would suggest that it should be a pressing strategic imperative for Indian decision-makers to work towards a military checkmating of China to neutralise 'The China Threat' and in turn the Pakistan threat assiduously nurtured militarily by China. But the follow-up question is whether India can ever hope to militarily checkmate China and improve India's security environment? Going by current trends of the Indian political leadership and the apex national security establishment of investing more on diplomacy than military preparedness to ward off 'The China Threat', the analytical answer is a big NO.

Checkmating China by India involves two major questions. Firstly, the political will and strategic audacity of India's leadership to adopt a 'hands-on' approach to checkmate China, not as a strategic subsidiary of the United States but standing tall on its own two legs. Secondly, does India have adequate financial resources to bankroll increased defence expenditure to acquire substantial nuclear and conventional military deterrence to checkmate China from its current strategy in South Asia?

The answer to the first question is that it is unlikely that the existing mind-sets of India's political leadership and apex national security establishment would undergo a change. Both these entities are likely to concentrate all strategic decision-making with themselves bypassing institutional inputs. Also keeping the Indian Armed Forces hierarchy out of apex level national security decision-making and more vitally nuclear weapons decision-making by these two entities leads to 'mentally challenged' strategic policy decisions. Political will and strategic audacity therefore cannot blossom in such a truncated decision-making environment.

The second question pertains to financial resources to bankroll sizeable defence expenditure to acquire substantial nuclear and conventional military deterrence against China. Financial resources are no longer a problem today for India. The Indian problem on increased defence expenditure is that massive amounts of the Indian budget are earmarked for non-productive political-populist schemes like NREGA and other subsidies which lead to substantial budget deficits and to offset which the Defence Budget becomes the notable casualty in terms of being asked to surrender thousands of crores of rupees every year before the presentation of the Budget. The existing mind-set of underwriting wasteful expenditures on political-populist measures at the cost of Indian national security requires a complete transformation of policy approaches.

So the final answer is that India will never be able to militarily checkmate China's enhanced military postures impinging on Indian security. If India's political leadership under different political dispensations had been imbued with the will of checkmating China, they would not have allowed India's slippage in its defensive postures and war preparedness, and kept pace with China's constant military expenditure increases, not in an arms race, but in a sincere effort to not to allow the strategic and military chasm between China and India in terms of nuclear and conventional military deterrence differentials to grow.

Concluding Observations

China's defence budgets every year have registered double-digit increases over the last two decades. This has facilitated China to emerge as the dominant military power in Asia and a contender capable of a serious challenge to United States global military predominance. China has achieved this posture by spending significant amounts on military expenditure facilitated by a booming economy. India in contrast also has a booming economy but it has been niggardly in its defence expenditures as defence expenditure is made subservient to political-populist schemes. Capital acquisition of critical military hardware are delayed for decades due to political indecision, bureaucratic lethargy and other considerations which view capital acquisitions of critical military equipment from abroad with extraneous perspectives.

Resulting from the above is the stark strategic reality that India will not be able to militarily checkmate China. In 1962, China militarily humiliated India due to lack of Indian defence preparedness in the preceding two decades. In 2012, with existing mind-sets at the highest-level in India and the slippage that has taken place in defence outlays in the last two decades, India risks a similar repeat 1962 performance of not a military debacle (thanks to the Indian Armed Forces used to making-do with military hardware available with them to defend India) but of a "strategic diminishment" of India on the global stage which India aspires to ascend.

THE DRAGON'S NEW TEETH

That China is rapidly modernising its armed forces is not in doubt, though there is disagreement about what the true spending figure is. China's defence budget has almost certainly experienced double digit growth for two decades. According to SIPRI, a research institute, annual defence spending rose from over $30 billion in 2000 to almost $120 billion in 2010. SIPRI usually adds about 50% to the official figure that China gives for its defence spending, because even basic military items such as research and development are kept off budget. Including those items would imply total military spending in 2012, based on the latest announcement from Beijing, will be around $160 billion. America still spends four-and-a-half times as much on defence, but on present trends China's defence spending could overtake America's after 2035.

All that money is changing what the People's Liberation Army (PLA) can do. Twenty years ago, China's military might lay primarily in the enormous numbers of people under arms; their main task was to fight an enemy face-to-face or occupy territory. The PLA is still the largest army in the world, with an active force of 2.3m. But China's real military strength increasingly lies elsewhere. The Pentagon's planners think China is intent on acquiring what is called in the jargon A2/AD, or "anti-access/area denial" capabilities. The idea is to use pinpoint ground attack and anti-ship missiles, a growing fleet of modern submarines and cyber and anti-satellite weapons to destroy or disable another nation's military assets from afar.

In the western Pacific, that would mean targeting or putting in jeopardy America's aircraft-carrier groups and its air-force bases in Okinawa, South Korea and even Guam. The aim would be to render American power projection in Asia riskier and more costly, so that America's allies would no longer be able to rely on it to deter aggression or to combat subtler forms of coercion. It would also enable China to carry out its repeated threat to take over Taiwan if the island were ever to declare formal independence.

China's military build-up is ringing alarm bells in Asia and has already caused a pivot in America's defence policy. The new "strategic guidance" issued in January by Barack Obama and his defence secretary, Leon Panetta, confirmed what everyone in Washington already knew: that a switch in priorities towards Asia was overdue and under way. The document says that "While the US military will continue to contribute to security globally, we will of necessity rebalance towards the Asia-Pacific region." America is planning roughly $500 billion of cuts in planned defence spending over the next ten years. But, says the document, "to credibly deter potential adversaries and to prevent them from achieving their objectives, the United States must maintain its ability to project power in areas in which our access and freedom to operate are challenged."

It is pretty obvious what that means. Distracted by campaigns in Iraq and Afghanistan, America has neglected the most economically dynamic region of the world. In particular, it has responded inadequately to China's growing military power and political assertiveness. According to senior American diplomats, China has the ambition—and increasingly the power—to become a regional hegemon; it is engaged in a determined effort to lock America out of a region that has been declared a vital security interest by every administration since Teddy Roosevelt's; and it is pulling countries in South-East Asia into its orbit of influence "by default". America has to respond. As an early sign of that response, Mr Obama announced in November 2011 that 2,500 US Marines would soon be stationed in Australia. Talks about an increased American military presence in the Philippines began in February this year.

The uncertainty principle

China worries the rest of the world not only because of the scale of its military build-up, but also because of the lack of information about how it might use its new forces and even who is really in charge of them. The American strategic-guidance document spells out the concern. "The growth of China's military power", it says, "must be accompanied by greater clarity of its strategic intentions in order to avoid causing friction in the region."

Officially, China is committed to what it called, in the words of an old slogan, a "peaceful rise". Its foreign-policy experts stress their commitment to a rules-based multipolar world. They shake their heads in disbelief at suggestions that China sees itself as a "near peer" military competitor with America.

In the South and East China Seas, though, things look different. In the past 18 months, there have been clashes between Chinese vessels and ships from Japan, Vietnam, South Korea and the Philippines over territorial rights in the resource-rich waters. A pugnacious editorial in the state-run *Global Times* last October gave warning: "If these countries don't want to change their ways with China, they will need to prepare for the sounds of cannons. We need to be ready for that, as it may be the only way for the disputes in the sea to be resolved." This was not a government pronouncement, but it seems the censors permit plenty of press freedom when it comes to blowing off nationalistic steam.

Smooth-talking foreign-ministry officials may cringe with embarrassment at *Global Times*—China's equivalent of Fox News—but its views are not so far removed from the gung-ho leadership of the rapidly expanding navy. Moreover, in a statement of doctrine published in 2005, the PLA's*Science of Military Strategy* did not mince its words. Although "active defence is the essential feature of China's military strategy," it said, if "an enemy offends our national interests it means that the enemy has already fired the first shot," in which case the PLA's mission is "to do all we can to dominate the enemy by striking first".

Making things more alarming is a lack of transparency over who really controls the guns and ships. China is unique among great powers in that the PLA is not formally part of the state. It is responsible to the Communist Party, and is run by the party's Central Military Commission, not the ministry of defence. Although party and government are obviously very close in China, the party is even more opaque, which complicates outsiders' understanding of where the PLA's loyalties and priorities lie. A better military-to-military relationship between America and China would cast some light into this dark corner. But the PLA often suspends "mil-mil" relations as a "punishment" whenever tension rises with America over Taiwan. The PLA is also paranoid about what America might gain if the relationship between the two countries' armed forces went deeper.

The upshot of these various uncertainties is that even if outsiders believe that China's intentions are largely benign—and it is clear that some of them do not—they can hardly make plans based on that assumption alone. As the influential American think-tank, the Centre for Strategic and Budgetary Assessments (CSBA) points out, the intentions of an authoritarian regime can change very quickly. The nature and size of the capabilities that China has built up also count.

History boys

The build-up has gone in fits and starts. It began in the early 1950s when the Soviet Union was China's most important ally and arms supplier, but abruptly ceased when Mao Zedong launched his decade-long Cultural Revolution in the mid-1960s. The two countries came close to war over their disputed border and China carried out its first nuclear test. The second phase of modernisation began in the 1980s, under Deng Xiaoping. Deng was seeking to reform the whole country and the army was no exception. But he told the PLA that his priority was the economy; the generals must be patient and live within a budget of less than 1.5% of GDP.

A third phase began in the early 1990s. Shaken by the destructive impact of the West's high-tech weaponry on the Iraqi army, the PLA realised that its huge ground forces were militarily obsolete. PLA scholars at the Academy of Military Science in Beijing began learning all they could from American think-tanks about the so-called "revolution in military affairs" (RMA), a change in strategy and weaponry made possible by exponentially greater computer-processing power. In a meeting with *The Economist* at the Academy, General Chen Zhou, the main author of the four most recent defence white papers, said: "We studied RMA exhaustively. Our great hero was Andy Marshall in the Pentagon [the powerful head of the

Office of Net Assessment who was known as the Pentagon's futurist-in-chief]. We translated every word he wrote."

CHINA'S SOLDIERS COME IN FROM THE COLD

In 1993 the general-secretary of the Communist Party, Jiang Zemin, put RMA at the heart of China's military strategy. Now, the PLA had to turn itself into a force capable of winning what the strategy called "local wars under high-tech conditions". Campaigns would be short, decisive and limited in geographic scope and political goals. The big investments would henceforth go to the air force, the navy and the Second Artillery Force, which operates China's nuclear and conventionally armed missiles.

Further shifts came in 2002 and 2004. High-tech weapons on their own were not enough; what mattered was the ability to knit everything together on the battlefield through what the Chinese called "informatisation" and what is known in the West as "unified C4ISR". (The four Cs are command, control, communications, and computers; ISR stands for intelligence, surveillance and reconnaissance; the Pentagon loves its abbreviations).

Just another corner of the network

General Chen describes the period up to 2010 as "laying the foundations of modernised forces". The next decade should see the roll-out of what is called mechanisation (the deployment of advanced military platforms) and informatisation (bringing them together as a network). The two processes should be completed in terms of equipment, integration and training by 2020. But General Chen reckons China will not achieve full informatisation until well after that. "A major difficulty", he says, "is that we are still only partially mechanised. We do not always know how to make our investments when technology is both overlapping and leapfrogging." Whereas the West was able to accomplish its military transformation by taking the two processes in sequence, China is trying to do both together. Still, that has not slowed down big investments which are designed to defeat even technologically advanced foes by making "the best use of our strong points to attack the enemy's weak points". In 2010 the CSBA identified the essential military components that China, on current trends, will be able to deploy within ten years. Among them: satellites and reconnaissance drones; thousands of surface-to-surface and anti-ship missiles; more than 60 stealthy conventional submarines and at least six nuclear attack submarines; stealthy manned and unmanned combat aircraft; and space and cyber warfare capabilities. In addition, the navy has to decide whether to make the (extremely expensive) transition to a force dominated by aircraft-carriers, like America. Aircraft-carriers would be an unmistakable declaration of an ambition eventually to project power far from home. Deploying them would also match the expected actions of Japan and India in the near future. China may well have three small carriers within five to ten years, though military analysts think it would take much longer for the Chinese to learn how to use them well.

A new gunboat diplomacy

This promises to be a formidable array of assets. They are, for the most part, "asymmetric", that is, designed not to match American military power in the western Pacific directly but rather to exploit its vulnerabilities. So, how might they be used? Taiwan is the main spur for China's military modernisation. In 1996 America reacted to Chinese ballistic-missile tests carried out near Taiwanese ports by sending two aircraft-carrier groups into the Taiwan Strait. Since 2002 China's strategy has been largely built around the possibility of a cross-Strait armed conflict in which China's forces would not only have to overcome opposition from Taiwan but also to deter, delay or defeat an American attempt to intervene. According to recent reports by CSBA and RAND, another American think-tank, China is well on its way to having the means, by 2020, to deter American aircraft-carriers and aircraft from operating within what is known as the "first island chain"—a perimeter running from the Aleutians in the north to Taiwan, the Philippines and Borneo.

In 2005 China passed the Taiwan Anti-Secession Law, which commits it to a military response should Taiwan ever declare independence or even if the government in Beijing thinks all possibility of peaceful unification has been lost. Jia Xiudong of the China Institute of International Studies (the foreign ministry's main think-tank) says: "The first priority is Taiwan. The mainland is patient, but independence is not the future for Taiwan. China's military forces should be ready to repel any force of intervention. The US likes to maintain what it calls 'strategic ambiguity' over what it would do in the event of a conflict arising from secession. We don't have any ambiguity. We will use whatever means we have to prevent it happening."

If Taiwan policy has been the immediate focus of China's military planning, the sheer breadth of capabilities the country is acquiring gives it other options—and temptations. In 2004 Hu Jintao, China's president, said the PLA should be able to undertake "new historic missions". Some of these involve UN peacekeeping. In recent years China has been the biggest contributor of peacekeeping troops among the permanent five members of the Security Council. But the responsibility for most of these new missions has fallen on the navy. In addition to its primary job of denying China's enemies access to sea lanes, it is increasingly being asked to project power in the neighbourhood and farther afield.

The navy appears to see itself as the guardian of China's ever-expanding economic interests. These range from supporting the country's sovereignty claims (for example, its insistence on seeing most of the South China Sea as an exclusive economic zone) to protecting the huge weight of Chinese shipping, preserving the country's access to energy and raw materials supplies, and safeguarding the soaring numbers of Chinese citizens who work abroad (about 5m today, but expected to rise to 100m by 2020). The navy's growing fleet of powerful destroyers, stealthy frigates and guided-missile-carrying catamarans enables it to carry out extended "green water" operations (ie, regional, not just coastal tasks). It is also developing longer-range "blue water" capabilities. In early 2009 the navy began anti-piracy patrols off the Gulf of Aden with three ships. Last year, one of those vessels was sent to the Mediterranean to assist in evacuating 35,000 Chinese workers from Libya—an impressive logistical exercise carried out with the Chinese air force.

Power grows out of the barrel of a gun

It is hardly surprising that China's neighbours and the West in general should worry about these developments. The range of forces marshalled against Taiwan plus China's "A2/AD" potential to push the forces of other countries over the horizon have already eroded the confidence of America's Asian allies that the guarantor of their security will always be there for them. Mr Obama's rebalancing towards Asia may go some way towards easing those doubts. America's allies are also going to have to do more for themselves, including developing their own A2/AD capabilities. But the longer-term trends in defence spending are in China's favour. China can focus entirely on Asia, whereas America will continue to have global responsibilities. Asian concerns about the dragon will not disappear.

That said, the threat from China should not be exaggerated. There are three limiting factors. First, unlike the former Soviet Union, China has a vital national interest in the stability of the global economic system. Its military leaders constantly stress that the development of what is still only a middle-income country with a lot of very poor people takes precedence over military ambition. The increase in military spending reflects the growth of the economy, rather than an expanding share of national income. For many years China has spent the same proportion of GDP on defence (a bit over 2%, whereas America spends about 4.7%). The real test of China's willingness to keep military spending constant will come when China's headlong economic growth starts to slow further. But on past form, China's leaders will continue to worry more about internal threats to their control than external ones. Last year spending on internal security outstripped military spending for the first time. With a rapidly ageing population, it is also a good bet that meeting the demand for better health care will become a higher priority than maintaining military spending. Like all the other great powers, China faces a choice of guns or walking sticks.

Second, as some pragmatic American policymakers concede, it is not a matter for surprise or shock that a country of China's importance and history should have a sense of its place in the world and want armed forces which reflect that. Indeed, the West is occasionally contradictory about Chinese power, both fretting about it and asking China to accept greater responsibility for global order. As General Yao Yunzhu of the Academy of Military Science says: "We are criticised if we do more and criticised if we do less. The West should decide what it wants. The international military order is US-led—NATO and Asian bilateral alliances—there is nothing like the WTO for China to get into."

Third, the PLA may not be quite as formidable as it seems on paper. China's military technology has suffered from the Western arms embargo imposed after the Tiananmen Square protests of 1989. It struggles to produce high-performance jet engines, for example. Western defence firms believe that is why they are often on the receiving end of cyber-attacks that appear to come from China. China's defence industry may be improving but it remains scattered, inefficient and over-dependent on high-tech imports from Russia, which is happy to sell the same stuff to China's local rivals, India and Vietnam. The PLA also has little recent combat experience. The last time it fought a real enemy was in the war against Vietnam in 1979, when it got a bloody nose. In contrast, a decade of conflict has honed American forces to a new pitch of professionalism. There must be some doubt that the PLA could put into practice the complex joint operations it is being increasingly called upon to perform.

General Yao says the gap between American and Chinese forces is "at least 30, maybe 50, years". "China", she says, "has no need to be a military peer of the US. But perhaps by the time we do become a peer competitor the leadership of both countries will have the wisdom to deal with the problem." The global security of the next few decades will depend on her hope being realised.

MILITARY BUDGET OF THE PEOPLE'S REPUBLIC OF CHINA

The military budget of the People's Republic of China (PRC) is the portion of the overall budget of China that is allocated for the funding of themilitary of the People's Republic of China. This military budget finances employee salaries and training costs, the maintenance of equipment and facilities, support of new or ongoing operations, and development and procurement of new weapons, equipment, and vehicles. Every March, as part of its annual state budget, China releases a single overall figure for national military expenditures. The Chinese government's published 2012 military budget is about US$106.4 billion, the second largest in the world and up about 11.2 % from 2011.

Unofficial estimates

Unofficial estimates place the total amount of military spending for the People's Republic of China higher than the Chinese government figures, but these calculations tend to differ between organizations. The last year that many international institutes provided estimates of Chinese military spending in comparable terms was 2003. In terms of the prevailing exchange rate, SIPRI,RAND, the CIA and the DIA estimated the budget to be between US$30–65 billion. In terms of purchasing power parity, or the relative purchasing strength of the expenditure, the SIPRI estimate was as high as US$140 billion. The Chinese government's published budget at that time was less than US$25 billion.

A RAND Corporation study for year 2003 estimated the People's Republic of China's defense spending to be higher than the official number but lower than United States Department of Defense calculations. The defense spending of the People's Republic of China was estimated, in the mid-range estimate, to be 38 billion dollars or 2.3% of China's GDP in 2003. The official figure was 22.4 billion dollars.

Nevertheless, Chinese military spending doubled between 1997 and 2003, nearly reaching the level of the United Kingdom and Japan, and it continued to grow over 10% annually during 2003-2005.

In 2010, the US Department of Defense's annual report to Congress on China's military strength estimated the actual 2009 Chinese military spending at US$150 billion. Stockholm International Peace Research Institute (SIPRI) estimates that the military spending of the People's Republic of China for 2009 was US$100 billion, higher than the official budget, but lower than the US DoD estimate. The International Institute for Strategic Studies in a 2011 report argued that if spending trends continue China will achieve military equality with the United States in 15-20 years.

Jane's Defence Forecasts in 2012 estimated that China's defense budget would increase from $119.80 billion to $238.20 billion between 2011 and 2015. This would make it larger than the defense budgets of all other major Asian nations combined. This is still smaller than the estimated United States defense budget of $525.40 billion for 2013. However, United States defense spending is slightly declining.

CHINA'S MILITARY BUDGET 2010

China announced (March 04) a 7.5% increase in its defence budget for 2010, breaking a double digit increase in declared military expenditure for a decade. At $ 78.25 billion (Yuan 532.11 billion), it is 1.4 per cent of the country's GDP, and 6.3 percent of the national budget, Chinese spokesmen argue. For the first time in several years this figure has fallen below 10 per cent of the budget.

Li Zhaoxing, a former Foreign Minister and spokesman for the 3rd plenum of the ongoing 11th Central Committee (CC) said that in addition to improving military response to a variety of security threats, some funds can be used to improve servicemen's lives. It is a fact that in the course of improvement of people's lives in general the military must have a slice of the pie. This has been happening since 1999 when the first major rise in China's military budget was announced.

China's "millet and rifle" People's Liberation Army has a known history of sacrifice and austerity. Since 1949 Mao Zedong's People's Army has undergone many internal revolutions of forms and strategy. Following 1978 "reform and opening up" policy when China decided to follow a market oriented economic path and advocated different entities including some ministries earn their keep, the PLA went into business. Such business was not limited to foreign military trade, but was spread over a large area including farming, property, civilian products, hotels and restaurants, and even Karaoke bars and massage parlours.

The PLA was getting rich, but money brought with it the usual evils. Corruption, non-military activities and huge pay gaps between the senior level and the lower levels. This led to demoralization at the fighting level.

Premier Zhu Rongji had the unenviable task to "de-commercialize" the PLA. A challenging task, Zhu succeeded to a great extent. By 1999, he significantly defanged the PLA's commercial teeth. But they had to be compensated. During the 60th anniversary of the PRC military parade last year, the women soldiers in their stylish uniform looked like models on a Parisian ramp!

Compared to their Indian military counterparts the life styles of the PLA officers have generally been better. About ten years ago, a PLA officer who was in a delegation visiting New Delhi in summer, went back and wrote an article comparing the two armies. He said he was appalled to see Indian officers travelling to work and back at the headquarters either in non-air conditioned buses or on their own two-wheelers in the height of summer. Whereas, the Chinese officers could not conceive of travelling in a non-air conditioned vehicle. Mercedes was their preferred transport.

This does not mean that a huge proportion of the PLA budget is spent on pay and perquisites. The drop in the increase in the 2010 budget is misleading. The real spending is, and always has been, much more than the declared figure. If the military arms and equipment displayed at the 60th anniversary parade last year is anything to go by, it will be evident that the declared budget could not cover them. And, the display, mainly meant for the people of the country, may be a glimpse of what is to come. Such developments require huge Research and Development (R&D) expenditure with a long gestation period. For example, the Chinese started the most modern nuclear submarine projects, the Type 093 and the 094 (which carries nuclear missiles), sometime in the late 1980s, and formalized in early 1990s. They came to the deployment stage around 2004-2006.

Similar is the case of the aircraft carrier project. It was conceived by Admiral Liu Huaqing, then the first Vice-Chairman of the Central Military Commission (CMC). A lot of money has already been invested including on the acquisition of the decommissioned Russian air craft carrier, the "Varyag". It is being used to study the designs, especially the hull. Similar has been the case of the development of the fourth generation aircraft, the J-10 and its export model the JF-17.

The long range missile, nuclear weapons advancement, research of space warfare are areas that require huge and long term investments. For example, the DF-31 ICBM and its separate version DF-31A, have emerged as a major challenge to the USA. It is not known if the DF-41 missile, a longer range missile has been scrapped or is still on the anvil. A new version of anti-ship missile to penetrate USA's anti-missile systems like the ship mounted Aegis system is at an advanced stage. A new exo-interceptor missile was tested recently.

One very important area the Chinese are working on is space warfare. There have been signals from Beijing on again and off again. But close observers of China's space programme have no doubts that the space warfare programme holds high priority in China's defence planning. China's shooting down of a defence satellite with a ground based missile in January

2007 is well known. But the scope that the PLA is looking at is much larger.

Micro satellites and Nano-satellites will have a much larger role to play in the future other than communications. These can be used as anti-satellite (ASAT) weapons. Other things at work are space based weapons like laser weapons.

In recent years, one of China's major focus has been on asymmetric warfare. A very wide definition, its philosophy is no-contact warfare and as camouflaged as possible. This is known as the "Assassin's Mace" weapon, where the assailant is invisible or deeply embedded in the opponent's court (society as one of them. The methods of operation are many, but the common factors are stealth, depth of penetration and deniability.

China's cyber warfare capability has sharply improved, and in technological sophistication it is catching up fast with the USA and Russia. Recent cyber attacks from China have demonstrated all three characters – stealth, depth and deniability. It is fully integrated into informationalized warfare now, and needs grounds abroad for testing or real attacks. Other areas in which they are acquiring sophistication include radiation warfare, electro-magnetic pulse (EMP) weapons and laser weapons to confuse and debilitate the enemy's network in battle field conditions.

The military sectors not reflected in the PLA include the Second Artillery (nuclear weapons and missiles), space warfare, asymmetric warfare, and foreign military acquisition among others. It is, however, understandable that the budget of the PLA's Second Department, the intelligence wing, is not reflected in the budget.

In assessing the size of the budget, comparative money value and cost perspective inside China and the West also need to be taken into account. What $ 78.25 billion will get in China is far more than it will fetch in the Wnest.

Basically, the declared budget takes care of the total livelihood (except pensions) of the largest armed force in the world, including an array of conventional weapons, logistics and systems, and their infrastructure projects.

In earlier years, the estimate made by the Pentagon, the SIPRI of Sweden and other varied between $160 to $220 billion. In looking at the 2010 budget, it would not be unsafe to estimate that an increasing amount of money is going into space R&D and asymmetric warfare. It would be safe to assume that the real military budget of China in 2010 would not be less $180 billion dollars at least. One word of caution here. In most international experts' writings on China's military, the comparison is made with the USA or the USA and NATO as a whole. The Australians are lately waking up to this, and Japan has a fair idea. Both Japan and Australia would be covered by the USA in the remote case of a Chinese attack.

But what about countries like India which fought a limited border war with China in 1962? True, the Chinese realize that the new India is no longer the India of 1962. Two Chinese colonels wrote a book "The Next War with India", which was seen in 1993. Brilliant strategists, the authors saw a future war with India will not be fought only on the ground, but in all the three dimensions – ground, air and sea.

It is, however, imperative that India's military planners add three more dimensions in their strategic calculations. One, which can be noted as a half dimension, is China's plans to produce medium to long term missiles with very high yielding conventional warheads. This can cause devastating destruction and not be called a nuclear war.

The next is China's nuclear doctrine. China's nuclear doctrine is shifting from "no first use" to use against the intention or preparation to attack of a nuclear equipped power. China's strike will depend on their perception of an imminent attack. Today, India is a nuclear equipped power with the nuclear capable Agni-III missile with a range of 3,500 kms.

The third is China's naval power projection in the Indian Ocean. China already has two naval ships patrolling the

Somalian coast against piracy. China's PLA Navy has now offered the European Union naval escorts of food shipment to Somalia with added deployment. This could start within a month. Finally, China is beginning to explore naval/military bases in littoral countries of the Indian Ocean. They can, at any time, avail of the Gwadar deep Sea Port in Pakistan which they built. Of the three services, the Chinese navy has been getting the biggest slice of the military budget.

India, therefore, needs to look at China realistically, and tailor its military strategy and diplomacy accordingly in the region.

5

Defence Expenditure and Spending of India

Defence expenditure is an important component of national security and every country allocates a significant portion of its resources for this purpose. However, given the scarcity of resources and the competing demands from other sectors, a nation's ability to meet all its Defence requirements is not unlimited. Even the United States, the only military superpower, is unable to afford many of its major programmes, forcing it to scale down the number of items to be procured. The sheer size of the Defence budget and its impact on other sectors of the economy thus, more often raises the question as to how much a country can afford for its Defence.

In the absence of any clear framework of evaluating affordability of Defence spending, many analysts tend to view the same from the perspective of a country's share of Defence in gross domestic product (GDP) over a period of time, or by comparing these shares with those of other countries. This method of relative measurement, however, suffers from ambiguities as it does not take into account a country's specifc security concerns and the economic compulsions in its totality. In the global context, the affordability of military spending of some of the world's major military spenders varies not only in degree but also from time to time. While the variation in the degree of affordability indicates the changing security threats that are perceived differently by countries, the fuctuation in affordability over time points to the fact that what may be affordable at one point in time, may not be so at another time. Among the major powers, except for Japan, no other country has been able to sustain consistently high level of Defence spending (in percentage of GDP) over a length of time. The macro economy, which guides major spending heads of the government, could be a factor in controlling Defence spending over a period of time. In the US, the present level of military spending has contributed to fiscal distress, raising doubts whether such large-scale military spending is affordable or sustainable in the future.

In the light of the above, the article tries to examine affordability of India's Defence spending. However, as illustrated above, there is no established or universally accepted framework of evaluating affordability as such, and the relative method of measurement does not take into account the economic aspects. The present article tries to approach the issue by taking into account different factors, but is restricted to an economic analysis. In particular, it examines Defence spending with respect to resource gap; estimates of the various Finance Commissions; fiscal responsibility of the government; the country's national resources expressed in terms of the GDP; total resources available to the government; the priority of resource allocation; and financing of Defence expenditure.

DEFENCE EXPENDITURE AND FINANCE COMMISSION OF INDIA

The Finance Commission of India, a statutory body under the Constitution, plays an important role in providing fscal recommendations to the Government. The body is tasked, among others, to review the state of fnances of the government, assess the requirements of the various sectors of the State and provide guidelines for distributing the State's resources among the Centre and States. The recommendations of the Commission provide the basic foundation for restoring 'budgetary balance, bringing macro-economic stability and equitable growth.'

The 11th Finance Commission, after reviewing the broad requirements of the economy, acknowledged the need for steady growth in Defence Capital expenditure, and accepted the need for overall Defence budget to grow by 15 per cent per year during the Commission's forecast period (2000-01 to 2004-05). Based on the projected 'fiscal profile' of the Central Government, the Commission assumed the Defence budget to reach the level of 3 per cent of the GDP by 2004-05, to meet the increased requirements of the Capital expenditure. However, at the end of the Commission's forecast period, Defence spending increased by only 10 per cent per year, while its share in GDP was much lower than the Commission's estimate of 3 per cent. As regards the growth of Revenue expenditure, the Commission also accepted a 10 per cent growth rate per year for the period from 2000-01 to 2004-05. Against this projected growth rate, the actual growth rate of Revenue expenditure during this period was 4.6 per cent. The corresponding growth figure for the Capital expenditure during this period was 21.4 per cent.

Unlike the 11th Finance Commission, its successor, the 12th Finance Commission, allowed for a relatively moderate growth rate of 6.5 per cent per year for the Revenue expenditure for the five-year period from 2005-06 to 2009-10. In three years – from 2005-06 to 2007-08 – the annual growth rate on this account stood at 6.6 per cent, which was close to the forecast range provided by the Commission. However, unlike its predecessor, the Commission did not link the Capital expenditure directly with GDP, which grew by 14.5 per cent per year, in nominal prices, between 2005-06 and 2007-08. Compared to this, the Defence Capital expenditure during this period was increased by annual average of less than 8 per cent.

If the recommendations of the past two Finance Commissions of India are taken into consideration, Defence spending has largely remained within the Commissions' projected range and within the country's macro-economic framework. The lesser percentage growth of Defence spending, when compared to its projected figures, suggests that the

Defence expenditure has remained within the government's desired objectives of budgetary balance, economic stability and equitable growth.

DEFENCE PROJECTION AND ALLOCATION

India's defence spending in current prices has increased substantially over the years, from nearly Rs. 1200 crore in 1970-71 to Rs. 1,05,600 crore in 2008-09 (this represents a five-and-a-half fold increase in constant prices, from nearly Rs. 13,418 crore to Rs 73,360 crore). In the last one decade, it has increased by an average of nearly 10 per cent per year from Rs. 47,070.63 crore in 1999-2000. A fgure depicting India's Defence spending since 1980-81. Notwithstanding the growth in Defence spending, the Defence outlays do not necessarily match the demands of the Defence establishment. For instance, in the last five years, the unmet demand by the Services/Departments varies between some Rs. 5,880 crore and Rs. 26,150.7 crore, which is nearly 6-27 per cent of the total projected demands. The shortfall on the Revenue side ranges between 4 per cent and 13 per cent, and that on the Capital side varies from as low as 6.9 per cent to over 49 per cent.

The lesser percentage of 'shortfalls' in Revenue expenditure compared to that of Capital expenditure shows that while the former is more or less fixed, the latter is relatively flexible. At the same time, the 'shortfalls' both in absolute and percentage terms indicate that all the demands made by the Defence sector are not fully in conformity with the resources available with the government. However, over the past five years, the percentage 'shortfalls' are coming down, indicating that the government has found the wherewithal to afford and meet the increasing requirements projected by the Defence establishment over the past five years.

DEFENCE EXPENDITURE AND GROSS DOMESTIC PRODUCT

The percentage share of Defence in GDP is considered as a common measure of a country's Defence expenditure and gives a fair idea about its affordability. On the basis of this, comparison is often made to see where a country stands vis-à-vis other countries, and also to arrive at a 'norm' by looking at a particular country's own past trends. Going by this indicator, India's current Defence affordability at around 2 per cent of GDP is less than its neighbours, especially Pakistan's nearly 3.5 per cent and China's over four per cent. Regarding the affordability 'norm' from the past trends, India's Defence spending as a proportion of GDP is fluctuating and more specifically, on a declining path in the recent past. Compared to the seventies and eighties, when the percentage share of Defence in GDP averaged 2.74 per cent and 2.95 per cent respectively, in the last one decade (1999-2000 to 2008-09), the average has come down to 2.18 per cent. Moreover, if the present growth rates of GDP and Defence spending continue, in the next one decade the share of the latter in the former will remain within 2 per cent of GDP. A matrix of projected GDP-Defence spending, at different growth rates.

The declining share of Defence in GDP can be ascribed, among others, to the strong performance of Indian economy in the recent years. For instance, the Indian economy in the last 5 years (2003-04 to 2007-08) grew by an average of more than 14 per cent per year, in current prices, compared to less than 9 per cent per year during the previous five years. The strong performance of the GDP over the years means an enhancement of the country's economic ability to afford more on various sectors including Defence. However, Defence, which earlier received a larger share of the national resources, is now receiving a declining share, and is consequently more affordable, in the relative terms.

CENTRAL GOVERNMENT EXPENDITURE

Unlike GDP, which gives the value of national resources generated in an economy in a given year, government expenditure gives the total resources available to the Government for allocation among different sectors. The pattern of allocations from the government expenditures suggests the priority attached on each allocation for each sector. Though this priority is best explained when Defence spending is expressed in terms of its share in Central Government expenditure, yet the analysis can further be extended to that of 'General Government' expenditure (central and state together) to see the priority at the national level.

During the past one decade (1997-98 to 2006-07), total 'General Government' spending and total Central Government spending have increased significantly, by nearly 188 per cent and 168 per cent, respectively. On the other hand, the Defence spending has grown relatively lower at 142 per cent, suggesting that allocation for other sectors have increased at a faster pace. Over the last 5 years Defence spending as a percentage of total Central Government expenditure has been reduced from the peak of 15.9 per cent during 2005-06 to the low of 13.0 per cent during 2007-08 (RE).

The faster growth of both central government and total 'General Government' expenditure compared to Defence expenditure suggests that despite increased level of Defence spending, the government has been able to spend more on the non-Defence sectors. In relative terms and from the point of view of resource allocation, the decreasing share of Defence shows that the allocation for it is easily provided (affordable) over the years.

FISCAL RESPONSIBILITY AND DEFENCE EXPENDITURE

The 'persistent fscal problems' of the country led the Government to pass the Fiscal Responsibility and Budget Management (FRBM) Act, 2003. The Act required eliminating the revenue deficit and bringing it below 3 per cent of GDP by 2008-09. A Task Force, which was constituted to ensure this fscal responsibility of the government, recommended a number of policy proposals pertaining to reforms in tax, and government expenditure. The 'fscal projections under the reforms scenario', as estimated by the expert group, was expected to accelerate the GDP growth to 13.0 per cent per year, in nominal prices, by 2008-09. The higher growth of the economy along with the proposals under 'reforms scenario' was also expected to take Defence expenditure to a higher level and 'stabilise' it at 2.3 per cent of the GDP from 2006-

07 to 2008-09. However, during this period, the growth of the economy though marginally outpaced the estimates of the Task Force, yet the percentage share of Defence in GDP fell short of 2.3 per cent of the GDP. If Defence were allowed to receive 2.3 per cent of the GDP, as projected by the Task Force, then between 2006-07 and 2008-09, it would have received nearly Rs. 95,000 crore, Rs. 1,08,000 crore, and Rs. 1,21,000 respectively. The Defence budgets for these three years are Rs. 89,000 crore, Rs. 96,000 crore, and Rs. 1,05,600 crores, respectively.

The higher growth of GDP and the reduced share of Defence in it means some of the funds meant for Defence are, in fact, transferred to other sectors (especially towards interest payments and subsidies) so as to keep the FRBM targets under control. From the Defence point of view, the increased allocations that were expected to accrue to it due to the proposed reforms, have not fully materialised while its own spending remaining well within the estimated range of the country's fscal responsibilities, as outlined by the Task Force.

GOVERNMENT EXPENDITURE AND DEFENCE EXPENDITURE

The major heads of government expenditure can broadly be classified into Developmental expenditure and non-Developmental expenditure. During the 10-year period since 1997-98, the annual average growth of Developmental expenditure of both the 'General Government' and Central Government has been more than on the non-Developmental heads. Among the 10 largest heads of the general Government expenditure, Defence has recorded the lowest annual growth rate after Administrative Services. For the same major heads of the Central Government expenditure, Defence, though, has exceeded the overall growth of non-Developmental expenditure, yet compared to the major heads under Developmental expenditure, it has recorded the lowest growth rate after that of Power, and Irrigation & Flood Control.

The relatively faster growth of major heads of Developmental expenditure compared to that of Defence expenditure during the past decade shows that the growth of the latter has not hindered the government's priority in terms of higher percentage allocation on major developmental goals. In other words, Defence, from the resource allocation point of view, has remained within the affordable limit, in the sense that it has not hampered the growth prospects of the economy.

ECONOMIC PARAMETERS EXAMINED

All the economic parameters examined in the article show that the allocations for Defence over the years have remained affordable, though, in some cases, in a relative sense. From the point of view of Defence requirements, the decreasing percentage shortfalls (between Defence projections and allocations to Defence) over the past five years indicate that the Government could increasingly afford the requirements projected by the Defence establishment. As far as the objectives of budgetary balance and fscal stability are concerned, the Defence expenditure has largely remained within acceptable limits set by various Finance Commissions and the Task Force on FRBM and therefore, could not be blamed for the budgetary or fscal imbalances, if any, in the economy. While the robust growth of the GDP and the consequent rise of Government revenues have significantly enhanced the country's spending ability, the decreasing share of Defence in these resources indicates that the burden of Defence has reduced significantly. In terms of resource allocation and its priorities, the growth of Defence spending has not caused retardation in growth of spending in other sectors of the economy, especially in the developmental sectors.

FINANCING DEFENCE EXPENDITURE AND GOVERNMENT EXPENDITURE

Financing of government expenditure, including Defence expenditure, constitutes an important aspect of public finance, considering the role of various sources of government earnings and their impact on the economy. Over the last 10 years (1997-98 to 2006-07), the government's total revenue earning has increased by nearly 216 per cent and, as a result, its share in the total government expenditure has increased from 68 per cent to nearly 75 per cent. The increase in revenue earning, which is mainly on account of increases in both tax and non-tax revenue, has helped the government in reducing the fscal deficit and lessen the debt burden on the economy. While the tax and non-tax revenue have increased by 228 per cent and 172 per cent, the debt burden and fscal deficits, measured by their percentage share in GDP, have decreased from 24 per cent to 16 per cent and from 4.81 per cent to 3.61 per cent, respectively. From the Defence point of view, the increase in the revenue earnings has lessened its percentage dependence on the latter, from 13.81 per cent to nearly 11 per cent. Besides, the surge in revenue earnings, which has reduced government's dependence on the debt financing, has also reduced the share of the Defence debt on India's "external outstanding debt". In other words, in last 10 years, the financing of the Defence spending has become relatively easier on account of the government's increasing earnings.

MEASURING MILITARY EXPENDITURE

The SIPRI military expenditure project was initiated in 1967 to study developments in worldmilitary expenditure. The current SIPRI database on military expenditure covers 172 countries and contains consistent data for the period since 1988. Data for the most recent 10-year period are published annually in the SIPRI Yearbook. Data from 1988 is available in the SIPRI military expenditure database online. SIPRI provides the only long-term, historically consistent series of military expenditure data with global coverage available today.

Defining military expenditure

There is no generally agreed definition of military expenditure worldwide. SIPRI seeks to include in its definition of military expenditure all costs incurred as a result of current military activities. The guideline definition used by SIPRI includes expenditure on the following actors and activities: (a) the armed forces, including peacekeeping forces; (b) defence ministries and other government agencies engaged in defence projects; (c) paramilitary forces, when judged to be trained and equipped for military operations; and (d) military space activities. It includes all current and capital expenditure on: (a) military and civil personnel, including retirement pensions of military personnel and social services for personnel; (b) operations and maintenance; (c) procurement; (d) military research and development; and (e) military aid (in the military expenditure of the donor country). It does not include civil defence and current expenditure for pastmilitary activities, such as for veterans' benefits, demobilization, conversion and weapon destruction.

Other organizations and countries employ varying definitions of military expenditure. Media reports on military expenditure, including in specialist publications, tend to report simply the defence budget of the country in question, although many countries have significant military expenditure in other budget lines. (Sometimes, a defence budget may also include items not included in the SIPRI definition, such as demobilization costs). The International Monetary Fund's *Government Financial Statistics Yearbook (GFSY)* collects expenditure data according to a functional classification; functional classifications typically place military pensions within the social security function, military healthcare within the health function, etc. Many countries likewise report military expenditure according to a functional definition. The NATO definition of military expenditure is similar to the SIPRI definition; however since 2004 NATO has changed its definition so as to exclude expenditure on paramilitary forces (even those with a national defence function in times of war) if they are not "realistically deployable". Meanwhile a number of governments, of which the UK was the first, have moved to a system of 'Resource Account Budgeting' across all areas of government, which involves accounting for expenditure on an accrual rather than a cash basis—whereby costs are accounted for when they are incurred rather than when they are paid—and including items such as a charge for capital employed (based on an assumed return that could be obtained were the capital otherwise employed). This is not included in the SIPRI definition. (The UK does however provide an alternative cash-based measure close to the SIPRI definition.)

Why measure military expenditure?

Military expenditure information is used by a wide variety of users, including governments, diplomats, academic researchers and students, non-governmental organizations, international organizations such as the World Bank and IMF, journalists, and interested members of the general public. Military expenditure data are for a variety of purposes, including;

- To assess the economic burden of a country's military forces on their economy.
- To assess a governments priorities, possibly by comparing spending on the military with spending on other sectors such as health and education, and changes in their relative levels over time.
- To assess a country's orientation as relatively peaceful or 'militaristic' (although one should be cautious in such an assessment, as this also depends on a country's security situation), or as a measure of how they view the various security threats and challenges they may face. Rapid increases in military expenditure over a short period of time may for example be a warning sign of possible internal or external conflict, although the connection is far from direct.
- To give a rough indication of the relative level of military capability or power of different countries – such a use is rather problematic, as there is no direct relationship between military expenditure – an input measure – and military capability or power, which are output measures.
- To conduct statistical research relating military expenditure across countries and/or over time to other economic, political and security variables. Such research may include:
  1. The impact of military expenditure on economic growth and development, or on other economic variables such as international debt or corruption.

2. The existence or otherwise of 'trade-offs' between spending on the military and other areas such as health and education.
3. The determinants of military expenditure, such as a country's economic wealth, armed conflict, political systems, and the military expenditure of neighbours and rivals.
4. The effect of military expenditure (along with other variables) on the risk of armed conflict.

SIPRI regards military expenditure as a measure of the economic resources devoted to the military. SIPRI presents military expenditure data for each country in three forms: first, in current-price, local currency terms, as this represents the primary raw data from which all others are calculated. Secondly, in constant price dollar terms. Constant prices allow meaningful comparisons of the resources consumed by the military over time, allowing for inflation, while conversion to a common currency allows some measure of cross-country comparison, although this is problematic as the market exchange rates used for conversion may not accurately represent the purchasing power of a currency, while alternative purchasing power parity rates are also subject to numerous difficulties. Conversion to a common currency also allows military expenditure to be aggregated globally or regionally, to gain a sense of the total volume of resources devoted to the military worldwide. Thirdly, SIPRI reports military expenditure as a proportion of each country's GDP (based on figures for each in current local currency). This figure, the 'military burden' is the most direct measure of the economic burden of the military sector. It may also give an indication of the degree of 'militarisation' of a country, although this should be treated with caution.

CONVERSION OF DATA INTO CONSTANT US DOLLARS

SIPRI places most emphasis on ensuring that its military expenditure series are consistent over time for each country. While comparability between countries is sought as far as possible, this is given lower priority, as consistency over time is necessary to be able to assess trends in spending, and as the variations in reporting data by different countries is so great as to render full cross-country comparability unachievable. This is reflected in the use of constant-price dollar conversions for military expenditure data. This means that each current price local currency series is first converted into constant price local currency for the chosen base year, (currently 2010), and then converted into US$ at the market exchange rate for the base year. For example, suppose that prices (measured by the CPI) in a particular country had risen by 20% between 1998 and 2010. Then to convert the 1998 figure to constant dollars, first we would add 20% to obtain a constant (2010) local currency price, then divide this figure by the dollar exchange rate in 2010 for that country's currency.

(For countries following a fiscal year other than the calendar year, current local price data for the fiscal year is first converted into calendar year data by assuming a constant rate of expenditure through each year, before conversion to constant dollars is carried out. An exception is the USA for which the original fiscal year data is used directly).

This ensures that we have a meaningful comparison between this country's military expenditure in different years, taking account of inflation-we have consistency over time. However, if we want to compare, say, this country's 1998 military expenditure with that of a neighbour for example, the comparison is distorted by the fact that we are converting at 2010 exchange rates-which may not have changed in the same way as relative prices between 1998 and 2010. If we wanted to properly compare two countries' expenditure in 1998, we should convert the figures at the 1998 exchange rate. (In fact, SIPRI does publish current dollar figures for the most recent year of data). Nonetheless, constant price conversions still allow a rough cross-country comparison, except where exchange rates have seriously diverged from relative price movements between the year of interest and the base year. Market exchange rates are determined by the supply and demand of currencies used in international transactions. However, the prices of many goods and services on domestic markets are determined in partial or complete isolation from the rest of the world. Therefore, the MERs do not always accurately reflect differences in price levels between countries.

An alternative is to use purchasing power parity (PPP) conversion factors (or PPP exchange rates). The PPP dollar rate of a country's currency is defined by the World Bank as 'the number of units of a country's currency required to buy the same amount of goods and services in the domestic market as a U.S. dollar would buy in the United States'. > The only PPP rates available for all countries are GDP-based basket of goods and services that are major components of the gross domestic product. Such GDP-based PPP rates are designed to control for differences in price levels and thus to provide a measure of the real purchasing power of the GDP of each country.

Using GDP-based PPP rates instead of MERs for currency conversion results in much higher output and expenditure figures for many developing and transition countries since they have relatively low prices for non-traded goods and services—thus giving the currency higher purchasing power. A unit of local currency therefore has greater purchasing power within a developing country (which is better reflected by using PPP rates) than it has internationally (which is what is reflected by using MERs). For those such developing and transition countries for whom data was available for 2008, the median increase in military expenditure figures from using PPP rates instead of MERs was around a factor of 2. Three-quarters of these countries would see their relative figures increase by at least two-thirds. Meanwhile, using PPP rates would cause the GDP and military expenditure figures of most 'developed' countries to fall relative to the USA, by a median rate of 17 per cent—reflecting the low value of the US dollar at market exchange rates in 2008. However, the reliability of such PPP rates is lower than for MERs, since PPP rates are statistical estimates, calculated on the basis of collected price data for a basket of goods and services for benchmark years. Between benchmark years, the PPP rates are extrapolated forward using ratios of prices indexes, either GDP deflators or consumer price indexes. Like all statistical estimates they are subject to a margin of error.

Furthermore, GDP-based PPP rates are of limited relevance for the conversion of military expenditure data into US dollars. Such PPP rates are designed to reflect the purchasing power for goods and services that are representative of spending patterns in each country, that is, primarily for civilian goods and services. Military expenditure is used to purchase a number of goods and services which are not typical of national consumption patterns. For example, the price of conscripts can be assumed to be lower than the price of a typical basket of goods and services, while the prices of advanced weapon systems and of their maintenance and repair services can be assumed to be much higher. The extent to which this data reflects the amount of military goods and services that the military budget can buy is not known. Due to these uncertainties, SIPRI uses market exchange rates to convert military expenditure data into US dollars, despite their limitations.

RELIABILITY OF MILITARY EXPENDITURE DATA

The great majority of countries nowadays make available at least basic military budget information, in many cases over the internet as well as in printed official documents. There are a few countries in the SIPRI database that at present make no data available at all: for the most recent years these are Cuba, Equatorial Guinea, Eritrea, Guyana, Myanmar, Turkmenistan and Uzbekistan. Also no data is available for Somalia due to the lack of a functioning central government.

However, even where military expenditure data is published by national governments, this data may be subject to a number of problems which may limit international comparability of data and a proper understanding of the economic burden of the military on the country. First of all there is the problem of different *definitions* of military expenditure in different countries. While SIPRI always seeks data as close as possible to the SIPRI definition, including by finding additional sources of data to the main published defence budget where possible, this is not always available. Secondly, there is the problem of currency conversion. In addition to these there are numerous issues relating to the *reliability, transparency and comprehensiveness* of military expenditure data. These issues were explored in a number of case studies conducted by SIPRI of African countries.

Reliability: In some countries, especially poorer countries with limited state capacity, there may be weak systems for financial monitoring and control in the military sector and elsewhere. Actual levels of expenditure may be incompletely recorded, or actively falsified due to corruption or otherwise. Some governments may also seek to disguise the true level of expenditure, for example for the benefit of donor countries and institutions. Poor financial discipline may allow ministries or armed services to overspend their budget without sanction. In a number of cases, only budgeted expenditure figures for the militarymay be available, rather than actual expenditure, which may be substantially different.

Transparency: Many countries provide only limited information on military expenditure, such as just a headline defence budget figure. This makes it hard to know just what is or is not included in military expenditure figures, whether definitions have changed over time, whether figures are for actual or budgeted expenditure, and so forth. Lack of transparency and detail may also call into question the reliability of the data provided.

Comprehensiveness: In many countries, published military expenditure figures systematically exclude significant items of military expenditure. In some cases this is due to a difference of definition, for example the exclusion of military pensions (for which figures may or may not be available elsewhere). In other cases, military expenditure may be funded from a number of extra-budgetary or off-budget sources. Many countries exclude expenditure on arms imports from their military expenditure figures for example. (This is the case in China for example, the world's second-largest military spender). *Extra-budgetary* military expenditure is spending financed from other lines within the overall state budget. In Russia for example, some spending on military research and development is financed through the budget for science and technology, with precise figures for how much of this is military-related unavailable. *Off-budget* spending is sources of revenue for the military outside the regular state budget. Frequently, arms imports and sometimes other military spending is financed from dedicated accounts for natural resource revenues. Chile for example has a dedicated fund for arms imports funded by 10% of the annual revenues of the state copper company, CODELCO (a rare case where the amount of the off-budget revenue for themilitary is publicly available). At the time of publication, a law was going through the Chilean Parliament to abolish this off-budget funding stream. Another common source of off-budgetary revenue is military-run business activities, for example in Indonesia.

Wherever possible, SIPRI seeks to find information on extra-budgetary and off-budgetary sources of military spending, or make estimates where precise figures are not available. In the cases of Russia and China, for example, SIPRI makes annual estimates based on methodologies developed by experts on military spending in these countries. However in many cases the missing expenditure is not available in any public source, and is not susceptible to a reasonable estimate.

SIPRI documents as far as possible known omissions and uncertainties in military expenditure data for each country in the footnotes to the military expenditure tables in the SIPRI Yearbook. Further information on issues relating to military expenditure data for individual countries is available on request.

MILITARY EXPENDITURE AND MILITARY CAPABILITY

While there may be other political or economic motivations, the primary reason countries carry out military expenditure is to acquire military capability of one sort or other. However, extreme caution should be exercised in drawing a link between a country's level of military expenditure and their degree of military power or military capability, as there are many other factors that contribute to military capability, and many intervening factors affecting the degree to which military expenditure succeeds in buying military capability.

Firstly, it should be recognized that military expenditure is a *flow* measure, that is a measure of current resources devoted to renewing, replacing and expanding military capability. It therefore does not measure the acquired *stock of* capabilities represented both by previous stocks of equipment, and by accumulated knowledge, experience, infrastructure, organization and doctrines (or lack thereof) within the military establishment. For example, when Russian military expenditure plummeted following the collapse of the Soviet Union in 1991, they retained the Soviet Union's nuclear arsenal, and much of their stocks of conventional weapons. Of course as such equipment has aged this may well have led to a commensurate drop in Russia's military capability.

Secondly, the value of military expenditure in creating military capability will vary enormously from country to country. An important factor will be whether the *mix* of military expenditure between, for example, personnel and equipment expenditure, is appropriate for the types of military task desired by the country. Many countries, for example, have sought to reduce the size of their armed forces since the end of the Cold War, seeking to create a smaller, but better trained and equipped force suitable for engaging in modern armed conflicts. Conversely, if a country has high levels of military spending, but most of this is going towards maintaining an excessively large army, this spending may not translate into much meaningful military capability. Another factor will be the *efficiency* of military expenditure; this may be adversely affected by corruption, for example, by poor management and organization of forces, or by poor planning and execution of equipment projects. A further factor is a country's *technological absorption* capability – large sums of money spent on major high-tech equipment may be of little value if a country lacks the trained personnel, military organization and doctrine to effectively use the equipment.

Thirdly, a country's military capability will depend also on factors which may be hard to measure in financial terms, such as morale, military preparedness, combat experience, doctrine and organization, etc. Even more so, a country's military *power* – its ability to use its military capability to achieve desired political goals – will depend on a whole range of other political, geographical and economic factors, such as the overall economic and industrial strength of a country, the size of a country in terms of borders and coastlines to be defended, the terrain in which armed forces may be expected to operate, the quality of communications between different areas of operation, the strength of their potential adversaries and alliances with other countries, a country's position within the international community, and many more.

Therefore, while one could be fairly confident that a country with annual military expenditure of $50 billion would almost certainly have considerably more military capability than one with annual expenditure of $5 billion. However, beyond these very broad and clear comparisons, attempts to draw conclusions about a country's level of military capability from its level of military expenditure should be regarded with considerable skepticism.

INDIA'S MILITARY SPENDING

Presenting the country's annual budget for 2012-13 in the Indian parliament earlier this month, Indian Finance Minister Pranab Mukherjee announced a massive 17 percent increase in spending on defence services, raising it to 1.93 trillion Indian rupees ($40 or 38.6 billion). Of this outlay, 41 percent would be spent on procuring modern weapons systems and military hardware. This year's rise follows a 12 percent increase in the previous year's budget. Mukherjee offered little explanation for this massive boost in military expenditure, apart from stating that the allocation was "based on present needs" and that "any further requirement will be met." India's actual military budget is even higher, as the figure for "defence services" does not include spending on its nuclear weapons programme, military pensions and the paramilitary forces.

Three days after India's budget was presented, the Stockholm International Peace Research Institute (SIPRI), a reputed think tank, released a study on global arms transfers according to which India has now overtaken China as the world's biggest importer of weapons. India purchased some $12.7 billion in weaponry during 2007-2011 from foreign countries and accounted for 10 percent of all arms imports during this period.

India's future arms acquisitions plans, as it goes on a major military spending spree to expand and modernise its armed forces, are even more staggering. In a report published last month, Jane's Defence Weekly estimated that India will spend $100 billion on defence procurement between 2011 and 2015.

In the past, India bought most of its advanced weaponry from Russia. This is changing now, as India increasingly looks to western countries in building up a modern arsenal. The US and other western countries have not only been aggressively marketing their military hardware, they have also feverishly been wooing Delhi politically in order to get a share of the Indian market for fighter jets, tanks, artillery, small arms, transport planes, submarines and a range of naval vessels. According to a Pentagon report, India was the third largest purchaser of US arms during fiscal 2011 – after Afghanistan and Taiwan – with contracts worth $4.5 billion.

In the largest-ever bilateral defence deal between India and the US, Delhi last year ordered 10 C-17 Globemaster-III strategic airlift aircraft for $4.1 billion. Together with the 12 C-130J Super Hercules India has ordered from the US, these aircraft will greatly enhance India's capability to swiftly move troops and equipment to forward areas. The Kargil airstrip is being extended to enable these large transport planes to operate from there.

The biggest prize in the Indian arms market, that for the supply of 126 multi-role fighter aircraft to replace the Soviet-era fleet of MiGs, has been won by Dassault Aviation of France, manufacturer of Rafale warplanes. The contract has an estimated worth of $12-15 billion. The addition of another 63 probably at a later stage would take the overall cost to over $20 billion.

Delhi's plans for a blue-water navy are also on track. India already has an old aircraft carrier, the Viraat, which will remain operational for some years to come. The refurbished Russian aircraft carrier Admiral Gorshkov, rechristened as the Vikramaditya, is expected to be delivered by the end of 2012. In addition, an indigenous aircraft carrier which is being built at the Cochin Shipyard is expected to become operational in 2015. The Indian navy is confident that it will have two full-fledged aircraft carrier battle groups by 2015 or so.

India is also going ahead with the development of its own nuclear-powered submarine. In December last year, it took delivery of an Akula II class nuclear-powered attack submarine on a 10-year lease from Russia. It is remarkable that there has been little public debate in India on the purpose or justification for the country's hugely ambitious military build-up plans. Anyone who questions the programme immediately risks being labelled as unpatriotic. Nor has the Indian Government ever clearly articulated the strategic priorities that drive its military expansion and modernisation programme or given a coherent rationale for its costly investment in military hardware.

In May last year, Defence Minister A K Antony expressed "serious concern" over growing defence ties between Pakistan and China and said that India would have to bolster its own military capabilities to meet the challenge. "The main thing," he said, "is we have to increase our capability. That is the only answer." Antony made these comments following reports China planned to accelerate the supply of 50 new JF-17 Thunder multi-role combat jets to Pakistan. Delhi's claim of a "challenge" from Pakistan is of course nothing but fiction in view of India's overwhelming conventional superiority over Pakistan, on land, in the air and on sea.

In testimony before the US Senate last January, James Clapper, Director of US National Intelligence, expressed the view that the Indian military was strengthening its forces "in preparation to fight a limited conflict along the disputed border, and is working to balance Chinese power projection in the Indian Ocean." Yet the fact is that the chances of even a "limited" military conflict between China and India are zero.

The People's Daily, mouthpiece of the Communist Party of China, came nearer to the truth in a commentary on December 18 last year titled "Risks behind India's military build-up". India, the newspaper said, had strategic ambitions and was strengthening its military clout to match its status as a major power. The newspaper advised India that instead of being hostile to its neighbouring countries, it should reduce its own "persecution mania".

The main reason for India's splurge on modern military hardware is that it wants to flex its military muscles to gain recognition as a major regional or even global power. India is particularly unhappy at Chinese influence in the Indian Ocean region and is having to play catch-up in what it likes to think is its own strategic backyard. To assert this claim, Delhi has gone into overdrive cultivating relations with countries up and down the length and breadth of the Indian Ocean. Last month, it hosted naval exercises with 14 Indian Ocean countries on the Andaman Islands. Pakistan and China were not invited. India is also spending $2 billion to set up a military command on Andaman Islands.

On a visit to India last year, Hillary Clinton publicly urged India to turn its "Look East" policy into one of "Act East." With Washington's encouragement, Delhi is now hoping to carve out a role for itself not only in the Indian Ocean but also in the South China Sea and the Western Pacific. For this purpose, India has struck a strategic partnership with

Vietnam, a country which has historically been distrustful of China. India's first foray into South China Sea did not end very happily though. An amphibious assault vessel, INS Airavat that sailed from the Andamans to Vietnam last July on a goodwill visit was challenged in the South China Sea by the Chinese navy which asked the Indian vessel to leave Chinese waters. Both sides later played down the incident but the message seems to have been registered.

One of the widely circulated myths about our defence expenditure is that we spend a far bigger portion of our GDP on our military than India does. The data published by SIPRI tell a different story. Pakistan's defence expenditure as a share of GDP for 2009, the latest for which data has been published by SIPRI, was 2.8 percent. India's defence expenditure was also 2.8 percent of the GDP for that year. The long-term trend in Pakistan is downwards. Defence expenditure fell from 6.2 percent of the GDP in 1988 to 2.8 percent in 2009. In India it has remained more or less constant. It was 3.6 percent in 1988 and 2.8 percent in 2009.

THE DRAG ON INDIA'S MILITARY GROWTH

India's rapid economic growth and newfound access to military technology, especially by way of its rapprochement with the United States, have raised hopes of a military revival in the country. Against this optimism about the rise of Indian military power stands the reality that India has not been able to alter its military-strategic position despite being one of the world's largest importers of advanced conventional weapons for three decades.

We believe that civil-military relations in India have focused too heavily on one side of the problem – how to ensure civilian control over the armed forces, while neglecting the other – how to build and field an effective military force. This imbalance in civil-military relations has caused military modernization and reforms to suffer from a lack of political guidance, disunity of purpose and effort and material and intellectual corruption.

The Effects of Strategic Restraint

Sixty years after embarking on a rivalry with Pakistan, India has not been able to alter its strategic relationship with a country less than one-fifth its size. India's many counterinsurgencies have lasted twenty years on an average, double the worldwide average. Since the 1998 nuclear tests, reports of a growing missile gap with Pakistan have called into question the quality of India's nuclear deterrent. The high point of Indian military history – the liberation of Bangladesh in 1971– therefore, stands in sharp contrast to the persistent inability of the country to raise effective military forces.

No factor more accounts for the haphazard nature of Indian military modernization than the lack of political leadership on defense, stemming from the doctrine of strategic restraint. Key political leaders rejected the use of force as an instrument of politics in favour of a policy of strategic restraint that minimized the importance of the military.

The Government of India held to its strong anti-militarism despite the reality of conflict and war that followed independence. Much has been made of the downgrading of the service chiefs in the protocol rank, but of greater consequence was the elevation of military science and research as essential to the long-term defense of India over the armed forces themselves. Nehru invited British physicist P.M.S. Blackett to examine the relationship between science and defense. Blackett came back with a report that called for capping Indian defense spending at 2 percent of GDP and limited military modernization. He also recommended state funding and ownership of military research laboratories and established his protégé, Daulat Singh Kothari, as the head of the labs.

Indian defense spending decreased during the 1950s. Of the three services, the Indian Navy received greater attention with negotiations for the acquisition of India's first aircraft carrier. The Indian Air Force acquired World War II surplus Canberra transport. The Indian Army, the biggest service by a wide margin, went to Congo on a UN peacekeeping mission, but was neglected overall. India had its first defense procurement scandal when buying old jeeps and experienced its first civil-military crisis when an army chief threatened to resign protesting political interference in military matters. The decade culminated in the government's 'forward policy' against China, which Nehru foisted on an unprepared army, and led to the war of 1962 with China that ended in a humiliating Indian defeat.

The foremost lesson of 1962 was that India could not afford further military retrenchment. The Indian government launched a significant military expansion program that doubled the size of the army and raised a fighting air force. With the focus shifting North, the Indian Navy received less attention. A less recognized lesson of the war was that political interference in military matters ought to be limited. The military – and especially the army – asked for and received operational and institutional autonomy, a fact most visible in the wars of 1965 and 1971.

The problem, however, was that the political leadership did not suddenly become more comfortable with the military as an institution; they remained wary of the possibility of a coup d'etat and militarism more generally.

The Indian civil-military relations landscape has changed marginally since. In the eighties, there was a degree of political-military confluence in the Rajiv Gandhi government: Rajiv appointed a military buff, Arun Singh, as the minister of state for defense. At the same time, Krishnaswami Sundarji, an exceptional officer, became the army chief. Together they launched an ambitious program of military modernization in response to Pakistani rearmament and nuclearization. Pakistan's nuclearization allowed that country to escalate the subconventional conflict in Kashmir while stemming Indian ability to escalate to a general war, where it had superiority. India is yet to emerge from this stability-instability paradox. We do not know why Rajiv Gandhi agreed to the specific kind of military modernization that occurred in the mid-eighties, but then stepped back from using this capacity in 1987 during the Brasstacks crisis. Sundarji later wrote in a veiled work of fiction and told his many friends that Brasstacks was the last chance India had to dominate a non-nuclear Pakistan.

The puzzle of Brasstacks stands in a line of similar decisions. In 1971, India did not push the advantage of its victory in the eastern theatre to the West. Instead, New Delhi, under *uberrealist* Prime Minister Indira Gandhi, signed on to an equivocal agreement at Simla that committed both sides to peaceful resolution of future disputes without any enforcement measures. India's decision to wait 24 years between its first nuclear test in 1974 and the second set of tests in 1998 is equally puzzling. Why did it not follow through after the 1974 test, and why did it test in 1998? .

Underlying these puzzles is a remarkable preference for strategic restraint. Indian leaders simply have not seen the use of force as a useful instrument of politics. This foundation of ambivalence informs Indian defense policy, and consequently its military modernization and reform efforts.

To be sure, military restraint in a region as volatile as South Asia is wise and has helped persuade the great powers to accommodate India's rise, but it does not help military planning. Together with the separation of the armed forces from the government, divisions among the services and between the services and other related agencies, and the inability of the military to seek formal support for policies it deems important, India's strategic restraint has served to deny political guidance to the efforts of the armed forces to modernize. As wise as strategic restraint may be, Pakistan, India's primary rival, hardly believes it to be true. Islamabad prepares as if India were an aggressive power and this has a real impact on India's security.

IMBALANCE IN CIVIL-MILITARY RELATIONS

What suffices for a military modernization plan is a wish list of weapon systems amounting to as much as $100 billion from the three services and hollow announcements of coming breakthroughs from the Defense Research and Development Organization (DRDO), the premier agency for military research in India. The process is illustrative. The armed forces propose to acquire certain weapon systems. The political leadership and the civilian bureaucracy, especially the Ministry of Finance, react to these requests, agreeing on some and rejecting others. A number of dysfunctions ensue.

First, the services see things differently and their plans are essentially uncoordinated. Coming off the experience of the Kargil war and Operation Parakram, the Indian Army seems to have arrived at a Cold Start doctrine, seeking to find some fighting space between subconventional conflict and nuclear exchange in the standoff with Pakistan. The doctrine may not be official policy, but it informs the army's wish list, where attack helicopters, tanks and long-range artillery stand out as marquee items. The Indian Air Force (IAF), meanwhile, is the primary instrument of the country's nuclear deterrent. The IAF's close second role is air superiority and air defense. Close air support, to which the IAF has belatedly agreed and which is essential to the army's Cold Start doctrine, is a distant fourth.

The Indian Navy wants to secure the country's sea-lanes of communications, protect its energy supplies and guard its trade routes. It wants further to be the vehicle of Indian naval diplomacy and sees a role in the anti-piracy efforts in the Malacca Straits and the Horn of Africa. What is less clear is how the Indian Navy might contribute in the event of a war with Pakistan. The navy would like simply to brush past the problem of Pakistan and reach for the grander projects. Accordingly, the Indian Navy's biggest procurement order is a retrofitted aircraft carrier from Russia.

India's three services have dramatically different views of what their role in India's security should be, and there is no political effort to ensure this coordination. Cold Start remains an iffy proposition. India's nuclear deterrent remains tethered to a single delivery system: fighter aircraft. Meanwhile, the Indian Army's energies are dissipated with counterinsurgency duties, which might increase manifold if the army is told to fight the rising leftist insurgency, the Naxalites. And all this at a time when the primary security threat to the country has been terrorism. After the Mumbai attacks, the Indian government and the people of India are said to have resolved to tackle the problem headlong, but today the government's minister in charge of internal security, Palaniappan Chidambaram, is more under siege himself than seizing the hidden enemy.

Second, despite repeated calls for and commissions into reforms in the higher defense structure, planning, intelligence, defense production and procurement, the Indian national security establishment remains fragmented and uncoordinated. The government and armed forces have succeeded in reforms primed by additions to the defense budget but failed to institute reforms that require changes in organization and priorities.

The Kargil Review Committee, and the Group of Ministers report that followed, for example, recommended a slew of reforms. The changes most readily implemented were those that created new commands, agencies and task forces, essentially linear expansion backed by new budgetary allocations. The changes least likely to occur were those required changes in the hierarchy.

The most common example of tough reform is the long-standing recommendation for a chief of defense staff. A military chief, as opposed to the service chiefs, could be a solution to the problem that causes the three services not to reconcile their priorities. However, political leaders have rejected the creation of the position of military commander-in-chief, mainly for fear of giving a military officer too much power. Instead of a chief of defense staff, the government has tried to install an integrated defense staff that is supposed to undertake reconciliation between the services, but which really is a toothless body with little influence.

Lastly, the Ministry of Defense has a finance section deputed by the Ministry of Finance. This section oversees all defense expenditures, even after they have been authorized. Once the cabinet has approved a spending item, what authority does the section have to turn down requests? However, the finance section raises questions of propriety, wisdom and policy that should under normal circumstances be under the purview of the defense minister.

No Legitimate Procurement Process

Corruption in weapons procurement has been a political issue since the mid-1980s, when allegations of a series of paybacks in the purchase of Bofors artillery, HDW submarines and other items mobilized an opposition that removed Rajiv Gandhi from power in 1989. Since then, Indian political leaders have tried hard not to appear to be corrupt, going out of their way to slow down new purchases.

However, corruption is still a problem, as shown in the 2001 Tehelka expose of political leaders accepting bribes in return for defense contracts. Recently, Uday Bhaskar, the Indian Navy officer and defense analyst, wrote bitingly that for a number of years now the armed forces, which desperately need modernization, have been returning unspent funds to the treasury.

There is widespread recognition that corruption is morally venal and detrimental to the cause of Indian security. We believe, however, that the second-and third-order problems of corruption have unacknowledged impact on military modernization and capacity. The Defense Procurement Manual and Procedures on the Ministry of Defense's website are the first steps in the right direction, but the Indian government has generally failed to build a transparent and legitimate procurement process.

The deep roots of corruption extend to military research and development and to the heart of India's foreign relations. Since the mid-1970s, however, the DRDO embarked on a number of ambitious and well-funded projects to build a fighter aircraft, a tank, and missiles. All three projects floundered.

While the aircraft and tank projects have largely failed, the missile program is considered successful. The reputation of the success carried the director of the missile program, A.P.J. Abdul Kalam, to the presidency. Yet in 2010, no Indian missile in the arsenal of the armed forces has managed to alter the strategic equation with Pakistan or China. The Prithvi short-range missile is not useful because of its range and liquid fuel needs. The longer-range Agni models have gone through numerous tests without entering the army's arsenal. Other variations, such as Nag and Akash, have limited strategic purpose.

The virtual monopoly over military research in state-owned labs has meant that the abundant energies of the Indian private sector have remained outside the defense industry. Where in the United States, small and medium-sized defense contractors form the backbone of the research complex, India is far from thinking along those lines. Despite recent efforts to include the private sector through various schemes, there continues to be distrust of private industry in the Indian defense establishment. We believe it is easier for a private foreign supplier to win a contract with the Ministry of Defense than it is for a small private Indian company to do so.

For decades, the Indian government has accepted dishonest promises made by DRDO as the basis for providing billions of dollars of support because of the persisting ideology of autarky. The greatest success of military research in India comes not from the DRDO, but from the Atomic Energy Commission, which built the nuclear devices. But the government has been unwilling to subject DRDO to public accountability. Instead, the head of DRDO serves as the defense minister's scientific adviser. The two positions – of supplier and adviser – bring inherent conflict of interest, but this has not been an issue in India at all.

The second pattern of systemic corruption comes from the inability of the Indian defense system to wean itself from the supply of Soviet/Russian equipment. The reasons why India initially went to the Soviet Union for weapons are well-known. The United States chose Pakistan, India went to the Soviet Union. But that political decision was reinforced by ideas about the corruption-free nature of the state-owned Soviet defense industry and the profit-mindedness of western, and especially American, firms.

This characterization has always been untrue. Soviet/Russian suppliers have engaged in as much corruption as western firms, but because the Soviet Union was a closed system, the corruption – which was reported first in the press in the supplier countries – was never really reported in the Soviet Union.

This tradition continues, though the Russian free press has been more critical of the country's defense deals. Indeed, those who served as Indian 'agents' for the Soviet firms have highlighted the better business practice of Russians, a laughable matter in light of India's recent travails with the retrofit and sale of the Russian aircraft carrier Admiral Gorshkov.

The tendency is reiterated in Indian preferences in dealing with the West as well. Western firms have always been seen as money-grubbing, an opinion that exists across the political spectrum and is prevalent in the civilian bureaucracy. New Delhi seems to prefer government-to-government foreign military sales, which are in turn causing some degree of protest from users who want longer-term maintenance arrangements with suppliers.

The political rapprochement between India and the United States has not yet filtered into the system for attitudes to change dramatically. India's growing military supply relationship with Israel is instructive. The most successful Israeli firm in the Indian market is Israel Aerospace Industries (IAI), a state-owned company. IAI was quick to adopt the Russian model of operation in India: offering the DRDO co-development opportunities to win contracts. In contrast, American firms are reluctant to work with, let alone transfer high-end technology to a state owned enterprise. They would prefer to set up a subsidiary in India, which could retain control of the technology.

India has been one of the biggest importers of advanced conventional weapons in the last thirty years, but this sustained rearmament has not altered India's strategic position. The armed forces push for modernization, but do not have the authority to mount the national campaign necessary for transforming the security condition of the country. Budget increases delivered by a rapidly expanding economy and access to western technology previously denied to India have led to optimism about Indian military power, but the dysfunction in India's civil-military relations reduces the impact of rearmament. Arming without aiming has some purpose in persuading other great powers of India's benign rise, but it cannot be the basis of military planning.

6

Practice in Budgeting for the Military Sector

Sound financial management of a country's entire security sector is essential if the country is to have effective, efficient and professional security forces that are capable of protecting the state and its population against internal and external threats. Highly autonomous security forces that are able to act with impunity in the economic and political spheres are invariably professionally weak and bad value for money. This chapter provides a perspective on how good practice can be achieved. It emphasizes adherence to public expenditure management principles and various elements of defence planning and budgeting.

GOOD PRACTICE IN THE MILITARY BUDGETARY PROCESS

From the perspectives of public policy and budgetary process, the military sector shares many of the characteristics of other sectors of government. This means that the citizens of any country will benefit from a military sector that is subject to the same broad set of rules and procedures that are applied to other sectors. It is therefore essential to give a high priority to principles such as transparency, accountability to elected civil authorities and comprehensiveness of budget coverage. In that respect, military budgeting should be no different from budgeting for other governmental sectors.

At the same time, it is often argued that the military sector is different from other parts of the public sector in at least two ways. The first is the need for confidentiality in the area of national security. The second is the highly political nature of expenditure decisions relating to the military sector, especially arms acquisition decisions.

It is clear that some degree of confidentiality is necessary in the area of national security. However, this should not be used to justify a lower level of oversight or a lack of adherence to internationally recognized standards of public expenditure management. Different forms of oversight may be necessary for some areas relating to national security. It is also important to be clear about the distinction between confidentiality and the lack of public scrutiny. It is possible to retain a high degree of confidentiality in highly sensitive areas without compromising the principle of democratic accountability. A subject may be sensitive—off-budget activities, for example—but it should not be kept secret. War plans, on the other hand, should be confidential. Even so, holding war plans in confidence does not mean an absence of democratic accountability. It simply requires appropriate systems of clearance and procedures for consulting the legislature and other oversight bodies.

All budgeting involves political decisions and trade-offs, but it is often argued that political considerations carry greater weight in defence than in other sectors. To the extent that this is true, provided that the political system is open, it should still be possible to contest the basis on which decisions are made and, in particular, to ensure that the principles of sound financial management are not violated. Thus, the highly political nature of decisions concerning the military sector should not prevent that sector from adhering to the important principles of transparency, oversight and accountability.

CONSTITUTES GOOD PRACTICE IN MILITARY BUDGETING

In order to develop an appreciation of good practice in the military budgetary process, it is important to consider: (*a*) the relevance of good practice; (*b*) the principles of sound public expenditure management; and (*c*) the key principles of democratic governance in the security sector.

The principles of sound public expenditure management

The 10 principles of public expenditure management are widely accepted as the basis for budgeting processes. It is important to understand that these are the ideals that public officials should have in front of them as a guide. No public expenditure system anywhere in the world gets top marks on all 10 principles. The point is to progressively improve adherence to them. There is no justification for the military sector to violate any of these principles. The way in which it implements some of them may be a little different from some other sectors, but the principles themselves must not be violated: they are all relevant to a well-managed budgetary process. The principles most frequently cited in relation to the military sector are transparency and accountability. The confidentiality suggest, transparency is the cornerstone on which an accountable military budgetary process is built. Transparency and accountability are crucial issues in the allocation and management of defence resources for all levels of planning, programming and budgeting. If the allocation and management of defence resources are not transparent, the military sector will never be able to achieve public support or the cooperation and support of broader government. If it is not accountable to government and the people, the military becomes a cause unto itself and will not be aligned with national interests and priorities. It will easily be corrupted and decision making will be easily diverted towards self-interest.

Civil involvement in and control of overall budget decisions, as well as careful auditing at all levels, can help ensure that resources are actually used to accomplish policy objectives. The most effective way to achieve this is to obtain at all levels a commitment to national interests and objectives and to develop clear and transparent planning, programming and budgeting processes and systems to implement them. These processes must of necessity be aligned with the national financial management framework. Transparency and accountability can be enhanced through a system of performance agreements. Such agreements rely on the definition of clear output objectives and performance standards and on agreement on the required resources. The system is also based on negotiation, ensuring better insight, understanding and cooperation. Important as transparency and accountability are, it is essential not to lose sight of the other principles of public expenditure management. In particular, attention should be given to: (*a*) the *comprehensiveness* of the budget; (*b*) the *predictability* of the level of revenues backing that budget and the macro-economic policies on which those revenues depend; (*c*) the *contestability* of the budget process; and (*d*) the *honesty* with which estimates of revenue and expenditure are developed.

The relevance of good practice

Good practice is based on adherence to principles of sound public expenditure management. One might well question the relevance of somewhat abstract principles when dealing with an issue like military spending, where actual practice diverges significantly from good practice and the conditions for achieving good practice are frequently not present, as is the case throughout much of Africa. The purpose of starting with good practice is that it provides a clear vision of the objectives of policy reform—in this case, a democratically governed military sector under civilian leadership that adheres to the principles of sound budgeting and financial management. Without such a vision, it is impossible to develop either a strategy for reaching the ultimate objectives or benchmarks to measure progress along the way. It is also impossible to determine where the problems lie with existing policy and practice.

The key principles of democratic governance in the security sector

The 10 principles of democratic governance in the security sector are increasingly widely accepted. They reflect the mutual obligations that civil authorities and security personnel have towards each other. Security forces have a responsibility to be accountable to civil authorities; to uphold the rule of law, including the protection of human and civil rights; and to carry out their professional duties to the best of their abilities. Civil authorities have the responsibility to avoid politicizing security bodies; to respect their professional prerogatives; and to provide them with a clear mandate and adequate resources and training to carry out that mandate. As in the case of the principles of public expenditure management, there is no justification for the military sector to violate these principles.

MILITARY BUDGETARY PROCESS INTO GOVERNMENT-WIDE PROCESSES

There are five crucial, interrelated components of the management of expenditure in any sector: (*a*) strategic planning; (*b*) review of the previous year's performance; (*c*) determination of what is affordable; (*d*) allocation of resources both between and within sectors; and (*e*) efficient and effective use of resources. The linkages between these components in the case of the military sector, with reference to the broader security sector.

For the budgetary process to be effective, every sector needs to follow good practices internally and to link with the broader, government-wide financial management and oversight process. All of this must occur within the framework of democratic governance and the principles of sound budgeting and financial management.

Strategic planning in the security sector

As in any other part of the public sector, military budgets should be prepared in accordance with a sectoral strategy. This involves identifying the needs and key objectives of the security sector as a whole and the specific missions that the defence forces will be asked to undertake.

The starting point for developing policies and strategies for the security sector is an understanding of the causes of insecurity and the identification of the instruments that government wants to employ to enhance security. Governments have various tools for strengthening security. Key among these are diplomacy; economic and political tools to reduce economic and social inequalities and tensions; mediation to resolve conflict domestically and regionally; and, of course, the country's security bodies. Once the broad areas of responsibility for the security forces are identified, governments should agree on the tasks that will be undertaken by the different bodies: armed forces, police, gendarmerie or paramilitary forces, and intelligence bodies. Based on these assessments, governments should develop a formal defence policy framework. This policy then informs planning, programming and budgeting. The planning and programming process, along with the linkages to the military budgetary process.

While it is true that 'policy is what government does, not what it says it wants to do', formal policies and plans to implement these policies are important. In the absence of well-thought-out and clearly articulated policies, it is impossible to manage the finances of the military sector in a rational manner. Budgeting becomes ad hoc. In the absence of a clear statement of which activities undertaken by the armed forces are included in the 'defence' function, it is impossible to develop adequate functional breakdowns of expenditure and to understand how much it costs to provide adequate military security. In addition, it is difficult to develop performance benchmarks and thus to assess the efficiency and effectiveness of expenditure in the military sector. In the absence of a strategic plan, countries risk not obtaining a level of military security commensurate with their financial outlays.

As the case studies in this volume illustrate, few governments in Africa have undertaken thorough, participatory strategic review processes of the sort outlined. What is more, defence policy and planning processes are rarely based on a broad evaluation of a country's security environment and a detailed assessment of the specific tasks that should be undertaken by the country's various security forces. A counter example is Uganda, which undertook a broad security assessment in 2002–2003. It identified 134 'threat agents', of which three were specific to the military. This result underscores the importance of not attempting to undertake defence planning in a vacuum, but of linking it with planning for the police, paramilitary forces, civilian intelligence and other state security forces, as well as with the country's economic and developmental objectives.

In highly resource-constrained countries, such as those in Africa, it is extremely important for governments and societies to use resources as efficiently and effectively as possible. The first step in this process is to engage in strategic planning. In doing so, it is important to ensure that the defence review process takes place in a manner consistent with the country's economic objectives and capacities. The demonstrates, economic considerations need to be taken into account at the beginning, the middle and the end of the review process. A defence force costs money. A country will not be secure if it develops a defence policy for which it cannot provide resources in an open, accountable and sustained manner. Thus, part of the guidance for the review process should include the financial framework for the security sector in general and the military sector in particular. Throughout the entire process, the finance minister and other key economic managers need to be informed and consulted. Options for force structures need to be developed within the context of the financial parameters and the risks associated with buying a certain level of defence. The final decisions must reflect economic realities.

Review of the previous year's performance in the security sector

While strategic reviews occur infrequently in African countries, it is important that the outcome of the previous year's financial planning and implementation period be reviewed at the beginning of the annual budget cycle. The efficient and effective management of resources in any sector, including the security sector, requires that information on performance be fed back into the budgeting process. While defining and measuring performance for the military sector is more difficult than for many other sectors, a focus on readiness or capability has been shown to be helpful for any discussion of the role, structure, performance and resource needs of the defence forces. However performance is defined, the review of the previous year's budgetary performance will be facilitated by a well-functioning financial management information system (FMIS).

Determination of what is affordable in the security sector

Government policies, whether in the security or any other sector, must be affordable. Affordable policies require a sustainable macroeconomic balance, which is critical to the long-term economic health of a country. To attain a sustainable macroeconomic balance, governments must give a high priority to exercising discipline over public expenditure.

Overall financial discipline is also critical because a ceiling on funding that can be easily raised allows governments to avoid firm decisions on priorities. At the other end of the spectrum, without a solid floor to the budget, resources become unpredictable and operational performance suffers. It is therefore extremely important to have in place institutions that can achieve long-term macroeconomic stability, determine the overall resource envelope for public expenditure and enforce government decisions on expenditure priorities and levels.

Financial discipline is weak in many African countries. While the military is by no means the only body that exceeds the agreed limits of the financial allocation in the course of the financial year, it frequently enjoys a privileged position. Government officials, military officers, and heads of state and government have intervened in the resource-allocation process with flagrant disregard for established procedures and predetermined spending priorities. Military officers have presented the treasury with invoices for expenses incurred outside the budget framework. Defence ministers have refused to share the details of defence spending with finance ministers and parliament. The full financial implications of arms-acquisition decisions, including debt incurred for military purposes, are often not reflected in budgets, which may eventually destabilize financial policy. This sort of behaviour contributes to the widespread problem in Africa of military budgets that cannot fully fund the defence function.

As far as the failure to respect lower limits on expenditure, the armed forces are less likely to have their allocations reduced during the course of a financial year than other security forces, such as the police or gendarmerie. Nonetheless, it is important to develop clear rules for any reallocation of resources during the financial year—including those occasioned by shortfalls in revenue—and to apply them across the board.

Medium-term expenditure frameworks (MTEFs) are one mechanism that can help reduce incentives to evade financial discipline. MTEFs have become popular with the development assistance agencies because they can help: (*a*) improve the linkage between policies and objectives and between inputs and outputs; (*b*) make the budgetary process more transparent, especially by improving monitoring; (*c*) focus on outputs and service delivery; and (*d*) increase ownership by sectoral ministries.

As several of the case studies in this book demonstrate, it can be difficult for African governments to develop realistic multi-year plans, given the lack of predictability in government revenues and the reliance on a strong institutional base. However, something like an MTEF is important because the military sector needs a time frame for planning and budgeting of longer than one year. As the case of South Africa demonstrates, adopting a multi-year framework is not impossible in the African context.

A specific benefit to the military sector of adopting a medium-term framework is that it encourages full costing of defence programmes, particularly outlays on arms acquisition and major construction projects. Irrespective of the difficulty in implementing an MTEF, it is still important to have a full costing of the different components of the defence programme. Full costing will help make the case for a particular level of funding. It will also clarify the sustainability of individual programmes and it will help maximize efficiency and effectiveness in those cases where budget cuts become necessary. Full costing is therefore critically necessary for the operational effectiveness of the defence forces.

ALLOCATION OF RESOURCES FOR THE MILITARY SECTOR

Once the overall resource envelope is agreed, resources must be allocated according to priorities both within the military sector and between the military sector and other sectors. Sectoral strategies and information on performance (outputs and outcomes) are critical components of the allocation process. It is important that assessments of past performance be fed into planning for the coming year (or years in the case of multi-year budgeting cycles). The key financial and economic managers plus the legislature must have the capacity to be fully involved in the resource-allocation process and the process must include all relevant actors. The central budget office should assess the appropriateness of the defence ministry's budget. The armed forces must compete fully with other sectors for funding. The legislature must have adequate time to review and comment on the proposed defence budget before the beginning of the financial year. Methods of incorporating public input into the allocation process can help build public support for the final budget.

In many African countries the conditions required for the effective allocation of resources are not present. Institutional capacity for military budgeting is weak in both the executive and legislative branches of government. Financial management and oversight within the armed forces are correspondingly inadequate. The military sector holds a highly privileged position compared with other sectors when the overall resource envelope is divided among sectors. Arms acquisition requests include neither justification nor full costing. The legislature frequently receives even less information on the defence budget than on budgets for non-security activities, and input from the public on spending priorities is actively discouraged or ignored. The challenges facing legislative oversight of the armed forces in West Africa.

While the military often enjoys a privileged position in terms of resource allocation, financial constraints have led some African governments to fail to provide the armed forces with adequate resources to carry out their assigned missions. This not only places at risk the safe and secure environment that is necessary for both economic and political development, but also creates frustration and resentment within the armed forces. Participants in a workshop on democratic governance in the security sector held in Dakar in October 2001 argued that adequate transparency in the military sector is critical so that the serious underfunding that afflicts armed forces throughout the region is clear for all to see. They suggested that there is both disdain for the military among civilians and a belief that military security is a comparatively low priority among those who control their countries' financial resources. In their view, this not only leads to inadequate defence budgets and thus inadequate external security but can also heighten internal insecurity through a threat of coups. For reasons of both financial and political stability, it is important that the military sector competes on an equal footing with other sectors and that the process of allocating resources among sectors takes place in a transparent and accountable manner.

EFFICIENT AND EFFECTIVE USE OF RESOURCES IN THE MILITARY SECTOR

Once a budget has been approved by the legislature and monies have been appropriated, the goal is to ensure the efficient use of resources to implement sectoral priorities. This requires careful monitoring and evaluation of operational performance both within the armed forces and by civil servants. As the case studies in this volume demonstrate, there are often significant deviations between the approved budget and actual expenditure in African countries. A well-functioning FMIS is critical if decision makers and public-sector managers are to obtain the financial data they require to control aggregate expenditure, prioritize among and within sectors, and operate in a cost-effective manner. Additionally, it is extremely important that irregularities identified in the course of monitoring are addressed, lest a climate of non-compliance be created or reinforced. Particular attention should be given to ensuring the transparency of procurement and acquisition processes and their conformity to good practices.

Accounting standards in the military sector should not deviate from those in other sectors. Defence ministries should have their own internal audit offices and the government's auditor-general should audit defence accounts on a regular basis. The results of the auditor-general's audits should be reported to the legislature in a timely fashion and irregularities addressed expeditiously. Cash flow and expenditures should be monitored closely. Methods of verifying the number of individuals employed in the armed forces and the defence ministry and of linking salary and wage payments to individual employees facilitate this monitoring process. Expenditure tracking studies can help determine whether resources are being spent as intended. Value-for-money audits by the auditor-general or other oversight bodies will help determine if resources are being spent efficiently. As in any other sector, the results of monitoring and evaluation work need to be fed back into strategic planning. Some of the specific issues that need particular attention in terms of strengthening the efficiency of resource use in the military sector.

The case studies in this volume demonstrate that the capacity for financial management in the military sector is weak in Africa. In part this is because overall financial management capacity is weak. At the same time, different standards are frequently applied to the military sector. The degree of transparency and accountability is often considerably lower in the military sector than in the government as a whole. Efforts are rarely made to identify deviations between approved and actual resource use; where such deviations are identified, problems are rarely corrected. If the defence forces are to be capable of fulfilling their mandated duties in a professional manner, however, it is important to use resources allocated to the military sector as effectively and efficiently as possible.

GOOD PRACTICE IN MILITARY PROCUREMENT AND ACQUISITION

There should be little difference between public expenditure management in general and public expenditure management in the military sector. Defence procurement and acquisition should accordingly be carried out according to the same principles that guide public sector procurement in non-military areas: fairness, impartiality, transparency, cost-effectiveness and efficiency, and openness to competition. In addition, it is essential that there be high-level consultation and evaluation of all major projects for all forms of public sector procurement and acquisition. A generic procurement process, applicable to all sectors of government.

At the same time, with the exception of procurement of works and commodities (such as construction, clothing, food, fuel, office equipment, general vehicles and consultancy services), defence procurement does exhibit some distinctive characteristics: (*a*) the relative importance of cost in determining which bid is accepted; (*b*) the confidentiality associated with national security considerations; (*c*) the time frame for major weapons procurement; (*d*) the complexity of defence procurement; and (*e*) the existence of international arms control treaty regimes and national legislation governing arms procurement. These distinctive characteristics are deviations in scale rather than principle. There certainly should be scepticism about any claims that procurement of relatively standard works, services and commodities for the military should be subject to different rules.

Cost considerations in bidding

While standard procurement practice in non-military sectors is giving increasing emphasis to value for money, defence analysts argue that factors other than cost are more frequently the major factors in accepting a bid for weapon procurement projects in the military sector. They point out, however, that national legislation can play an important role in regulating the part that cost plays in weapon procurement processes in the military sector. In South Africa, for example, the 1998 Defence Review and the 1999 White Paper on defence-related industries spell out which technologies are considered 'strategically essential capabilities' and thus exempt from lowest-cost considerations. The South African Parliament has approved both policy documents.

Confidentiality

Transparency in defence procurement must be limited by national security interests. Confidentiality clauses will be required in the arms procurement process. This, too, can be regulated by national legislation. The South African Defence Review lists a number of reasons for confidentiality in defence procurement. These include: the protection of third-party commercial information, the national security of South Africa, prevention of harm to South Africa's ability to conduct international relations, and the protection of South Africa's economic interests and the commercial activities of government bodies.

The time frame for major weapons procurement

From inception to final acceptance of the product, procurement of major weapon systems may take as long as 15 years. Some flexibility needs to be built into the procurement process to take account of contingencies such as fluctuations in currency exchange rates.

This long time frame also makes it essential that quality control takes place throughout the procurement process, rather than when the product is ready for delivery. Arms procurement projects should also take into account full life-cycle costs and support for the acquired systems. The long time frame also makes it essential to attempt to forecast spending farther into the future than in non-defence sectors. The UK, for example, has a 10-year 'long-term costing' system for defence.

The complexity of arms procurement

Because of the complexity of arms procurement, sound management of the procurement process requires interdisciplinary project teams. Such teams should have expertise on engineering, resource management, contracting, quality assurance and design assurance. In addition, because of the particular complexity of the procurement of major weapon systems, which can involve a substantial number of subcontractors, opportunities for corruption are great. These projects therefore require the highest level of management and scrutiny by governmental accountability mechanisms. For example, South Africa has three levels of approval for major arms procurement projects within its Department of Defence. For major projects, parliamentary approval may also be required.

International arms control treaty regimes and national legislation governing arms procurement Procurement in the military sector is distinct from general government procurement in being subject to international treaties and specific national legislation. Some defence

STRATEGIC DEFENCE PLANNING

Too often the defence debate is dominated by short-term perceptions of security, based on snapshot views of the world and the cost of defence. The argument is 'there is no threat, so why spend?'. Strategic situations change rapidly, but the building of defence capabilities and expertise takes time. All strategic defence planning must therefore be done with a long-term view. To do so it is necessary to understand the major variables in defence planning: the ends, ways and means of defence. Government and defence planners share the responsibility for the determination of these ends, ways and means.

The scales show that what government requires from defence (the ends), taking into consideration the approved defence posture (the ways), must be balanced by defence capabilities (the means) and that this requires a determined amount of resources. The scales can be brought into balance by either reducing ends, adapting the defence posture (moving the pivot to the left) or increasing means and thus resources. If there is an imbalance or inconsistency between ends, ways and means, this will result in a strategic gap between what needs to be done and what can be done.

The ends of defence

Defence ends are the required defence outputs in support of the government's goals and objectives, which include peace, security, stability and public safety. The primary responsibility for determining the ends of defence rests with the government (the parliament and cabinet). Examples of defence outputs (ends) are: (*a*) provision of deterrence through the existence of mission-ready forces; (*b*) the meeting of international obligations such as search-and-rescue and disaster relief; (*c*) participation in peace missions; (*d*) peacetime border control and protection against non-military threats; (*e*) support to the police; and (*f*) support to civil authorities.

Ways of defence

The ways of defence are military strategic and operational concepts and are influenced by the government's national security and foreign policy as well as its strategic defence posture. The responsibility for determining the ways of defence is a dual responsibility of the government and the military, with the military primarily responsible for providing expert advice to the government. Examples of strategic and operational defence postures (ways) are: (*a*) non-offensive defence or forward mobile defence postures; (*b*) a strategic defensive or offensive posture; (*c*) defence through regional defence cooperation and alliances or through self-defence.

Means of defence

The means of defence are essentially the operational capabilities of the defence force, as expressed in the force design. The determination of the force design is primarily the responsibility of defence planners and must be in alignment with the ends and ways as prescribed by policy. Examples of force design elements are: infantry units, armour units, artillery units, naval surface combatants, naval sub-surface combatants, air force fighter squadrons, air force transport squadrons, air force helicopter squadrons, operational medical units and military attachés. These defence means are the real cost-drivers of defence. The creation, maintenance and development of these capabilities are the primary consumers of defence resources.

DEFENCE BUDGETING : PLANNING AND PROGRAMMING

No meaningful programming or budgeting can be done without the existence of a long-term or strategic defence plan, just as no meaningful plan can exist in the absence of a guiding policy. The development of both policies and plans in the military sector as part of the government-wide and sectoral budgetary processes was outlined above. The planning and programming process in more detail and then links it back to the budgetary process.

The defence plan

Essentially, the defence plan is the document that specifies the measurable outputs that the military sector will produce in pursuit of the government's objectives, measured against the identified financial allocation within the medium-term expenditure framework of three to five years. The defence plan incorporates the strategic plan, the defence programmes and the budget. The plan should also cover longer periods (up to 30 years) for matters such as capital acquisition, infrastructure and personnel planning.

The nature of the protective functions of government—which include intelligence, policing, justice and correctional services (or prisons) as well as defence—means that planning is always contingent. Requirements are driven by unpredictable factors such as internal crime levels and external instability. In the case of defence, planning must be done for a very uncertain future environment. This is complicated by the long period required to build and prepare defence capabilities, which implies the maintenance of certain capacities purely for possible future eventualities (i.e., defence contingencies).

The defence plan provides the framework for the performance agreement between the defence minister, the political leader of the ministry, and the permanent secretary, who heads the ministry and is its chief accounting officer. The performance agreement should be a written document that clearly specifies the outputs required from the ministry, the associated resource allocations and the performance measurements that will be employed. This serves as the contract between the minister and the permanent secretary. It must of necessity be a product of negotiation between these two individuals. There are three primary outputs that must be specified in the defence plan.

Defence administration. This covers the top-level administrative outputs required for the management of the defence function. It includes the provision of defence policy, strategy, plans, programmes and budgets.

Defence commitments. These are the identified short-to medium-term operational force-employment tasks and objectives.

Defence capabilities. These include the force design, with the required readiness states as well as the supporting force structure. Defence capabilities are the main cost-drivers of defence.

The determination of the first two outputs is relatively simple, being based mostly on current and short-to medium-term future requirements. The determination of defence capabilities is, however, much more complex and long-term in nature.

Defence administration

Defence administration outputs are determined by an analysis of the legislative, policy and management framework within which the military must function. This analysis will be strongly influenced by the demands and requirements of government, specifically those emanating from the defence ministry and other national ministries such as the finance ministry and the public service and administration ministry. This programming function will identify specific objectives to be reached within a one-to three-year timescale.

These objectives are mostly determined, managed and coordinated by the policy and planning, finance and other staff divisions at the defence ministry or defence headquarters. The resources allocated to these activities are relatively small and are mostly associated with the personnel costs of the associated staff divisions, administrative costs and the costs for professional services.

Defence commitments

Short-to medium-term defence commitments or operational outputs are determined through a military operational assessment. This process will rest heavily on the intelligence forecasts of the internal and external security environment for the short to medium term. It will also be strongly influenced by the objectives of the foreign affairs ministry and the internal safety and security ministry. This programming function will identify specific objectives to be reached within a one-to three-year timescale. These activities are mostly determined and managed by the joint operations division at defence headquarters. The resources allocated to these activities are dependent on their scale, duration and intensity. These should include all employment costs, such as increased maintenance, fuel, ammunition, rations and operational allowances among others.

Defence capabilities

The determination of defence capabilities. The establishment, development and maintenance of defence capabilities constitute the main cost element of defence. The determination of the force design and structure is thus the prime area of debate between defence planners and political decision makers, including those responsible for financial management. In the defence plan the determined force design and the structure of the defence force must be clearly stated in terms of quantity (number of units) and quality (readiness states and preparedness). The development and maintenance of this force design and structure constitute a specific objective for the ministry. The staff work for the determination of this objective is primarily undertaken and coordinated by the policy and planning and joint operations divisions at the defence ministry or defence headquarters.

The defence programmes

As defence ministries and forces are large organizations, the management of the top-level objectives is largely delegated to subordinates at the second level of management. These are typically service chiefs and chiefs of staff divisions at the ministry or defence headquarters. Each of these delegated managers will be responsible for a specific defence programme. These defence programmes essentially convert the strategic defence plan into a format where clear responsibility and accountability of the programme managers—who are also referred to as the principal budget holders—are established.

Defence administration programme

The defence administration programme will identify those activities that are essential for the professional, efficient, transparent and accountable management of the defence function and will be coordinated at defence headquarters by the chief of staff responsible for the integrated functioning of all headquarters staff divisions. This programme should include, among others, sub-programmes for political direction (in the office of the defence minister), day-to-day running of the ministry (in the office of the permanent secretary), policy development, corporate departmental planning, strategic intelligence, defence foreign relations, financial management, corporate communication (public relations and internal communication), and internal auditing and inspection.

Objectives for this programme are derived from the top-level administration objectives in one of three ways. First, a top-level objective can be directly delegated to a programme manager at the second level. For example, the objective to 'develop the defence budget for financial years (X) to (Y) for presentation to the finance ministry by (date)' can be delegated to the chief of staff for finance.

Second, a top-level objective may lead to secondary objectives that can be divided among two or more programme managers at the second level while overall responsibility is maintained by the permanent secretary. For example, the objective to 'do a complete defence review for presentation to parliament by (date)' can be subdivided and delegated to the chief of staff for intelligence ('do a strategic intelligence assessment'), the chief of staff for policy and planning.

Third, the permanent secretary should determine his or her own developmental objectives to ensure the continued improvement of the performance of the ministry. These could include objectives to improve the management processes of the ministry (delegated to the chief of staff for policy and planning), to improve information technology systems (delegated to the chief of staff for joint support), and to improve the command and leadership practices of the ministry (delegated to the chief of staff for joint support).

Force-employment programme

The force-employment programme will derive its objectives directly from the top-level defence commitments in the plan and will be coordinated at defence headquarters by the chief of staff for joint operations. This programme should also include sub-programmes for operational intelligence and counter-intelligence, joint force preparation, and command and control. Objectives for these sub-programmes are developed by the chief of staff for joint operations.

Other than those objectives derived directly from defence commitments in the top-level plan, typical force-employment objectives may include objectives to develop command-and-control skills through war gaming and exercises, objectives to prepare and exercise joint formations through military exercises, and objectives to ensure the intelligence for and security of operations.

The force-provision programmes

The force-provision programmes are the domain of the chiefs of the combat services (the army, the air force and the navy), who are responsible for the establishment, development and maintenance of combat-ready forces as agreed in the approved force design. These programmes derive their objectives directly from the approved force design and structure and will include sub-programmes for each of the capability areas as defined in the approved force design as well as for service-specific training and force preparation. Examples of these capability areas are: infantry, armour, artillery, anti-aircraft, engineering, special forces, fighter aircraft, air reconnaissance, helicopters, air transport, submarines, surface combat ships and sea mine-warfare vessels.

Joint force-support programme

The joint force-support programme will identify those joint activities that are essential for the support of the defence administration, the force-employment programmes and, most importantly, the force-provision programmes of the services. The joint force-support programme will be coordinated at defence headquarters by the chief of staff responsible for the coordination of the supporting functions.

Most of the objectives for this programme will be derived through service agreements between the chief of staff for joint support and the other programme managers. This implies that, as certain functions can be executed more efficiently in a centralized manner, such functions should be identified and contracted to joint support by the service chiefs and other divisional chiefs by means of service agreements specifying the level and the cost of services required. This programme should include sub-programmes for personnel management, logistic services, including acquisition and procurement, and military health services.

Resource allocation to the defence programmes

The defence programmes provide the basis for performance agreements between the permanent secretary and the chiefs of staff of the combat services and headquarters staff divisions. Performance agreements basically consist of the objectives to be achieved along with the time frame, the expected standards, the associated level of resource allocation and the required delegations of powers. In addition, these programmes include the service agreements negotiated directly between programme managers. These service agreements also consist of the objectives to be achieved with the time frame, the expected standards, the associated level of resource allocation and, where applicable, the required delegations of powers. As such, these programmes are the product of negotiations between the permanent secretary and subordinate chiefs as well as directly between programme managers.

This process of negotiation is iterative in that each objective must be evaluated for cost and then be either agreed or changed, as required. A change could be an increase in resources or a downscaling of an objective. In order to ensure efficiency, the permanent secretary (and other clients) must demand that programme managers accurately determine the cost of achieving set objectives and provide proof that all efficiency improvements have been considered. The cost of all activities should be regularly compared against a benchmark. The permanent secretary should consider increasing resources or downscaling the requirement only when convinced that the objective is being pursued in the most efficient way possible.

The defence programmes, in the final instance, provide the starting point for the detailed development of the defence budget down to unit level.

The budget

The strategic defence plan specifies the required outputs of the military sector at the highest level as well as the broad level of resource allocation envisaged over an extended period. The defence programmes, in turn, specify outputs in the form of objectives at the next lower level as well as planned allocations to the programme managers for producing these outputs. These must now be converted into business plans where specific activities for reaching these objectives are specified and accurately costed. These business plans are made at unit level (including directorates or sections at defence headquarters) and are in turn the basis for the performance agreements between the programme managers and unit commanders or section chiefs as well as for directly negotiated service agreements. The same considerations raised of performance and service agreements at the next higher level are valid for these agreements.

These business plans are written annually for the next financial year as well as for the subsequent years covered by the MTEF. The defence budget is the total of the business plans expressed in financial terms. It is the ministry's income and spending plan for a set period of time. It is a quantitative expression of the proposed plan of action for the reaching of defence objectives for that time period.

Budgeting is done at unit level, where all inputs that are required to execute the delegated activities must be accurately determined and costed. These input costs (budget items) will include: (*a*) personnel expenditure, such as salaries, allowances, bonuses and gratuities; (*b*) administrative expenses, such as subsistence and travel, transport, membership fees and registration, study expenses, and communications; (*c*) stores, including ammunition and explosives, spares and components for normal maintenance, construction and building material, office supplies, fuel and clothing, among many others; (*d*) equipment, such as vehicles, weapons, machinery and furniture; (*e*) rental of land and buildings;

A PRACTICAL MODEL FOR THE DETERMINATION OF OPTIMAL DEFENCE CAPABILITIES

The determination of optimal defence capabilities to be developed and maintained, along with the associated states of readiness, is the major challenge to the defence planner. This is because defence planning is premised on an uncertain future, is severely constrained by the availability of resources, will always be contested by sectional interests within the defence establishment and is extremely difficult to justify to a populace concerned with more immediate social and personal security issues. Furthermore, the potential consequences of being wrong are enormous in their implications for the future security and well-being of the state.

The development and maintenance of defence capabilities are also the main cost-drivers of defence. The solution of the defence capabilities equation, therefore, requires the major effort in the defence planning process. It is also the prime area of debate between the defence planner and political decision makers. Political decision makers cannot be expected to simply decide on the ends and ways of defence without major inputs regarding the implications of their decisions, especially the implications for the security of the state and the financial implications.

This poses the challenge to the defence planner of finding a rationale for the determination of defence capability requirements that will elicit the understanding and support of political decision makers and civil society. Obviously, such a rationale must be based on the need for efficiency in defence expenditure.

Defence value

If it is accepted that the primary objective of the defence force is to defend and protect the state, its territorial integrity and its people through the provision of contingency-ready military forces and that this is to be done within given financial restrictions, then, the most efficient solution must be sought. Efficiency implies the optimal output for any given input; that is, the best value for money.

This raises the question of how to determine defence value. As defence is concerned with possible future events or threats (defence contingencies), each of which carries an implied risk to the state, *defence value is proportional to risk reduction*. Each defence contingency carries with it an associated risk. If the value of the relative risk of such contingencies can be determined, then this will allow for the development of a system for determining relative defence value.

Defence contingencies

The first step in the defence planning process is the determination of defence contingencies. This entails describing in some detail the possible future events that the defence force might have to deal with. In this process there are no limits and the more contingencies that are accurately described the better. This list should not be restricted to probable events, as these will be determined in the next step; instead, it should contain as many possible defence contingencies as can be imagined. Examples include: (*a*) invasion of the national territory by a foreign power; (*b*) punitive military action against the state; (*c*) coercive military action against the state; (*d*) disruption of national maritime lines of communication and trade; (*e*) military naval, air and land blockades; (*f*) border violations and cross-border crime; (*g*) natural and other disasters that defeat the means of civil society; and (*h*) peace missions in alignment with international and regional obligations.

Risk

Defence primarily concerns possible future events (defence contingencies) and the preparation to successfully counter them when they occur. For each such contingency a statistical probability of occurrence can be determined as well as the potential impact that the occurrence of such a contingency might have on the country. Obviously, contingencies of high probability and major impact carry more risk to the state than contingencies of low probability and minor impact: *risk is proportional to probability and impact*. High-risk contingencies have a high probability of occurrence and the potential for grave impact and vice versa.

The determination of probability

The determination of probability is the most difficult exercise in defence planning, as it is the most subjective and is somewhat like crystal ball gazing. It cannot be an exact science as it deals with an uncertain and ever-changing future. However, without considering probability it is extremely difficult to plan for the future and to determine priorities for defence capabilities to be maintained and developed. An exact formula for determining probability, but it does give guidance regarding some factors to be considered. In 'real life' the determination of the probability of occurrence of a contingency is mostly a task of the intelligence community, consisting of national intelligence, foreign affairs, and military intelligence and strategists. There are three guides to the determination of probability.

1. Evaluate the historic frequency of occurrence (both internationally and nationally) over a very long period.
2. Use a wide spread of probability over a range that is nearer 0.001 to 1 than 0.1 to 1. This ensures greater discrimination in the calculation of probability. As an example, the probability of an invasion could be nearer 0.001 than 0.1.
3. Since absolute probability is all but impossible to calculate, effort should concentrate on the determination of relative probabilities between various contingencies. The involvement of politicians, academics and civil society organizations in this exercise will greatly enhance the quality of the resulting product.

The determination of impact

The determination of impact is less subjective that of probability. Nonetheless, this is not an easy exercise and the involvement of civil society and, in particular, academics in this endeavour is strongly recommended. The potential impact of a contingency that cannot be successfully countered can be calculated using the following parameters: (*a*) the potential loss of life; (*b*) the potential loss of infrastructure; (*c*) the potential loss of economic production and trade; (*d*) the relative loss of sovereignty; (*e*) the relative loss of national image and prestige; (*f*) the relative loss of international confidence; and (*g*) the effect on national morale.

Once the list of contingencies and their relative risk value (probability and impact) have been determined, the value part of the 'value for money' formula has been established. What remains to be done is to calculate the cost of dealing with these potential contingencies. This is another complex exercise.

CONCEPTS OF OPERATIONS AND FORCE DESIGN

For each of the defined contingencies, the best operational concept to counter such an eventuality and the corresponding required capabilities (the 'mini-force design') must be determined. War gaming or simulation processes are the best tools for doing this. Once this has been done, each mini-force design must be costed accurately. This is a major exercise that requires the full and honest participation of the combat services and units down to the lowest level as well as of financial experts. If this is not accurately done, the basis for decision making is seriously undermined.

Costing

Each element of the mini-force design must be fully costed over its life cycle in order to be able to determine cost/benefit ratios for optimization. This cost consists of: (*a*) the annual personnel cost, (*b*) the annual operating cost and (*c*) the annualized capital cost. The annual personnel cost is the full cost of all personnel-related expenses such as salaries, allowances, bonuses and gratuities. The annual operating cost is the full cost of the normal day-to-day running of the unit. This includes administrative expenses, transport, subsistence and travel, provisioning, day-to-day maintenance, fuel, and professional and specialist services. The annualized capital cost is calculated by adding the full procurement cost and the mid-life upgrade cost of capital equipment and dividing it by the expected number of years of operational life of the equipment.

The emphasis on full life-cycle cost is to ensure sustainability of the end result. If this factor is ignored, decisions will be taken that will prove to be unaffordable in the future. This is the cause of many militaries in the developing world having large inventories of unserviceable, unsupportable and unusable equipment.

Optimizing

Once the list of contingencies, the defence value calculations (relative risk-reduction values) and the cost of the elements of the force design are available, calculation of the best value for money can be done.

It must be emphasized that this process will not provide precise, scientifically accurate answers, but it will provide insight into the problems of defence planning and a good basis for discussion with decision makers. It removes the subjectivity of arguments by the individual combat services that their requirements be prioritized. It provides a menu for decision making in which the services that can be ordered can be compared against cost and from which the implications of decisions can be seen. It should be emphasized that the more inclusive the participation in this process is (by political decision makers, other government departments, academics and civil society organizations together with defence experts), the better and more credible the results will be.

FORCE DESIGN AND SUPPORTIVE PLANNING

The above process must culminate in the approval by government of the force design of the armed forces. This also implies a clear commitment by the government to provide funds to the defence ministry for the development, preparation and maintenance of such forces. Without this, no meaningful long-term planning or medium-term programming and budgeting can be done. The force design, together with the required support structures, will form the basis for the development of other long-term plans such as a capital acquisition plan, a facilities or infrastructure plan and the personnel plan. These are long-term plans providing for the procurement of weapon systems, facilities and personnel and the development, preparation, maintenance and eventual disposal of such assets. All of these plans should have a long-term horizon commensurate with the life cycles of these assets. There are, of course, many practical challenges to this planning process.

BUDGETING FOR THE MILITARY SECTOR

Two interrelated developments gave rise to this study. The first was the result of a SIPRI study on the military expenditure of African states. This study concluded that an examination of the processes of budgeting for the military sector in African countries would provide a better understanding of the influences on the levels of military spending in those countries than a simple search for the final budget figure for the military sector. The second was the initiation of the security sector reform debate at the February 2000 symposium organized by the British Department for International Development (DFID). The emphasis of this new debate was on the process of managing military expenditure, in place of donors' earlier, narrow focus on the level of military spending.

While these developments provided the immediate motivation for undertaking this study, the central role played in the 'African problem' by security— or its absence—meant that the need for a study of military budgetary processes in Africa went much deeper, being intertwined with the whole problem of governance and development in Africa. Issues such as the diversion of resources for defence purposes and the proper balance between expenditure on security and on development were part of the disarmament discourse in the developing world as far back as the 1970s. These issues returned to the centre stage from the late 1980s as a result of widespread conflict on the continent, the phenomenon of failed states, the international financial institutions' public expenditure management reforms and bilateral donors' concerns about how their economic assistance was used by poor states.

Donors attempted to impose a predetermined ceiling (or 'acceptable level') on the military expenditure of states. These attempts were directed especially at those states deemed to be engaged in 'excessive' or 'unproductive' expenditure on the military at the expense of the social sector and economic development, and they paid little regard to local security concerns. They also failed to yield the expected results. Instead they led to two unintended consequences: (*a*) the deliberate manipulation of military expenditure figures; and (*b*) the resort to

off-budget spending, which further compounded the problem of public expenditure management. These unintended consequences arose primarily because recipient countries disagreed with the donors on the issue of overspending on the military. In addition, the recipient countries did not accept that their military expenditure constituted unproductive spending.

To promote an understanding of the problems caused by this approach, donors convened several meetings between 1990 and 2000 with a specific focus on the issue of military expenditure and development in developing countries. These meetings and commissioned studies reached fundamental conclusions, which can be summarized as follows.

1. The data on military expenditure, on which judgement on excessive military expenditure was based, were very weak and needed improvement.
2. Even though it could be excessive or inappropriate, military expenditure is not necessarily unproductive expenditure if it leads to an improvement in the well-being of citizens.
3. The focus should be on the process that decides the level of military expenditure rather than on the level of spending per se.
4. Defence should be treated no differently from other parts of the public sector in terms of policy formulation, budgeting, implementation or monitoring. In other words, the key governance principles of transparency, accountability, discipline and comprehensiveness in planning should apply to the military sector just like any other sector.

These conclusions found some resonance at the International Monetary Fund (IMF) and the World Bank, which had started to use the opportunities provided by the end of the cold war to take a critical look at the issue of military expenditure in member countries. By the mid-1990s, both organizations had started to include military expenditure issues in their dialogue with recipient countries. Given the pre-eminent roles played in development cooperation by the IMF and the World Bank, this development encouraged other donors, especially member countries of the Organisation for Economic Co-operation and Development (OECD), to do the same with the recipients of their development assistance. Partly as a result of this and, more significantly, of the problems of widespread conflict and post-conflict public security, donors began to understand the central role played by security in development. Donors realized that some level of military expenditure is needed by states to meet their legitimate security needs and to provide the secure environment necessary for the sustainable development that is the goal of development assistance.

The 'process' approach

The conclusion of the 2000 DFID meeting on Security Sector Reform and Military Expenditure—that an integrated approach should be taken to the management of military expenditure in particular, and of the security sector in general—proved to be a major reason for the shift in some donors' approach to military expenditure. The new approach, known as the 'process' or 'governance' approach, combines good governance practices and sound financial management principles with security considerations and 'focuses attention on the institutional framework for both managing trade-offs between different sectors and for the effective management of the resources devoted to the defence sector'. There is no guarantee that the new approach will lead to an immediate reduction in military expenditure; on the contrary, in the short to medium term military expenditure may appear to increase, as previously off-budget military spending is brought on budget, and expenditure may rise in real terms as the armed forces are made more professional through training and the modernization of equipment. Ultimately, however, reduced military expenditure may be achieved once proper governance principles are entrenched in the system. The process approach offers three main potential advantages to both donors and recipient countries. First, it has the potential to reveal the exact process of budgeting for the military sector, the actors involved and the kinds of trade-off made between the military and other sectors. Ultimately, it can show whether the level of resources allocated to the military is justifiable. Transparency in the decision-making process can also reveal how reliable data are. Second, for recipient countries the process approach provides a unique opportunity to justify—to donors and their own citizens—the level of military expenditure and the extent of military needs, especially where spending limits imposed by donors mean that the basic security needs of the state cannot be met. Third, if donors focus on the application to the military sector of good governance principles, rather than the level of spending, the argument of political interference in domestic affairs of recipient countries carries much less weight and even becomes less sensitive.

These new ideas are gradually gaining ground, although donors still hesitate to adopt an approach that involves greater engagement out of fear of being accused of interfering in the internal political affairs of recipient states or of becoming entangled in their often complex security situations. An increasing number of donors are becoming involved in efforts to improve the security sector in recipient countries. An indication of how far this process has developed is the fact that such engagement is now discussed at meetings of the OECD's Development Assistance Committee. At these meetings, the possibility of counting support for the security sector as part of official development assistance is becoming a major issue.

METHODOLOGY AND SCOPE OF BUDGETING

In order to apply the process approach to the study, a framework of an ideal process is needed. The study uses an analytical framework that is an amalgamation of: (*a*) internationally accepted standards of sound public expenditure management, which includes good governance principles and sound financial management practices; and (*b*) an ideal policy, planning, programming and budgeting framework for armed forces. In other words, it combines economic and security considerations as the basis for determining and managing military expenditure. This balance is important for both the finances and the security of the state. The overarching principle of the framework is that the military sector should be treated no differently in terms of policy development, planning and budgeting from any other part of the public sector. It requires an integrated set of policy principles that involve the military and other sectors in the national policy framework and reflect the country's social, economic and political environment. The translation of this policy into a defence plan allows for the appropriate allocation and efficient use of resources. This framework is based on the assumption that all armed forces have a constitutional role, which enjoins them to serve as guarantors of the territorial integrity and the sovereignty of the nation.

According to this analytical framework, the budgetary process involves a number of institutions and actors that differ from country to country. In an ideal situation, however, the stages involved in the process remain basically the same. The overall policy direction and economic policy framework of the government have a major influence on the process. The objective is to ensure that government allocates resources appropriately to the military sector within the bounds of what the state can afford. It is also important that the process is transparent and participatory—since the approach will be most successful in a democratic environment—and that the military sector competes on an equal footing with all other government sectors.

A participatory process means that economic managers and oversight bodies such as the legislature and the auditor-general play a central role and that non-state actors are consulted. The various stakeholders in the process should receive the amount and type of information required to ensure that appropriate decisions are made. They also need to receive it in timely fashion. Accountability and control are essential; thus, the last three stages in the process outlined below—output monitoring, accounting for expenditure and evaluating results—are an important part of the process approach. The following are the main elements of an acceptable budgetary process for the military sector.

1. The financial envelope for the security sector is defined by the government and communicated to those responsible for overseeing strategic planning for the defence sector.
2. The security environment is analysed.
3. The constitutional and legal framework within which the decision is to be made and implemented is identified.
4. The challenges for the armed forces are defined. These are usually articulated in a defence White Paper or similar policy paper.
5. The types of military capability required to manage the challenges are identified and the options weighed.
6. The size, shape and structure of the armed forces are defined.
7. Resources are allocated and the military budget prepared.
8. Planned activities are implemented and functional areas aligned and rationalized in order to produce an effective defence organization.
9. Outputs (results) are monitored.
10. Expenditure is accounted for properly.
11. Outputs are evaluated and audited, and results are fed into future plans and reported to the relevant legislative and executive bodies.

While it is recognized that the framework may not be applicable in its entirety to all existing military budgetary processes across Africa, two compelling reasons make the use of an ideal process framework attractive (in this case for research). One is the need for a standard measure of good practice in the military policy, planning and budgeting process that will serve as the basis for assessing practice in a number of Africa states. Without such a measure it becomes difficult to assess performance in the sector. The other is that it provides conceptual support for the study on which to anchor the analyses in the case studies. A common conceptual approach provides a good basis for a comparative analysis in the whole study and helps point the way to how processes might be strengthened. In a number of African states the gap between formal and actual processes for determining military expenditure is currently significant. The study therefore examines both the de jure and de facto processes of decision making for military budgeting.

Research design

In view of the perceived sensitive nature of the study and the need to gain access to information, two researchers were commissioned for each case study: an academic researcher and a military practitioner, serving or retired. This proved quite useful in three seemingly difficult case studies. Two workshops were held as part of the study. The first, at the beginning of the study, was to familiarize the researchers with the methodology of the study, in particular the analytical framework, the research questions and what to expect in the field. The second was to discuss the findings of the study at the completion of the country studies.

To define the conduct of the actual research, a set of research questions was discussed and refined at the first workshop. These questions served as the main guide for the conduct of the research in the countries. The researchers supported the structured questions with documentary analysis and interviews with key actors in the budgetary process.

The essence of the structured approach was to provide a basis for the comparative analysis of the country studies according to the respective adherence of the eight countries to the principles of defence planning and programming and public expenditure management. Their adherence is categorized as 'high', 'medium' or 'low' and is used to identify patterns, find explanations and develop recommendations on how to improve the level of adherence.

Throughout the project an international advisory group, comprised of experts in security analysis, supported the study team. The advisory group helped in many respects, including the initial drawing up of research questions, the identification of country researchers from their existing networks.

Regional and country coverage

This study covers eight African countries: Ethiopia, Ghana, Kenya, Mali, Mozambique, Nigeria, Sierra Leone and South Africa. Key background facts about these countries. These countries do not fully reflect the diversity of the African continent in linguistic, cultural or geographic terms. Nor do they adequately capture the various budgetary traditions or practices found in Africa. Their choice became inevitable owing to the severe constraints encountered while conducting the study in the 14 countries which formed the ideal selection for the original project plan.

First, there was a dearth of qualified researchers to carry out the study in a number of the countries. Second, there were indications that some of the countries were hostile to the conduct of this kind of research. As well as the researchers' safety being put at risk if the study were to continue in those countries, access to information seemed likely to be denied. As a result, a number of countries where research proved impossible were either dropped or replaced. Given the circumstances, the original criteria for selecting case studies—geographical distribution, language (both anglo-and francophone), data availability, the nature of the state and the availability of researchers—were amended: the availability of researchers and of an environment conducive to research became the two most important criteria.

Regardless of the criteria, South Africa was chosen as a subject for study because of its success in the post-1994 transformation of its government in general and its budgetary process in particular.

THE OBJECTIVE AND FOCUS OF THE BUDGETING

This study is a pioneering effort to apply the process approach to an assessment of military expenditure management. Eight countries are used as case studies: Ethiopia, Ghana, Kenya, Mali, Mozambique, Nigeria, Sierra Leone and South Africa. The study is concerned not so much with the level of spending in these countries—even though this is touched on—as with the processes by which these countries arrive at their levels of spending. In using this approach to examine the processes of allocating resources to the military sector, the extent of adherence to the principles of defence planning and programming and sound public expenditure management is a major focus.

The guiding principle for the book is that the military sector should be treated no differently from the other parts of the public sector and should be subjected to the same standards, rules and practices. Various studies have shown that military budgets in Africa lack scrutiny by the various oversight bodies and are often protected against cuts when there is a shortfall in expected government income, making the military sector better resourced in comparison to other sectors. While the military sector does differ from other sectors in that certain aspects require some form of confidentiality, this should not confer any special status upon it in terms of resource allocation, transparency, accountability and oversight.

Thus, the main objective of this study is to critically examine the military budgetary processes of a sample of African states with a view to identifying the main actors and institutions in the budgetary process and their roles. Different actors and institutions play different roles in the budgetary process which affect both the level of expenditure and the reporting and auditing of expenditure. The other objective of this study has been to contribute to building local (African) capacity in the area of defence analysis through the use of local researchers. These two broad objectives are set against the background of: (*a*) highly unreliable official military expenditure data; (*b*) presumed off-budget military expenditure; and (*c*) the scarcity of local researchers with expertise in defence analysis.

The focus

Two issues about this study's use of the process approach need to be flagged from the outset. One is the seemingly narrow focus of the study on the *military* budgetary process. A focus on the wider security sector could have been more appropriate and would perhaps have provided a slightly different set of conclusions. However, since this is a ground-breaking study and since what is true for the military sector is largely true for the whole security sector, nothing has been lost by focusing on the military, which, in any case, is generally assumed to consume the most resources and to be the least transparent of the security forces. Indeed, to ensure that the study did not lose its focus, it was decided early in the project to use a word with an unambiguous meaning to describe the section of the security sector on which research attention was to be directed: hence the use of the term 'military' rather than 'defence', which has a much broader meaning in many African states. Where, following local terminology in particular countries, the term 'defence' is used in this book, it refers to the military as defined here.

The second issue is that the adoption of the process approach should not be assumed to imply general support for the belief subsisting in many circles, including the donor community, that African states spend, relatively speaking, too much on the military sector. Across Africa, there is a general underfunding of the public sector, including the military sector. While other sectors in poor states receive support from external sources, the military sector receives little such support, especially since the end of the cold war. Yet African military forces are increasingly being used for internal security purposes and international peacekeeping operations without any corresponding increase in resources. One of the reasons for the prolonged conflicts in weak African states is the national armies' lack of superior firepower that could put down armed rebellions at an early stage. Indeed, the ramshackle state of many military establishments in Africa is as much evidence of underfunding as a reflection of mismanagement of resources. The lack of adequate resources for the armed forces is glaring in some of the African states that are undertaking reforms of their military sectors. For instance, Uganda's defence review showed the need for reform in several key areas of the military sector. However, the costs of the reforms are quite high and Uganda cannot carry them out without external support.

The proportion of Africa's gross domestic product (GDP) absorbed by military expenditure with that in other regions of the world. Compared with Asia, Latin America, Oceania and Western Europe, Africa's military burden is high. However, it should be borne in mind that a handful of Africa's 53 states account for a disproportionate share of its military expenditure, while the majority are barely able to take care of their militaries due to a dearth of resources. Africa's military expenditure per capita is the lowest in the world; below the average for low-income countries, the category to which the majority of countries on the continent belong. In their resource-constrained environment, many African states feel that they cannot afford both security and development.

Although it is commonly acknowledged that military means are not the only way to provide security, the link between security and development is well established and so critical choices have to be made between investing available resources in security and in other sectors and on how best to synthesize security and development objectives. The trade-offs that are inevitable in the process may not meet the expectations of donors but may be unavoidable given domestic realities. Within the context of resource constraints, however, there is a need to ascertain the level of mismanagement of resources: what proportion of the, sometimes bloated, military budget actually goes towards the maintenance of the military, and what proportion falls into private hands owing to opaque management practices.

The adoption of the process approach, with its emphasis on adherence to sound public expenditure management principles and due consideration of the security environment, may aid the resolution of this dilemma.

BUDGET 2012: IN DEFENCE OF A STRONG RUPEE

On a cool late-winter evening 20 years ago, India's finance minister pulled a rabbit out of the hat. Dr. Manmohan Singh was delivering his second Union Budget on February 29, 1992. The first had been an interim budget on July 24, 1991 to stitch together an economy battered by near-financial bankruptcy with 67 tonnes of treasury gold mortgaged by the Indian government to the Bank of England and the Union Bank of Switzerland under the stern gaze of the IMF.

The rabbit Dr. Singh pulled out that evening was the Liberalised Exchange Rate Management System (LERMS) which created a dual exchange rate for the rupee. The reformist finance minister, demonstrating early signs of the gentle political guile that would stand him in good stead as prime minister in UPA-I and UPA-2, dubbed it "a partial float of the rupee". He was being economical with the truth. The partial float of the rupee was a fig leaf for one of the steepest controlled rupee devaluations in Indian history. On July 1, 1991, the exchange rate was Rs. 18 to the dollar. By March 1993, the exchange rate had plunged to Rs. 32 to a dollar – a decline of 77% in a little over 18 months.

The "partial float" of the rupee led eventually to current account convertibility but not to the full capital account convertibility the finance minister had promised. Despite the Tarapore Committee and others backing the idea (with riders), the rupee 20 years later remains partially convertible on the capital account with the Reserve Bank of India allowing Indians to remit only up to $2,00,000 a year for capital investments abroad.

Dr. Singh's leap year Budget on February 29, 1992 did not celebrate its 20th anniversary this year. The five state assembly elections pushed the Budget to March 16, much to beleaguered finance minister Pranab Mukherjee's relief. He received an additional fortnight to balance the nation's books and use creative accounting to keep the central fiscal deficit from spiralling into dangerous territory – roughly defined as anything above 6% of GDP.

Since Dr. Singh's interim Budget of July 1991 and his magical leap year Budget of February 1992, the rupee has depreciated by nearly 100% in 20 years (from Rs. 25.95 in February 1992 to just under Rs. 50 today). That's a compounded annual depreciation of 3.6%. On the face of it, that doesn't seem too steep. But a constantly weakening rupee pushes up the cost of imports, widens the trade and current account deficits, raises the external debt burden (currently over $320 billion), makes pertroproducts more expensive and fuels inflation.

Votàries of a weak rupee point to the example of China which – to the rest of the world's annoyance – has deliberately kept the yuan undervalued, forcing US legislators to consider officially declaring Beijing a "currency manipulator". The comparison with India though is not valid. China is the manufacturing workshop of the world. Exports comprise nearly 30% of its GDP. Last year it displaced Germany as the world's largest exporter (with annual exports of $2 trillion). In contrast, exports account for only 18% of India's GDP. A weak rupee does not help the other 82% of India's economy. Quite the contrary: an import bill of $470 billion (over 25% of Indian GDP) pushes up inflation and lowers competitiveness.

A stronger rupee will not only trim our trade and current account deficits and temper inflation, it will attract more FDI and FII. Today foreign investors factor in an historical 4% annual depreciation of the rupee when computing their return on investment (RoI). Were the rupee to strenghten, dollar returns would rise concomitantly. Average central bank lending rates in the west and Japan are between 0.25% and 3%. In India, the RBI's repo rate, at which it lends funds to banks, has averaged 7.00-8.50% in the recent past. The gap mirrors precisely the historical annual depreciation of the rupee against the dollar. A stronger rupee would reduce that gap and bring India in line with advanced economies.

Most crucially, a stronger rupee would bring down India's gargantuan – and rising – oil and gas import bill. A failure of our oil and gas exploration effort over the past two decades has led to India importing 80% of its crude oil requirement. This amount is nearly equal to the country's expected trade deficit in 2011-12 of $180 billion. A stronger rupee would significantly cut the trade deficit, even after netting the value of refined petroproduct exports. The saving, in the region of Rs. 1.20 lakh crore, could shave a quarter off India's fiscal deficit. Wouldn't Indian services – especially IT software – suffer if the rupee hardens? Service exports sell increasingly on quality, not price. Many (especially refined petroproducts and polished diamonds) have high import content. The biggest long-term beneficiaries of a stronger rupee would be India's manufacturing productivity. Cheaper imports would allow companies to ramp up foreign technology and build infrastructural and manufacturing assets. These in turn would lead to a spike in competitiveness, boosting exports based on quality, not marked-down prices. This would create a virtuous cycle of high productivity and quality allied with low inflation and deficits.

So what should be the value of a more muscular rupee? The *Economist's* latest Big Mac Index shows that the rupee is undervalued vis-à-vis the US dollar by 61% while the yuan is undervalued by 41%. While the *Economist's* Big Mac Index does not take into account lower national labour and ingredient costs, it has over the years been a surprisingly accurate indicator of exchange rate trends. Discounting the *Economist's index* for India's low-cost economy, the rupee is probably currently undervalued against the dollar by around 25%. A fair value for the rupee would therefore be just under 40 to a dollar. Our former finance minister, now prime minister, who 20 years ago said 25 to a dollar was fair value for the rupee in pre-reform India, might well agree.

7

Economic Aspects of Military Expenditure and Arms Transfers

The experiences in many countries, which have cut their armed forces, arms production and military expenditures, are that these cuts have had adverse economic effects, in terms of economic decline, especially on a local and regional level, and in terms of unemployment. Such negative economic consequences constitute obstacles to reductions in military expenditure even if there is scope for cuts from a security perspective. The question at stake is whether cuts in military expenditure lead to the release of economic resources for other competing demands? Is there a so-called *peace dividend*? This question can be perceived in two parts, the more long-term and the short-term. First, are there economic gains in the long term from reductions in military expenditure? This question can be analysed by looking at the economic impact of current military expenditure. If the overall impact is negative, there should be something to gain by reducing them. Second, what are the nature and costs of the adjustment process involved in transferring economic resources from military use to non-military use?

From a purely theoretical perspective, there is no consensus on the economic effects of military spending: the two main existing schools (neo-classical and Keynesian) provide different answers. Applied empirical studies show that in advanced economies military expenditure has a negative effect on economic growth through its effect on investment. Empirical studies for developing countries suggest that there is no evidence of a positive effect of military expenditure on economic growth and that a negative impact is likely. In general, these conclusions refer to a *ceteris paribus* comparison, when nothing else is changed. They do not assume a policy of conversion to redirect the saved money from reduced military expenditure into alternative uses, such as non-military government expenditure or investment.

Since military expenditure has no positive effect on the economy, it follows that there should be no negative impact on the economy of cuts in military expenditure in the long term, that is, after the completion of cuts. In this sense there is a *peace dividend* (an economic gain) to realise from cuts in military expenditure. This has also been demonstrated in a series of case studies using input-output simulations of military expenditure reductions. However, this does not mean that reductions in military expenditure are without negative economic consequences. During the period of adjustment to a situation with a lower level of military spending, a multitude of adverse economic consequences are likely to be confronted, on the macroeconomic, regional and local levels, on the company level and on the labour market. Such short-term economic adjustment problems have led many analysts to conclude that there is no peace dividend to be achieved from reduced military expenditure, while the proper conclusion to draw is that such reductions have not been associated with the proper policy, a policy directed at facilitating the conversion of military resources to civil purposes, that is, an active conversion policy.

Conversion policies can address anything from the demobilization of soldiers, base closures, diversification of arms-producing companies, transfer of military technology to civilian purposes. Such activities, which are annually documented by the Bonn International Centre for Conversion (BICC) had given extensive results by the late 1990s. In its most recent survey of disarmament and conversion the achievements through 1998 were summarized as follows: '...

while a reversal of the disarmament and conversion process in some countries or regions cannot be excluded, it must be emphasized that behind the noisy headlines of the many conflicts, there exists a string of positive, often silent achievements. Clearly, in total the 1990s balance sheet of disarmament and conversion is positive. Global disarmament continued even in 1997 and 1998, although at a slower pace, and so did conversion. Despite the difficulties of implementing disarmament, numerous practical conversion projects are underway or have already been completed.'

While efforts at the micro level to convert military bases, retrain former soldiers and diversify arms-producing companies are important contributions to the adjustment involved in reallocating military expenditure to sustainable non-military use, these efforts alone are not sufficient. This can be clearly seen from the Russian experience, where the ambitious conversion plans of the early 1990s faltered primarily because of the lack of two basic elements: investment capital and a functioning market for civil goods and for labour. Diversification of production requires a significant amount of investment, both for the conversion of production facilities and labour through reconstruction and retraining, which seldom occurs, and even more so for the expansion of civil production by new investment and new recruitment, which is the more feasible strategy. Therefore, the adjustment from military to civil use of economic resources, in addition to practical conversion measures, 'requires a more general policy which sees conversion as an integral part of a policy of industrial restructuring and regeneration'. Conversion must be seen as an investment process.

This conclusion applies in particular to the arms-producing industrial countries. However, it is also of relevance for developing, although in a somewhat modified form, since most of these have no arms production, and since the large part of their military expenditure is spent on military personnel. 'Thus, their adjustment problems will involve either releasing military personnel on to the labour market, or, in the case of conscription, not recruiting labour. In the short run, the result is likely to add to the substantial employment problems of developing economies. There are also likely to be implications for accommodation and for the provision of social services previously supplied by the armed forces.' Therefore, abrupt declines in military expenditures, 'when combined with conditions of economic decline stemming from low prices of exports, reduced foreign assistance and poor macroeconomic policies would lead to high costs, a long transition period, low benefits, and thus a low (or even negative) return from disarmament., This may be the case in several such countries today, unless countered by international technical and financial assistance and informed national macroeconomic, trade and defence economic policies. In the developing countries, through, the prospects of achieving a peace dividend might be improved because they probably have smaller stocks of military capital and relatively greater flows of resources into and out of the military sector.

Few studies have been made on the actual reallocation of public expenditure from civil to military purposes. However, a recent survey by the International Monetary Fund showed that reductions in military spending in some countries have been accompanied by increased public expenditure on health and education. In 61 countries for which health and education data were available for the period 1993– 97, the share of these expenditures increased during the period, both as a share of GDP and of total government expenditures, while the shares of military expenditures declined. The tabular data provided indicate that the increased shares of health and education were the result of the fact that expenditure on health and education did not decline as much as military expenditures.

KEY CHALLENGES

Our current world is one in which military activities annually absorb an amount of economic resources corresponding to the annual income of half of the world population, while at the same time there is an enormous need for these resources to stave off poverty, hunger and preventable diseases. Furthermore, in spite of the amount of resources spent ultimately for security purposes, the actual security of states and human beings in many regions is extremely low. The overall challenge lies in how to reduce military expenditure and international arms transfers and channel the released resources into economically and socially more beneficial uses, while at the same time not reducing, but rather enhancing the security of the world population. An insurmountable challenge it appears, but it still has to be addressed.

Any policy aimed at the reduction of military expenditure and international arms transfers, on a worldwide scale, or regionally or locally, would clearly have to address a whole range of factors which contribute to sustain current levels of military expenditure and arms transfers. This would involve at least six different levels: *(i)* the root causes of the need for military forces; *(ii)* a whole set of security-related factors behind military expenditures; *(iii)* the organization of the military sector itself; *(iv)* vested economic and political interests to sustain military expenditure; *(v)* arms control and disarmament agreements and activities; and *(vi)* the planned transfer of released resources to productive or social use. A condition for being able to address most of these challenges, is an open and democratic political decision making process for issues related to these.

The basic challenge is how to address the root causes of military forces, and in particular the more ominous ones. Again, these are multifold and not comprehensively explored. Among the more important factors today, at least in large parts of the developing world, is the existence of armed conflict. Thus, one of the basic challenges is how to address the root causes of armed conflict. Existing theories and empirical studies attribute armed conflict to a complex of economic, political, social, environmental, religious and other cultural factors. Causation is difficult to establish in social sciences and causes are working on different levels. On the systemic level it has been shown that there is a clear relationship between political system (as measured by human rights abuse) and armed conflict and between economic development (and the distribution of economic resources) and armed conflict but a less clear relationship between ethnic diversity and armed conflict.

A second challenge is how, given the need for military forces, to develop policies and measures which improve security regimes and security in all its aspects: international, regional, national and human, and in particular, to develop new nonmilitary policies and measures of providing security. These are factors traditionally belonging to the domains of national and international security, but increasingly also other domains, with the current transformation of the security concept to a broader scope, including not only military security of the state but also economic, social, and environmental security for both states and people. In particular there is a need to develop non-military methods of peace enforcement and to avoid the use of military means to prevent the outbreak of armed conflict or stop its continuation. The new phenomenon of using private security groups or forces for the provision of military security, particularly in Africa, deserves special attention. These security groups are primarily private companies providing security services to foreigners for profit. The main tasks of these companies is to fill the void created by inefficient armed forces.

Many of them have been involved in one way or the other in the region's many conflicts, supporting either government or the rebels. However, since they are profit oriented there are doubts about their sincerity in bringing about an enduring peace where they operate. How to regulate their activities is a source of concern for the international community. A third challenge is to ensure that there is a proper match between existing security requirements and the size of the military establishment and to reduce waste and inefficiencies which is common in the military sector and often made possible by the fact that military establishments are shrouded in secrecy and often politically and economically protected.

A fourth challenge is how to remove obstacles to reductions in military expenditures, which stem from domestic and personal, economic and political rather than international security-related factors. These refer to the vested interests not only of the military establishment itself, but also of the ruling regimes in many countries, of the companies and countries involved in the production and sales of military goods and services, and of the politicians with electorate constituencies in regions depending on military contracts. Vested interests in war, as described by Kaldor is an increasing challenge, primarily for the prospects of conflict resolution and successful peace settlements. Both these challenges can be met only by studying the causes and mechanisms of vested interests and devise measures addressed at the causes, not their effects.

The fifth challenge is to cement any progress reached into international agreements on arms control and disarmament, primarily because this creates some resistance against any reversal of progress. In particular there is a need to develop new forms of arms control measures that are relevant in the new post cold war environment.

While traditional arms control that developed during the cold war, was designed to manage arms competition among antagonistic states, what is needed today are arms control measures which can be applied in the context of internal armed conflict fought by substate or nonstate actors, in particular to maintain peace and resolve conflict in countries where civil wars have been settled by peace agreements.

Although much remains to be done in this area, some experience have been gained and analysed. A study by the Lessons Learned Unit of the UN Department of Peacekeeping Operations on the Disarmament, Demobilisation and Reintegration has developed a number of recommendations which also include the need to address the new channels of financing war and the conversion of military forces through their reintegration and rehabilitation. These are measures which requires significant assistance from the international community, both in terms of sanctions and financial assistance. Another summary has identified several categories of arms control mechanisms that are particularly well suited to post conflict environments: disengagement, demilitarization, disarmament, and confidence-building measures.

A sixth challenge, finally, and related to the above, is to find policies to redirect economic resources that have been released from cuts in military expenditure into uses which are beneficial to economic and social development in the long run. The transfer of resources from military to non-military uses requires a conversion policy for its implementation. It also requires financial capital for investment in alternative economic activities. Many countries in the developing world would require development aid to assist in the conversion process.

There are no easy solutions to this broad range of challenges The identification of such solutions is also beyond the scope of this paper. However, an important condition for their solution is increased transparency in the military sector in order to promote democratic and participatory decision-making in setting the priorities between military and non-military expenditure in the allocation of central government expenditure. In addition, increased information and knowledge about the characteristics and functioning of the military sector and about the relationship between military expenditure, conflicts, and economic developments are essential for any future change, whether in the short or medium term. Thirdly, the nature of these challenges, and the state of the economies in the most seriously affected countries, are such that any progress in addressing these require the involvement of the international community.

Such involvement includes many different types of activities. The most difficult to achieve is probably the commitment of economic resources for the various ends outlined above. Perhaps the most immediate task is to make a convincing argument for such financial commitments: one of the main proarguments is that the long run cost of not addressing these challenges is likely to exceed by far the short run costs of addressing them today.

Another overall challenge is a reconsideration of the relationship between security and economic development. These two issue areas have been and are still to a great extent treated as entirely separate fields, they are dealt with by different organizations, both nationally and internationally, and also within the UN system, and by different types of policies and measures. In practice, however, they are increasingly intertwined. Military expenditure constitutes a significant economic burden in many developing countries, which inhibits economic and social development. Lack of security inhibits economic activities and armed conflict exerts a disastrous negative impact on economic development.

The World Bank has created a Post-Conflict Unit to facilitate assistance in reconstruction activities after the cessation of hostilities. Security can no longer be understood mainly as military security. An expanded security policy should integrate also development policy in terms of a global security policy which covers economic, social, ecological and political relationships in other regions of the world. It is possible that the UN could have a role to play to promote the needed fundamental change in security policy which is already emerging.

The Need for Increased Transparency in Military Matters

Openness and democratic participation in the formation of defence and security policies, in arms procurement decision-making, and budgeting processes constitutes an overall challenge. Transparency in defence budgeting and the activities financed by defence budgets is important for two major reasons:

1. For establishing national priorities between military and non-military sectors in the allocation of public expenditures.
2. For building confidence and security between neighbour states.

Domestic transparency in military matters facilitates the identification of excessive military spending and can in itself lead to reductions in military expenditure in cases where other than security-related factors determine the amounts of money allocated to defence.

This facilitates the identification of excessive military expenditure and the establishing of priorities in the allocation of public resources between military and non-military purposes that are in line with the interests of the population. In many countries there is extremely little information available about the military sector, not only for the tax-payers and the electorate, but also for the members of parliament with the task to approve or reject government proposals on military matters.

Information exchanges with neighbour states can also lead to reduced levels of military expenditure by reducing threat perceptions and preparing the ground for arms control and disarmament agreements. While increased transparency on the national and sub-regional level is the most important, international initiatives may reinforce demands for national transparency and also contribute to the provision of data. Here, the international community and the United Nations have a role to play in promoting the concept of transparency and setting the standards. Existing initiatives include those of the United Nations for reporting military expenditure and international arms transfers. While the response rate to the latter is relatively high, the reporting of military expenditure has a much lower turn-out and this measures is currently therefore under review by member governments.

The UN Reporting Instrument on Military Expenditure

The UN call on its member states to report annually the size and structure of their military expenditure-which originally was established as a first step to reduction of military budgets-is currently a rather lame measure. The response rate is low, averaging around 30 countries out of a total of 187 UN member states and these are to a great extent those which already are most transparent in military matters. Some improvement is required and the reporting instrument is therefore currently under review. The most important changes required are:

a) A more active approach by the UN Secretariat to encourage member states to report;

b) Some political momentum behind the initiative.

Today the UN Secretariat is not authorized to do much more than passively receive and file the reports. The much greater response rate by other organizations, including SIPRI, shows that a more active approach could give rather prompt results. However for broad participation in the UN reporting system, this would not suffice. Incentives to report require a political context.

Information exchanges on a regional basis for confidence building, modelled after the OSCE system could provide one such context. Broader proposals to reduce military expenditure by specific percentages, as was the original intention with the UN system and as are still kept alive in the academic community, may be too crude and general to be feasible. However, it could be possible to develop similar proposals on a regional basis and including measures which are tailored to the security environment of a particular region. Another useful initiative would be to set up some kind of transparency institutes with the task to compile and provide information on military matters, and provide support to parliamentarians, civil society for an informed debate on budget priorities, arms procurement, arms imports, economic impacts, etc. Today the most basic information for an open debate on these issues is lacking in many countries.

The UN Register on Conventional Arms

The response rate to the UN Register on Conventional Arms (initiated in 1991)39 is higher: 97 member states reported in 1998. The report for 1999, which was released in August 1999, included responses from 64 countries with some additional replies expected later. Much remains to be improved, however. Transparency in the international arms trade is still very limited. The UN Register provides little detail on the items which are reported. Small arms and weapons of mass destruction are not included at all, neither are technology transfers for the manufacture of weapons.

Reporting on procurement from national production and on military holdings which have been included in the reporting to the UN Register since 1998 is still unsatisfactory. The Group of Government Experts with the task to review the Register will convene again in year 2000 and it is hoped that the gradual improvement of the Register will continue.

Transparency in Arms Production

The area in which there is the least transparency is arms production. This is so basically for commercial reasons. Arms producing companies release little information on their arms sales and governments are reluctant or unable to put pressure on them. With the internationalization of arms production, this becomes even more difficult on the national level. Still, arms producing companies are powerful actors and will probably have significantly increased leverage in the evolving international system for arms production and exports. With arms sales ranging up to 15-20 billion dollars per year and with an increasingly oligopolistic industrial structure, the power balance between state and industry is shifting to the detriment of the former. There is a need therefore, for policy proposals to introduce some transparency in the activities of the arms industry, with the long term view towards some type of regulatory measure of their activities, preferably on an international basis.

MILITARY BUDGET OF THE UNITED STATES

The military budget is that portion of the United States discretionary federal budget that is allocated to the Department of Defense, or more broadly, the portion of the budget that goes to any defense-related expenditures. This military budget pays the salaries, training, and health care of uniformed and civilian personnel, maintains arms, equipment and facilities, funds operations, and develops and buys new equipment. The budget funds all branches of the U.S. military: Army, Navy, Air Force, and Marine Corps.

Budget for 2010

For the 2010 fiscal year, the president's base budget of

the Department of spending on "overseas contingency operations" brings the sum to $663.84 billion. When the budget was signed into law on October 28, 2009, the final size of the Department of Defense's budget was $680 billion, $16 billion more than President Obama had requested. An additional $37 billion supplemental bill to support the wars in Iraq and Afghanistan was expected to pass in the spring of 2010, but has been delayed by the House of Representatives after passing the Senate.

Emergency and supplemental spending

The recent invasions of Iraq and Afghanistan were largely funded through supplementary spending bills outside the Federal Budget, so they are not included in the military budget figures listed below. Starting in the fiscal year 2010 budget however, the wars in Iraq and Afghanistan are categorized as "Overseas Contingency Operations" and included in the budget.

By the end of 2008, the U.S. had spent approximately $900 billion in direct costs on the Iraq and Afghanistan Wars. Indirect costs such as interest on the additional debt and incremental costs of caring for the more than 33,000 wounded borne by the Veterans Administration are additional. Some experts estimate these indirect costs will eventually exceed the direct costs.

Other defense-related expenditures

This does not include many military-related items that are outside of the Defense Department budget, such as nuclear weapons research, maintenance, cleanup, and production, which is in the Department of Energy budget, Veterans Affairs, the Treasury Department's payments in pensions to military retirees and widows and their families, interest on debt incurred in past wars, or State Department financing of foreign arms sales and militarily-related development assistance. Neither does it include defense spending that is not military in nature, such as the Department of Homeland Security, counter-terrorism spending by the FBI, and intelligence-gathering spending by NASA.

Audit of Implementation of Budget for 2010

The US Government Accountability Office (GAO) was unable to provide an audit opinion on the 2010 financial statements of the US Government because of 'widespread material internal control weaknesses, significant uncertainties, and other limitations'. The GAO cited as the principal obstacle to its provision of an audit opinion 'serious financial management problems at the Department of Defense that made its financial statements unauditable'.

In FY 2010 six out of thirty-three DoD reporting entities received unqualified audit opinions. Chief Financial Officer and Under Secretary of Defense Robert F. Hale acknowledged enterprise-wide problems with systems and processes, while the DoD's Inspector General reported 'material internal control weaknesses... that affect the safeguarding of assets, proper use of funds, and impair the prevention and identification of fraud, waste, and abuse'. Further management discussion in the FY 2010 DoD Financial Report states 'it is not feasible to deploy a vast number of accountants to manually reconcile our books' and concludes that 'although the financial statements are not auditable for FY 2010, the Department's financial managers are meeting warfighter needs'.

Audit of 2011 Budget

Again in 2011, the GAO could not "render an opinion on the 2011 consolidated financial statements of the federal government", with a major obstacle again being "serious financial management problems at the Department of Defense (DOD) that made its financial statements unauditable". In December 2011, the GAO found that "neither the Navy nor the Marine Corps have implemented effective processes for reconciling their FBWT." According to the GAO, "An agency's FBWT account is similar in concept to a corporate bank account. The difference is that instead of a cash balance, FBWT represents unexpended spending authority in appropriations." In addition, "As of April 2011, there were more than $22 billion unmatched disbursements and collections affecting more than 10,000 lines of accounting."

Support Service Contractors

The role of support service contractors has increased since 2001 and in 2007 payments for contractor services exceeded investments in equipment for the armed forces for the first time. In the 2010 budget the support service contractors will be reduced from the current 39 percent of the workforce down to the pre-2001 level of 26 percent. In a Pentagon review of January 2011, service contractors were found to be "increasingly unaffordable."

Military Budget and Total US Federal Spending

World War II commenced a new era of permanency in the United States defense budget. With the advent of the Cold War, the United States began to maintain a standing army and a permanent state of readiness for war that permanently elevated national defense expenditures. At the conclusion of his second term, President Eisenhower, wrote:

Our military organization today bears little relation to that known by any of my predecessors in peacetime, or indeed by the fighting men of World War II or Korea. Until the latest of our world conflicts, the United States had no armaments industry. American makers of plowshares could, with time and as required, make swords as well. But now we can no longer risk emergency improvisation of national defense; we have been compelled to create a permanent armaments industry of vast proportions. Added to this, three and a half million men and women are directly engaged in the defense establishment. We annually spend on military security more than the net income of all United States corporations. This conjunction of an immense military establishment and a large arms industry is new in the American experience. The total influence — economic, political, even spiritual — is felt in every city, every State house, every office of the Federal government. We recognize the imperative need for this development. Yet we must not fail to comprehend its grave implications. Our toil, resources and livelihood are all involved; so is the very structure of our society. In the councils of government, we must guard against the acquisition of unwarranted influence, whether sought or unsought, by the military industrial complex. The potential for the disastrous rise of misplaced power exists and will persist. We must never let the weight of this combination endanger our liberties or democratic processes. We should take nothing for granted. Only an alert and knowledgeable citizenry can compel the proper meshing of the huge industrial and military machinery of defense with our peaceful methods and goals, so that security and liberty may prosper together.

The U.S. Department of Defense budget accounted in fiscal year 2010 for about 19% of the United States federal budgeted expenditures and 28% of estimated tax revenues. Including non-DOD expenditures, defense spending was approximately 28–38% of budgeted expenditures and 42–57% of estimated tax revenues. According to the Congressional Budget Office, defense spending grew 9% annually on average from fiscal year 2000–2009.

Because of constitutional limitations, military funding is appropriated in a discretionary spending account. (Such accounts permit government planners to have more flexibility to change spending each year, as opposed to mandatory spending accounts that mandate spending on programs in accordance with the law, outside of the budgetary process.) In recent years, discretionary spending as a whole has amounted to about one-third of total federal outlays. Department of Defense spending's share of discretionary spending was 50.5% in 2003, and has risen to between 53% and 54% in recent years.

For FY 2010, Department of Defense spending amounts to 4.7% of GDP. Because the U.S. GDP has risen over time, the military budget can rise in absolute terms while shrinking as a percentage of the GDP. For example, the Department of Defense budget is slated to be $664 billion in 2010 (including the cost of operations in Iraq and Afghanistan previously funded through supplementary budget legislation), higher than at any other point in American history, but still 1.1–1.4% lower as a percentage of GDP than the amount spent on defense during the peak of Cold-War military spending in the late 1980s. Admiral Mike Mullen, former Chairman of the Joint Chiefs of Staff, has called four percent an "absolute floor". This calculation does not take into account some other defense-related non-DOD spending, such as Veterans Affairs, Homeland Security, and interest paid on debt incurred in past wars, which has increased even as a percentage of the national GDP.

Comparison with other Countries

The 2009 U.S. military budget accounts for approximately 40% of global arms spending. The 2012 budged is 3-4 times larger than the 240 billions of the military budget of China (compared at the nominal US dollar/Renminbi rate, not the PPP rate which would make more sense), and is more than the next twenty largest military spenders combined. The United States and its close allies are responsible for two-thirds to three-quarters of the world's military spending (of which, in turn, the U.S. is responsible for the majority).

In 2005, the United States spent 4.06% of its GDP on its military (considering only basic Department of Defense budget spending), more than France's 2.6% and less than Saudi Arabia's 10%. This is historically low for the United States since it peaked in 1944 at 37.8% of GDP (it reached the lowest point of 3.0% in 1999–2001). Even during the peak of the Vietnam War the percentage reached a high of 9.4% in 1968. Countries like Canada and Germany spend only 1.4% of GDP on their military.

Recent Commentary on Military Budget

In February 2009, Congressman Barney Frank, D-Mass., called for a reduction in the defense budget: "The math is compelling: if we do not make reductions approximating 25 percent of the military budget starting fairly soon, it will be impossible to continue to fund an adequate level of domestic activity even with a repeal of Bush's tax cuts for the very wealthy. I am working with a variety of thoughtful analysts to show how we can make very substantial cuts in the military budget without in any way diminishing the security we need...[American] well-being is far more endangered by a proposal for substantial reductions in Medicare, Social Security or other important domestic areas than it would be by canceling weapons systems that have no justification from any threat we are likely to face."

Republican historian Robert Kagan has argued that 2009 is not the time to cut defense spending, relating such spending to jobs and support for allies: "A reduction in defense spending this year would unnerve American allies and undercut efforts to gain greater cooperation.

There is already a sense around the world...that the United States is in terminal decline. Many fear that the economic crisis will cause the United States to pull back from overseas commitments. The announcement of a defense cutback would be taken by the world as evidence that the American retreat has begun."

Secretary of Defense Robert Gates wrote in 2009 that the U.S. should adjust its priorities and spending to address the changing nature of threats in the world: "What all these potential adversaries—from terrorist cells to rogue nations to rising powers—have in common is that they have learned that it is unwise to confront the United States directly on conventional military terms. The United States cannot take its current dominance for granted and needs to invest in the programs, platforms, and personnel that will ensure that dominance's persistence. But it is also important to keep some perspective. As much as the U.S. Navy has shrunk since the end of the Cold War, for example, in terms of tonnage, its battle fleet is still larger than the next 13 navies combined—and 11 of those 13 navies are U.S. allies or partners." Secretary Gates announced some of his budget recommendations in April 2009.

The Congressional Research Service has noted a discrepancy between a budget that is declining as a percentage of GDP while the responsibilities of the DoD have not decreased and additional pressures on the defense budget have arisen due to broader missions in the post-9/11 world, dramatic increases in personnel and operating costs, and new requirements resulting from wartime lessons in the Iraq War and Operation Enduring Freedom.

GAO Audits

The Government Accountability Office was unable to provide an audit opinion on the 2010 financial statements of the U.S. government due to "widespread material internal control weaknesses, significant uncertainties, and other limitations." The GAO cited as the principal obstacle to its provision of an audit opinion "serious financial management problems at the Department of Defense that made its financial statements unauditable."

In Fiscal Year (FY) 2011, seven out of 33 DoD reporting entities received unqualified audit opinions. Under Secretary of Defense Robert F. Hale acknowledged enterprise-wide weaknesses with controls and systems. Further management discussion in the FY 2011 DoD Financial Report states "we are not able to deploy the vast numbers of accountants that would be required to reconcile our books manually". Congress has established a deadline of FY 2017 for the DoD to achieve audit readiness. In addition to FY 2011, the Department of Defense's financial statements were either unauditable or such that no audit opinion could be expressed for FYs 2010-1998.

Reform

In a statement of 6 January 2011 Defense Secretary Robert M. Gates stated: "This department simply cannot risk continuing down the same path-where our investment priorities, bureaucratic habits and lax attitude towards costs are increasingly divorced from the real threats of today, the growing perils of tomorrow and the nation's grim financial outlook." Gates has proposed a budget which, if approved by the Congress, would reduce the costs of many DOD programs and policies, including reports, the IT infrastructure, fuel, weapon programs, DOD bureaucracies, and personnel.

ARMS INDUSTRY

The arms industry is a global industry and business which manufactures and sells weapons and military technology and equipment. It comprises government and commercial industry involved in research, development, production, and service of military material, equipment and facilities. Arms producing companies, also referred to as defence contractors or military industry, produce arms mainly for the armed forces of states. Departments of government also operate in the arms industry, buying and selling weapons, munitions and other military items. Products include guns, ammunition, missiles, military aircraft, military vehicles, ships, electronic systems, and more. The arms industry also conducts significant research and development.

It is estimated that yearly, over 1.5 trillion dollars are spent on military expenditures worldwide (2.7% of World GDP). This represents a decline from 1990 when military expenditures made up 4% of world GDP. Part of this goes to the procurement of military hardware and services from the military industry. The combined arms sales of the top 100 largest arms producing companies amounted to an estimated $315 billion in 2006. In 2004 over $30 billion were spent in the international arms trade (a figure that excludes domestic sales of arms). The arms trade has also been one of the sectors impacted by the credit crunch, with total deal value in the market halving from US$32.9bn to US$14.3bn in 2008. Many industrialized countries have a domestic arms industry to supply their own military forces. Some countries also have a substantial legal or illegal domestic trade in weapons for use by its citizens. An illegal trade in small arms is prevalent in many countries and regions affected by political instability.

Contracts to supply a given country's military are awarded by the government, making arms contracts of substantial political importance. The link between politics and the arms trade can result in the development of what US President Dwight D. Eisenhower described as a military-industrial-congressional complex, where the armed forces, commerce, and politics become closely linked. The European defence procurement is more or less analogous to the U.S. military-industrial complex. Various corporations, some publicly held, others private, bid for these contracts, which are often worth many billions of dollars. Sometimes, such as the contract for the new Joint Strike Fighter, a competitive tendering process takes place, where the decision is made on the merits of the design submitted by the companies involved. Other times, no bidding or competition takes place.

In the Cold War Era, arms exports were used by both the Soviet Union and the United States to influence their standings in other countries, particularly Third World Countries.

Land-based Weapons

This category includes everything from light arms to heavy artillery, and the majority of producers are small. Many are located in Third World countries. International trade in handguns, machine guns, tanks, armored personnel carriers and other relatively inexpensive weapons is substantial. There is relatively little regulation at the international level, and as a result, many weapons fall into the hands of organised crime, rebel forces, terrorists, or regimes under sanctions.

Small Arms

The Control Arms Campaign, founded by Amnesty International, Oxfam, and the International Action Network on Small Arms, estimated in 2003 that there are over 639 million small arms in circulation, and that over 1,135 companies based in more than 98 different countries manufacture small arms as well as their various components and ammunition.

Aerospace Systems

Encompassing military aircraft (both land-based and naval aviation), conventional missiles, and military satellites, this is the most technologically advanced sector of the market. It is also the least competitive from an economic standpoint, with a handful of companies dominating the entire market. The top clients and major producers are virtually all located in the western world, with the United States easily in first place. Prominent aerospace firms include Dassault Aviation, Sukhoi, EADS, Finmeccanica, Thales Group, Lockheed Martin, Boeing, and BAE Systems. There are also several multinational consortia mostly involved in the manufacturing of fighter jets, such as the Eurofighter. The largest military contract in history, signed in October 2001, involved the development of the Joint Strike Fighter.

Naval Systems

All of the world's major powers maintain substantial maritime forces to provide a global presence, with the largest nations possessing aircraft carriers, nuclear submarines and advanced anti-air defense systems. The vast majority of military ships are conventionally powered, but some are nuclear-powered. There is also a large global market in second-hand naval vessels, generally purchased by developing countries from Western governments.

Next to SIPRI there are several other sources that provide data on international transfers of arms. These include national reports by national governments about arms exports, the UN register on conventional arms and an annual publication by the US Congressional Research Service that includes data on arms exports to developing countries as compiled by US intelligence agencies. A list of such sources can be found at the SIPRI website. Due to the different methodologies and definitions used different sources often provide significantly different data. For example, according to Statistisk sentralbyrå (Norway state statistics), Norway exports a greater value (in USD) of arms than many of the nations listed above.

Some of the differences are possibly due to deliberate over-or under-reporting by some of the sources. Governments may claim high arms exports as part of their role in marketing efforts of their national arms industry or they may claim low arms exports in order to be perceived as a responsible international actor.

As of 2008 Britain has become the worlds leading developer of arms with British company BAE Systems. Defence group

BAE Systems is the first company outside the U.S. to reach the top position,thanks to a deal with the Pentagon for mine-resistant vehicles to be used in Iraq and Afghanistan. According to the Stockholm International Peace Research Institute, a defence think tank, the former British Aerospace group's arms sales are ahead of American market leaders Lockheed Martin and Boeing. The report reveals BAE's U.S. subsidiary was alone responsible for 61.5 per cent of the group's arms sales and around 58.5 per cent of total group sales. This demonstrates BAE's increasing reliance on orders for conventional weapons as the U.S. cuts back on its nuclear arsenal. The British figures were also boosted by orders for Eurofighter Typhoon jets from Saudi Arabia.

After the success of Pakistan's major developments in the defence industry the Defence Export Promotion Organisation (D.E.P.O.) was created to promote Pakistani defence equipment to the world by inviting major and small players to the I.D.E.A.S. Exhibition, which is held annually at the Karachi expo center. In recent reports, the defence exports were worth over $500 million USD in 2006 and growing annually.

THE MILITARY SECTOR AND THE POLITICAL ECONOMY OF MILITARY EXPENDITURE

While Ethiopia has a long military history, the emergence of a modern military force in Ethiopia, through centralization and professionalization, is a 20th century phenomenon. Beginning in the 1920s efforts were made to establish infantry battalions with some level of professional training. Russian military experts were first engaged in the 1920s, and in the 1930s Ethiopian soldiers were sent for training to the French military academy in Saint Cyr. In 1934 a military training school was established in the country, at Holata, with the assistance of a Swedish military mission. The soldiers trained at this local military institution provided the leadership core of a group called the Black Lion Organization, which led the resistance to Italian occupation of the country. The efforts to modernize the Ethiopian military received a boost after World

War II. First, the air force and the navy were established with the help of Sweden and Norway, respectively. The British played a key role in the modernization of the army in terms of training and equipment, while a new military academy was established in Harar, modelled on the British Royal Military Academy, Sandhurst, and commanded by Indian officers. In spite of these foreign connections and in contrast to other African countries, Ethiopia did not inherit its armed forces from a period of colonial rule; they were indigenous. The size of the military at the time of the collapse of Haile Selassie's rule in 1974 was estimated to be about 40 000, while the military budget was estimated to be $50 million in 1973.

Dramatic shifts occurred in the nature and size, and consequent cost, of the Ethiopian military from the 1970s onwards, coinciding with the establishment of the socialist regime of Mengistu in 1974. Various factors accounted for this. The first was the political ideology of Marxism-Leninism adopted by the government in which the economy and polity were centrally controlled and public expenditure rose significantly. Public expenditure as a percentage of gross domestic product was 13 per cent in the 1960s but rose to 34 per cent by the 1980s. The second factor was the culture of militarism that accompanied that ideology. In an effort to build a 'people's army', massive military recruitment was undertaken. As well as the usual channels of recruitment, such as the introduction of national military service from 1983, less orthodox methods were

also adopted, such as the recruitment of peasant militias. The third factor that inflated the size and cost of the military under the Dirgue regime was incessant conflict, domestic and external. Armed domestic opposition groups which waged war against the regime included the Eritrean Liberation Front and the Eritrean People's Liberation Front, both fighting for self-determination for Eritrea, the TPLF, the Oromo People's Liberation Front and the Ethiopian Democratic Union. On the external front, Ethiopia was confronted with a conflict with Somalia over the Ogaden region. Ethiopia's relationship with Sudan was also fraught with tension and conflict.

At the height of its strength, the Dirgue army was nearly 500 000 strong (including militia), consisting of infantry and mountain divisions, motorized divisions and a large number of tank battalions. It also had an air defence system, which deployed Russian anti-aircraft guns and surface-to-air missiles (SA-2, SA-3 and SA-7). The air force had 85 combat aircraft consisting of MiG-23 and MiG-21 fighters, bombers, and armed and transport helicopters. The navy had 32 craft in total, including 2 Russian-made frigates, 4 torpedo boats, 4 missile boats, 3 minesweepers (one of which was ocean-going) as well as 3 auxiliary ships for transport, 12 fast patrol boats and 2 minesweepers.

The EPRDF, which took over power from the Dirgue in 1991, disbanded the old army and grounded the air force. With the independence of Eritrea, the Ethiopian navy ceased to exist. The EPRDF converted its own force into a new army and started to rehabilitate the air force. By 1998 Ethiopia found itself engaged in a massive war with Eritrea and was forced to hurriedly mobilize a large army and acquire new and sophisticated equipment. The size of the Ethiopian armed forces in 2001 was 252 500, the largest in sub-Saharan Africa at the time. The estimated strength of the armed forces in Ethiopia and its neighbouring states. It shows that, before the demobilization that followed their border war, Ethiopia's military far outnumbered Eritrea's. These two countries continue to have the two largest armed forces in sub-Saharan Africa; indeed, in 2004 Ethiopia's military was 74 per cent larger than that of Sudan.

The inevitable result of the events of the past three decades was that military expenditure in Ethiopia skyrocketed. Military expenditure increased from 1625 million birr ($413 million in constant dollars) in 1990 to peak at 5589 million birr ($719 million) in 1999 at the height of the war with Eritrea. Military expenditure fell for only a few years after the collapse of the Dirgue in 1991; it started to rise again from 1993. Two immediate factors account for this. The first was the border war with Eritrea. The war occasioned massive recruitment and deployment of troops and the diversion of resources for military purposes. The unstable nature of Ethiopia's relationship with Eritrea persists even after the signing of a peace agreement in

December 2000. Second, in the post-Mengistu era the country still has to contend with internal civil strife in the south, the south-east and the south-west, where the Ogaden National Liberation Front and the Oromo Liberation Front are active. The military, therefore, still occupies a central position in the public profile and expenditure plans of the government, and so continues to consume enormous resources.

These two factors notwithstanding, the missions and roles of the armed forces have hardly changed under the last three regimes, except perhaps for some shifts in ideological emphasis. The army's role has always been to protect the territory of the country from external threat, to enforce security measures against internal insurgency, and to plan and organize civil defence, participate in civic construction projects and provide emergency relief during national disasters in peacetime. The air force's role has been to maintain air superiority within the country's airspace, defend the country from external aggression by air, provide air support for the army (and the navy before Eritrean independence) and during peacetime provide aviation services as required. During the imperial and Dirgue regimes, the armed forces had overtly or covertly assumed

the role of agents of social and political change. Partly as a result of Emperor Haile Selassie's belief in collective security (first through the League of Nations, then the United Nations), a belief shared by subsequent governments, Ethiopia participated in international missions in Korea, the Congo (Leopold-ville), Rwanda and Burundi. The past decade has been a period of transformation for the Ethiopian armed forces: one of its major tasks has been to build capacity.

THE NATIONAL BUDGETARY PROCESS IN DEFENCE EXPENDITURE

Ethiopia has a dual budgeting system in which recurrent and capital expenditure are considered separately. Until recently these two budgets were prepared separately by the Ministry of Finance and the Ministry of Economic Development and Cooperation, respectively. In October 2001 these two ministries were merged to form the Ministry of Finance and Economic Development. The new ministry determines budget ceilings for federal ministries and agencies and for the regions. In doing so, it takes stock of the performance of the economy for the previous year and makes economic projections for the following year in terms of growth, revenue, and so on. The MOFED does this in consultation with other state agencies, such as the National Bank of Ethiopia and the Central Statistical Authority. It is this macroeconomic framework that, when approved by the Council of Ministers and the Office of the Prime Minister, forms the background to the budgetary process in Ethiopia. At the federal level the amount to be allocated to recurrent and capital expenditure is determined by government priorities, ongoing projects, non-discriminatory expenditure and institutional capacity.

The implementation phase

The implementation phase of the budgetary process covers not only measures for disbursing funds already allocated but also the monitoring of how funds are spent to ensure that they are used judiciously and for the intended purposes. Following the notification and publication of the budget the various ministries are required to prepare a fund disbursement chart that specifies salary allotment, a work plan and a cash flow and to submit the chart to the MOFED. These charts are verified by the MOFED, which then authorizes the Treasury to release the funds (both recurrent and capital) to the line ministries.

Funds are dispersed to ministries each month on the basis of the allotted budget. Every ministry is required to submit a 'monthly disbursement request' in which it reports the previous month's expenditure, detailing what was spent and how it was used, and makes a request for the next month's allocation through a work plan. The requests for fund disbursement by line ministries usually contain three main components: the payment of salaries, a request for operational expenditure (according to the cash flow plan) and a request for payment of capital grants. The MOFED's Fund Disbursement Department handles the process of fund disbursement for the ministries and keeps records of all transactions. The budget registrar in the Disbursement Authorization Department of the MOFED records the original budget, all transfers and supplementary budgets, the disbursements made and any undisbursed allocation.

Fund disbursement is cumulative and undisbursed funds for a particular month can be used in another month in the same financial year. Funds unused by ministries at the end of the financial year have to be transferred to the Treasury, although transfer to other activities is also allowed. With regard to capital projects, ministries are expected to prepare a schedule of advance payments compatible with the amount of work to be carried out on the various projects. This schedule is consolidated and approved by the MOFED and passed to the Disbursement Authorization Department for further action.

During implementation of the budget, new or unforeseen requirements may necessitate a request for a supplementary budget; this is permitted by regulations on the financial administration of the federal government. The Council of Ministers establishes a committee that includes representatives of the Office of the Prime Minister, the MOFED and the line ministry. This committee first assesses the new or unforeseen requirements, based on policy decisions at the highest executive level. Once approved at this level, it is submitted to the House of Peoples' Representatives for approval, after which it is passed back to the MOFED for authorization of disbursement.

The MOFED coordinates the management and control of public funds in Ethiopia. It is this ministry that keeps the accounts of the federal budget and prescribes regulations on financial management and control for ministries and government agencies. In addition, ministries are required to manage and control funds allotted to them following the central regulations and directives on financial management set out by the MOFED. The regulatory mechanisms of the budget include requirements that: (*a*) budgetary receipts be recorded in the appropriate budgetary account as prescribed in the financial regulations and in a timely manner; (*b*) collected revenue be recorded under the appropriate revenue account; (*c*) expenditure only be made in compliance with the financial regulations; (*d*) all books of accounts be closed each month and a monthly receipt and disbursement be prepared and submitted to the MOFED at the centre and regional finance bureaux in the regions; (*e*) periodic financial statements be prepared and submitted to the Council of Ministers and regional executive committees by the MOFED at the centre and regional finance bureaux in the regions; (*f*) a consolidated annual report be prepared and sent to the Council of Ministers and regional executive committees by the MOFED and regional finance bureaux.

The MOFED can be seen to play a central role in the budgetary process of the country. It controls the formulation and implementation of the budget of line ministries at various levels. During the writing of the Budget Calls it is instrumental in the setting of budget ceilings. It can make changes in the budget allocation of line ministries after review and analysis of the budget estimate submitted by the ministries. It decides the level of the budget to be recommended to the Council of Ministers. During implementation, it has the power to disburse funds. Through the monthly accounting reports, it scrutinizes the performance of the ministries in budget implementation, and it can decide on the level of funding to be authorized for disbursement. It can also approve transfers and recommend supplementary allocations.

Reporting and auditing

According to the proclamation establishing the post, the Office of the Federal Auditor-General is tasked with the responsibility of undertaking financial and performance audits of the offices and organizations of the federal government. It does this by auditing the accounts of all federal ministries and agencies. The proclamation stipulates the penalties for anyone who obstructs the work of the Auditor-General through deliberate presentation of false documents or denial of access to required information. The annual report of the Auditor-General details his or her findings on the accounts audited. Unfortunately, the reports are usually late in arriving, sometimes by as many as three years. For instance, the report for financial year (FY) 1999/2000 was not presented to Parliament until June 2003. This delay diminishes the significance of the report since any recommendation for remedial action to rectify an error arrives too late to avoid repetition of that error in intervening years. A lack of adequate staffing has been given as the main reason for this major lapse in the auditing process.

The formulation phase

The MOFED is the major clearing house for the preparation of the federal budget in Ethiopia, although this is done in consultation with the various ministries that are the beneficiaries of the budget. The responsibilities of the Minister of Finance and Economic Development, as stipulated in the Council of Ministers Financial Regulations, consist of formulating and issuing directives that detail government financial policies in all areas of government finances; developing and maintaining appropriate standards of work and conduct for application throughout all public bodies; internal auditing functions; and preparing a financial plan for the country. In addition, the minister now has the duty to initiate policy proposals that help to define the country's long-term development perspective; prepare and follow up implementation of long-, medium-and short-term development plans; and prepare the annual development programme. The various steps involved in the process of budgeting. The first step in the process is the sending of Budget Calls and ceiling notifications to line ministries by the MOFED. The Recurrent Budget Call provides basic information such as the macroeconomic environment, aggregate recurrent budget ceiling and priorities for which the ministry must budget. The

MOFED then prepares a proposed total recurrent budget, which is reviewed and vetted by the Office of the Prime Minister and on which the line ministries' budget proposals are based. For the capital budget, the process for a particular budget cycle begins with an assessment of the economic situation and by determining the financial balance. At this stage, the macroeconomic framework is reviewed, economic priorities in terms of capital expenditure are set and national goals are defined with respect to economic development. This is followed by the issuance of the Capital Budget Call, which provides detailed guidelines to line ministries regarding the capital budget ceiling and how to prepare their budget proposals.

The next step in the process is the submission of budgetary requests by the various ministries to the MOFED's Budget Department following established regulations and ensuring appropriate budget sub-heading classification. A line ministry may have formal pre-budget discussions with MOFED officials in order to clarify some issues or to justify certain budget claims that the line ministry may wish to make. Line ministries may overshoot their budget ceiling when they prepare their budgets; however, such an action has to be justified for it to be considered by the MOFED.

The budget hearing at the MOFED follows the submission of budgetary requests. This is the component of the process that reflects the democratic nature of the budgetary process. The minister or vice-minister of the line ministry or the head or director of a department or agency is called to defend its budget before the MOFED. The budgetary request of the line ministry is prepared in an issue paper, which is normally the subject of discussion at the budget hearing. The basic issues that are raised in the budget hearing include policies, programmes and cost issues. When necessary the budget request presented by a line ministry. In addition, for the capital budget the MOFED, through its Capital Budget Steering Committee, holds budget hearings at which the line ministries defend their proposals. The key issues that form the core of the capital budget hearing and defence process include a focus on the status of projects; the implementation capacity of the country's development strategy and the projects' compatibility with the strategy; the cost structure of the projects; and the regional distribution of the projects. In other words, the development potential and cost implications of the projects are put under scrutiny.

After the budgetary hearing, the MOFED's Budget Committee reviews the exercise and prepares its recommendations, including the proposed sources of finance. Funds are allocated from internally generated revenue, from foreign assistance and from the central Treasury. The total amount to be disbursed to the line ministry in the recurrent budget is the sum of these three sources of finance. Should the MOFED recommend a rise in the ceiling, this has to be approved by the Office of the Prime Minister first. After the MOFED has reviewed the budget proposal, it is submitted to the Deputy Prime Minister for Economic Affairs. The Deputy Prime Minister then calls on line ministry representatives to further discuss the recommended budget before it is submitted to the Prime Minister. The Prime Minister may or may not authorize changes. From the Office of the Prime Minister, the draft recurrent budget is sent to the Council of Ministers for deliberations. The draft capital budget is also submitted to the Council of Ministers after a review and recommendations have been made by the Capital Budget Steering Committee.

The approval phase

Supreme authority for budget appropriation is vested in the House of Peoples' Representatives. The Prime Minister presents the budget recommended by the Council of Ministers to the House. After deliberation in a parliamentary session, it is sent to the Budget and Financial Affairs Standing Committee for review and recommendation. This committee reviews the budget in the presence of members of various other committees, receives written explanations from experts from the MOFED and makes its recommendation to the House. The entire House thereafter deliberates on the recommendations of the budget standing committee before the appropriation bill is approved. The House of Peoples' Representatives considers both the current and capital expenditure budgets as well as subsidies to the regions.

After the House of Peoples' Representatives approves the budget, it is signed by the President and is then made public through publication in the *Federal Negarit Gazeta*, the Ethiopian national gazette. Following this, the line ministries receive formal notification from the MOFED of their budget allocation for the next financial year. The MOFED then directs the Treasury to release the funds to the line ministries.

THE MILITARY BUDGETARY PROCESS AND SYSTEMS

The military budgetary process in Ethiopia is an integral part of the annual national budgetary system of the country. The line ministry for the military is the Ministry of National Defence. According to the MOFED budget classification, the MOND is classified as a programme and the whole military budget is classified as recurrent expenditure, following the United Nations's classification. The MOND is divided into sub-programmes. In FY 1991/92 these sub-programmes were: (*a*) administrative and general services (MOND headquarters); (*b*) the ground force; (*c*) the air force; (*d*) the navy; and (*e*) defence construction. Essentially, this reflected the classification that existed during the Dirgue regime.

In FY 1992/93 a new sub-programme was introduced for the Political Organization Army Department, which was established to carry out the demobilization and resettlement of the EPRDF troops who left the army. When this department had accomplished its task, it ceased to be a component part of the military budget after FY 1995/96. In FY 1994/95 when the Navy Department had been closed and the navy disbanded, it also ceased to be part of the MOND budget. Defence construction was also withdrawn from the MOND and now operates independently, along business lines, under the supervision of a government department responsible for nationalized enterprises. However, a new sub-programme was added in FY 1994/95: Project 40720, a vast repair and maintenance complex for heavy armaments, tanks and military vehicles built by the Soviet Union during the Dirgue regime which also includes some other unfinished projects. In FY 2001/2002 three new sub-programmes were added: the Defence Engineering College, the Health College and the Dejen Defence Project Coordination Office. The last of these oversees the management of a number of factories established to provide the military sector with material and equipment, such as quartermaster items and mechanical tools. In FY 2002/2003 more radical changes were made in the programme classifications, leaving eight sub-programmes: (*a*) administration and general services; (*b*) the office of the minister; (*c*) defence procurement; (*d*) the ground force; (*e*) the air force; (*f*) the Defence University; (*g*) Project 40720; and (*h*) the Dejen Defence Project Coordination Office. The components of each sub-programme consist of item expenditures which include personnel services (emoluments, allowances and pension contributions), goods and services (materials and supplies, travel, maintenance and contracted services), fixed assets and construction, and other payments (subsidies, investments, grants and miscellaneous payments).

In terms of administration, the Minister of National Defence is the political head of the ministry, although in reality the Prime Minister exercises considerable influence. The federal constitution requires that the Minister of National Defence be a civilian. At present the Budget Department, the Finance Department, the Procurement Agency, and the Administration and General Services Section of the MOND are all the responsibility of a minister of state, a civilian who is responsible directly to the Minister of National Defence. A civilian vice-minister heads the Defence Project Coordination Office. The head of the Budget Department, who is responsible for the formulation and administration of the budget, is also a civilian. In terms of the budgetary process, at least in the formal sense, civilian control appears to predominate.

Budget formulation

There is little or no difference between the budgetary

process for the military and those of the other ministries. The military budget begins at zero every year; in other words, the sector undertakes only annual budgeting. There is no medium-term perspective to military budgeting. The budgetary procedure is described in this and the following subsections; a diagram of the process and the calendar of the process.

The MOFED sends a Recurrent Budget Call, which includes a budget ceiling, to all ministries, including the MOND. The MOND headquarters, in turn, issues a Budget Call to the heads of the various sub-programmes, with a ceiling for each sub-programme, calling their attention to various directives. In the Budget Calls it is stressed that the budget preparation process should strictly follow existing budget preparation regulations, take account of policy decisions, meet budget standards, take account of the current price of goods and services, and so on. The budget proposals from sub-programmes include not only expenditure but also revenue. The Budget Calls also specify a deadline for the submission of budget proposals from sub-programmes. The prepared budget estimate is submitted for a budget hearing at the sub-programme level to determine the final estimate that will be sent to MOND headquarters.

Following the submission to MOND headquarters of the budget proposals by the sub-programmes, budget review and analysis are carried out by experts in the Budget Department of the MOND. This involves detailed analysis to establish that the budget estimates have been prepared in accordance with the Budget Calls. It also involves an assessment of whether the activities proposed in each sub-programme can be accomplished during the financial year, whether old and new projects have been clearly identified, and whether the budget estimate has been prepared by comparison with the previous year's performance and takes account of inventories. The objective of the exercise is also to enable the budget experts to prepare an accurate, realistic and credible consolidated budget estimate.

After review and analysis of the budget, a budget hearing

is held at MOND headquarters, at which the sub-programmes are represented and the Minister of National Defence and the Chief of Staff are present, to decide on the budget level to be recommended for each sub-programme and for the military sector as a whole. Immediately after the budget hearing and on the basis of the decisions taken during that hearing, the MOND Budget Department prepares a consolidated military budget, which also includes revenue estimates—services may collect revenue from the sale of surplus property, medical services, aviation services and items from welfare stores or canteens.

Approval

The Foreign, Security and Defence Standing Committee of the House of Peoples' Representatives scrutinizes the defence component of the national budget submitted by the Prime Minister before passing it on to the whole House for approval. After the budget appropriated by the House of Peoples' Representatives has been passed on to the MOND by the MOFED, the final exercise in the budget formulation process is the budget distribution (or recast), which allows each sub-programme to adjust the approved budget according to their actual revised requirements.

Implementation

Once the budget recast is approved by the MOFED, the process of budget implementation starts with the monthly requisition by the MOND for its allotted funds. At this stage all the control mechanisms that apply to other ministries and agencies of the federal government also apply to the MOND. This includes the monitoring of the execution of the budget on a monthly basis. It is doubtful, however, whether this applies to the procurement of major military weapons.

Reporting and auditing

The role of the Office of the Federal Auditor-General in the budgetary process of the military sector is to audit its financial accounts annually and at other times when it deems it necessary. The auditing, as in other ministries, is performed at three levels: internal audit by the ministry, auditing by the MOFED and auditing at the federal level by the Auditor-General's office. By law, all persons appointed as auditors (including internal auditors) should be approved by the Federal Auditor-General.

ISSUES ARISING FROM THE BUDGETING PROCESS

There are several issues arising from this study that indicate the limitations of the research and of the policy issues arising from it. Owing to the nature of the subject area (i.e., excessive confidentiality) and because of limited access, it has not been possible to unravel the informal processes and politics of the military budgetary process. Emphasis is placed more on the formal mechanisms and processes of the military budget and their critique.

Military budgeting starts at zero each year; there are no medium-or long-term strategic budget plans. Equally, there is no evidence of the existence of mechanisms for coordinating the planning organs and the Budget Department of the MOND. In the process of issuing Budget Calls in the MOND, decisions on increases or decreases in manpower strength, variations in budget standards and capacity building are made. However, it is unlikely that decisions on major defence policy issues (which will be converted into specific goals and programmes) are communicated to the head of the Budget Department who will have to apply them in the budget. Extra-or off-budget spending for the military is often not disclosed by the state or the military sector.

Organizational changes in the armed forces as different regimes take power, either through coup or armed struggle, tend to be motivated by a desire for regime stability. This has an effect on the continuity and development of the armed forces and deprives the nation of an experienced and disciplined professional armed force.

External assistance in the form of loans and grants, both bilateral and multilateral, is detailed in the revenue side of the national budget by source, but it is not shown on the recurrent expenditure side for any sector, including the military. Budget allocations for demilitarization and demobilization after the EPRDF took power from the Dirgue regime are reflected in the government budget proclamations. They do include a foreign aid component, but this is not recorded in the recurrent budget.

The Civil Service Reform Budget Design Team—a body representing the former ministries of Finance and of Economic Development and Cooperation and the Decentralization Support Activity Project—was established in 1997 to recommend reforms in the budget processes and structure for the federal government. It made proposals on how best to coordinate the preparation of the recurrent and capital budgets. Among the study's recommendations were changes in the format of the budget to promote consistency in the presentation of the recurrent and capital budgets and, most importantly, the preparation of the budget on a cost-centre basis. The latter proposal would bring together recurrent and capital expenditure so that budget managers could immediately see the total cost of a project or an administrative unit. Unit costs are used in the cost build-up of these cost centres. The team regards the use of these unit costs as a key technique for determining cost build-up and as a norm reference for costing the budget. The costs that the team have in mind are not the prices of items or services but ratios such as cost of transport per passenger or cost of education per pupil. Unit costs are developed for each major area of service and are calculated by dividing the total outlay by the output. Aside from the fact that the output of the military sector, in most cases, is not quantifiable, the necessary expertise for such an exercise does not exist in the MOND. In fact, the ministry has not yet set up a unit to undertake such a task. The measurement of costs and effectiveness in defence is very difficult, and the team's requirement for the calculation of unit costs would demand sophisticated cost-effectiveness analysis currently far beyond the capability of the MOND.

Reforms that have arisen from the recommendations of the Civil Service Reform Budget Design Team include organizational restructuring and a redistribution of duties and responsibilities in the MOND. Organizationally, a 'flatter' structure has been instituted, reflecting a move towards more decentralization. For example, budget and finance administration have been decentralized, as has local purchasing. Foreign purchasing remains centralized.

Redistribution of duties and responsibilities has meant that the Budget Department has been renamed the Plan and Budget Department and is now accountable directly to the Minister of National Defence, instead of the minister of state. The Material and Inventory Control Department has been separated from the Budget Department and made accountable to the minister of state. Inventory control will be undertaken once a year and will be computerized. Other reforms include: (*a*) the appointment of a new civilian vice-minister for policy and human resource development; (*b*) the initiation of the preparation of a strategic plan for the MOND; (*c*) in the future, annual and six-month performance reports will be presented to Parliament, and (*d*) the Hormat and Gafat engineering factories have been incorporated as sub-agencies of the MOND.

Significant as this reform is, it falls far short of a planning, programming and budgeting system. However, even with the existing system of budget preparation and implementation, the research indicates that, if the suggested reforms are to bring about the expected benefits, it will need to be complemented with training of personnel at all levels to upgrade the standard of budget administration in the MOND. Additionally, the ministry will need to establish a cost-evaluation unit staffed with highly educated and experienced professionals.

There is a paradox in the military budgetary process in Ethiopia. While Ethiopia has an established military culture which should provide a basis for a well-structured, cumulative and entrenched tradition of military budgeting, the political instability that has plagued the country has tended to undermine this. Different regime types with different ideological orientations, governance models and world views impose different management patterns on the military. In the current liberal democratic dispensation, the military budgetary process is carried out by different organs of government spanning the executive, legislature and bureaucracy (specifically, the Ministry of Finance and Economic Development and the Ministry of National Defence). As well as the MOND, the MOFED plays a key role in the military budgetary process in preparation, implementation, monitoring and evaluation. A zero-sum budgetary system has been adopted in military budgeting in Ethiopia.

While the formal process of military budgeting in Ethiopia is well laid out, it is accompanied by an informal process. Yet a strictly formal process is important in determining who actually does what and how it is done, and who wields what power and how it is wielded. For instance, while the legislature is formally conferred with wide powers in budgetary matters, in practice little of it is exercised with regard to the military sector; instead, the Prime Minister plays a pivotal role in the military budgetary process.

Similarly, the input of civil society is still very limited in the military budgetary process. Although Parliament conducts public hearings on budgetary matters for the different sectors of governmental activity, including defence, this does not usually result in any significant public or civil society input into the military budgetary process. Military issues generally remain 'sensitive' and largely classified, so any participation by civil society organizations in necessarily limited and uninformed. Moreover, only a few civil society organizations have the competence and expertise to analyse the intricacies, mechanisms and processes of military budgeting. The perceived 'sensitive' nature of military budgeting also discourages the public disclosure of off-line or extra-budgetary expenditure by the state.

There is a need to further democratize the process of military budgeting in Ethiopia (and in most other African countries). The budgetary process should be open to public scrutiny and discourse in order to improve the techniques used, ensure greater efficiency and better resource allocation, and extend the accountability of the nation's military sector.

ASSESSING THE MILITARY BUDGETARY PROCESS AND SYSTEMS

The Ethiopian military budgetary system suffers from a number of deficiencies that hamper efficient allocation and use of resources. Among these are: a lack of continuity in the process; the lack of a well-articulated defence policy and strategic plan; inefficient implementation of the budget; emphasis on input rather than output; over-centralization of authority; and relatively strong yet opposing influences on the level of military spending.

The first thing to note about the Ethiopian armed forces is that, when the Dirgue regime collapsed, the army was not simply disbanded. The EPRDF also discarded well-established doctrine on military operations, logistics and training along with the organizational structure and all the rules, regulations and standing operating procedures, and it closed training and other facilities. It was as though Ethiopia had never had an armed force. Moreover, the replacement was not a modern armed force; it was a guerrilla force, with all that that implies in terms of doctrine, organization and weaponry. The EPRDF retained a handful of officers and men from the old force, but otherwise it had to start afresh, establishing a new organizational structure and operating procedures and re-establishing facilities that it had closed when it took over. The EPRDF army started out with principles and a value system that were the antitheses of those of a modern professional army. Over time all this has changed. Since 1991 the government has focused on the re-establishment of a professional army. During this process, the new armed forces had to engage Eritrea in a border war. It is against this background that the budgetary process should be evaluated.

One of the methods of modern budget administration is 'planning, programming and budgeting', although the Ethiopian military has not adopted it. A particular advantage of this method in the Ethiopia situation is the analysis of defence capability that it requires; such an analysis is important in a defence system in the process of transformation. However, the planning, programming and budgeting method assumes that there are already short-, medium-and long-term plans and that the major budget centres are structured in such a way that they functionally reflect national defence objectives. Ethiopia may have strategic plans but, since the planning, programming and budgeting method has not been implemented, if these plans exist, they do not play an important role in the budgetary process because there is no mechanism for coordinating the activities of those who plan and those who prepare the budget. Lack of transparency in the process does not allow for an understanding of the basis of defence allocations.

It is known that the level of budget allocation to ministries is determined through the prior setting of ceilings by the MOFED. This does not contribute to budget discipline or efficient management of the budget or the defence system in general. On the contrary, in the administrative environment it may encourage the padding and inflating of budgets. For this reason, and others to do with efficiency, the MOFED should study the pros and cons of the setting of budget ceilings as a budgetary tool in the absence of a defence policy and of overarching national priorities and policy goals.

Except for the past few years, actual expenditure on defence in Ethiopia has exceeded appropriations. This may be largely owing to the fact that the MOND does not formulate its budget on the basis of medium-and long-term plans and may also be the result of the frequent external and internal conflicts. Long-term stability and the existence of medium-and long-term plans seem to be necessary conditions for budget ceilings to be an effective tool of the budgetary process.

In general, there are two possible approaches to budget formulation when attempting to achieve a goal. In the first approach, those responsible set budget ceilings and direct the implementing agencies to operate within the ceilings. There will of course be legal and administrative controls to ensure that implementing agencies with approved budgets adhere to the directives sent. This approach is usually less effective in maintaining budget discipline, as there is little basis for the ceilings.

The second and perhaps more useful approach is for the line ministries to first submit their spending estimates, without a ceiling being set beforehand. These estimates should give detailed justifications (usually on the basis of objectives or policy goals) for increases or decreases in budget, and should detail any new activities or programmes that are to be undertaken, such as fresh troop recruitment, the purchase of armaments or the construction of new facilities. Authorization may then be obtained from the government for the new or additional programmes and activities and for any cost increases after analysis of past budget performance. The emphasis is on justifying the new requirements, clearly indicating how they would enhance the readiness or capacity of the combat or support element concerned and, if the requirements arise during a period of conflict, how acquiring the new capability would contribute to the war effort.

This second method was used during the Dirgue regime, but it was still a 'line item expenditure' approach. It fell far short of enabling decision makers to be able to use the budget as a tool to achieve national defence goals. If the method were suitably refined (with a strategic plan and policy), it would allow for systematic analysis of defence requirements in terms of system costs and defence objectives. Since the method is iterative, it allows closer scrutiny of the objectives themselves, making it possible to consider alternative defence systems or postures. With the establishment of proper criteria it would be possible to select the optimum defence package. For these reasons, the Ethiopian Government should consider implementing the planning, programming and budgeting method, with the requisite analytical tools to ensure that the national defence goals are achieved and optimal use of resources is made.

A major activity of the budgetary process is the biannual

taking of inventories of stocks of materials and supplies. This exercise is an integral part of budget preparation, as budget estimates take into account the balance of the stocks. Procurement plans are also reviewed on the basis of inventory results. Existing stocks are redistributed so as to avoid excessive concentration of stocks in one unit or shortages in another—this is done in order to reduce the size of the budget estimates, and it is accordingly regarded as a very important part of the budgetary process. However, if this aim is to be achieved effectively and a substantial budget reduction is to result from the exercise, then an efficient control system must be put in place with trained personnel to operate it. Owing to staff turnover and reorganization, this may not be practicable. Under these circumstances, it is to be expected that there will be a bias in favour of underreporting stock levels, in the hope that budget ceilings will be increased or at least maintained. In short, the overall picture is that conditions in Ethiopia are not conducive to the efficient implementation of the budgetary process in the MOND.

As far as the administration of the budget is concerned, apart from ensuring that salaries and benefits are paid and that materials and supplies are procured in accordance with organization and equipment tables, the overriding emphasis is on control: not enough attention is paid to efficiency. In fact, there does not even appear to be a mechanism that could contribute to achieving efficiency. The budget consists of line item expenditure calculated on the basis of budget standards, the established civil service salary scale and the lowest possible prices for goods and services. Such an exercise in itself and in isolation cannot ensure that the goals of the defence system or its sub-systems are cost-effective, nor can it assist in measuring mission effectiveness.

Furthermore, the recent changes in classification in the military budget with the introduction of the defence procurement sub-programme, which is centrally planned and administered, are leading to over-centralization of authority and a reduction in the powers of the service units, which can only have a negative effect on the optimal use of resources.

New sub-programme has been allocated over 40 per cent of the total military budget. While supplies of materials and equipment constitute a significant portion of

the input to the military sector and there is a need to control costs (e.g., through taking advantage of bulk purchasing), this does not justify the classification of procurement as an independent category in the budget. Doing so is tantamount to taking from the service units (the ground and air forces) control over a significant portion of their resources: it deprives them of the opportunity to manage themselves efficiently and effectively. The service units are the best judges of their requirements and they should be allowed to make the necessary choices independently. Since some of the requirements of a service can be highly specialized, the right to manage its own financial resources is an integral part of a service's ability to manage itself efficiently. While central procurement need not mean that the budget for procurement is centrally planned and administered in the MOND, the recent change in budget classification is retrograde. It has come as a result of an overemphasis on cost reduction, to the exclusion of considerations of efficiency.

Ministry of National Defence expenditure increased by more than 180 per cent in real terms over the period 1992–2004. This partly reflects the strategic importance that the new regime attaches to the sector and the level of threat perceived by the state. However, allocations for defence remain high even after the reductions that followed the formal end of the Eritrea–Ethiopia War, in December 2000. There are two major factors that will affect Ethiopia's military expenditure in the future, aside from the actual performance of the economy itself. The level of foreign aid to Ethiopia, especially that from the World Bank and the International Monetary Fund, has in the past been contingent on reduction in the size of the armed forces. Consequently, the high level of expenditure may not continue. On the other hand, the Ethiopian military sector is in the process of transformation; this essentially means capacity building, with perhaps some change to the structure of the forces. Whatever the actual outcome of the opposing trends for capacity building and force reduction, there will be a need for a qualitative change in the management of the armed forces if undue burden on the economy is to be avoided and if the cost-effectiveness of the defence system is to be improved.

The role of the House of Peoples' Representatives in the budgetary process is minimal, even though the constitution grants the legislature a great deal of power. The President's role in the process is purely ceremonial; he has no constitutional power to influence the way in which the budget is formulated. While the House is the supreme body in terms of budget appropriation, the extent to which it exercises this authority is debatable. Although there is a standing committee for the budget, which is expected to study the budget proposals in detail and to submit its recommendations to the House, committee members lack the expertise to scrutinize the military budget properly and they do not have the services of experts at hand. In any case, the budget estimates are scrutinized as a whole, rather than by sector. The government announces through the media that budget hearings are going to be held and invites the general public to attend the hearings. Various interest groups have the opportunity

to submit their views to the standing committee and many actually do so, but this is little more than a formality: the committee deals with the budget proposals in their entirety and, in general, the recommendations presented to the House are identical to those presented by the executive. The committee cannot therefore be said to be as accountable to the public as its constitutional role demands. In fact it is the Ministry of Finance and Economic Development and the Office of the Prime Minister that have the decisive role in the budgetary process. It is therefore important to devise means of enhancing the competence of the Budget and Financial Affairs Standing Committee.

8

Defence Planning, Programming and Budgeting

No meaningful programming and/or budgeting can be done without the existence of a long term or strategic defence plan, just as no meaningful plan can exist in the absence of guiding policy. Within the protective function of government, which includes intelligence, policing, justice and correctional services (or prisons) as well as defence, planning is contingent by nature. This means that requirements are driven by outside factors such as internal crime levels and external instability. In the case of defence, planning must be done for a very uncertain future environment. This is complicated by the long period required to build and prepare defence capabilities, which implies the maintenance of certain capacities purely for possible future eventualities (defence contingencies).

THE BUDGET AND STRATEGIC DEFENCE PLAN

The strategic defence plan specifies the required outputs of defence at the highest level as well as the macro envisaged resource allocation to defence over an extended period. The defence programmes, in turn, specify outputs in the form of objectives at the next lower level as well as planned allocations to the programme managers for producing these outputs. This must now be converted into business plans where specific activities for reaching these objectives are specified and accurately costed from zero in terms of the required inputs. These business plans are done at unit level (including directorates or sections at headquarters) and are in turn the basis for the performance agreements between the programme managers and unit commanders/section chiefs as well as for service agreements directly negotiated. The same considerations as discussed in the previous paragraph on performance and service agreements at the next higher level are valid for these agreements.

These business plans are done annually for the next financial year as well the subsequent years covered by the Medium Term Expenditure Framework (MTEF). The defence budget is the sum-total of the business plans expressed in monetary (financial) terms. It is the department's income and spending plan for a set period of time. It is a quantitative expression of the proposed plan of action for the reaching of defence objectives for that time period.

Budgeting is done at unit level where all inputs that are required to execute the delegated activities must be accurately determined and costed from zero. These input costs (budget items) will include:

- Personnel expenditure such as salaries, allowances, bonuses and gratuities.
- Administrative expenses such as subsistence and travel, transport, membership fees and registration, study expenses and communications.
- Stores including ammunition and explosives, spares and components for normal maintenance, construction and building material, office supplies, fuel and clothing amongst many others.
- Equipment such as vehicles, weapons, machinery and furniture.
- Rental of land and buildings.
- Professional and specialist services such as consultation, outsourced services and research and development.

THE DEFENCE PROGRAMMES

As defence departments and forces are large organisations,

the management of the top-level objectives is largely delegated to subordinates at the second level of management. These are typically service chiefs and chiefs of staff divisions at the ministry or defence headquarters. Each one of these delegated managers will be responsible for a specific defence programme. These defence programmes essentially convert the strategic defence plan (departmental outputs as required and funded by Government) into a format where clear responsibility and accountability is established against the programme managers who are also referred to as the principal budget holders.

The Defence Administration Programme. The defence administration programme will identify those activities that are essential for the professional, efficient, transparent and accountable management of the defence function and will be co-ordinated at defence headquarters by the Chief of Staff responsible for the integrated functioning of all headquarter staff divisions. This programme should include sub-programmes for political direction (office of the Minister of Defence), departmental direction (office of the Head of Department), policy development, corporate departmental planning, strategic intelligence, defence foreign relations, financial management, corporate communication (public relations and internal communication) and internal auditing and inspection amongst others.

Objectives for this programme are derived from the top-level administration objectives in one of three ways.

- Firstly, a top-level objective can be directly delegated to a programme manager at the second level. For example the objective to "develop the defence budget for fiscal years (XXXX) to (YYYY) for presentation to the Department of Finance by (date)" can be delegated to the Chief of Staff for Finance.
- Secondly, a top-level objective may lead to sub-objectives that can be divided amongst two or more programme managers at the second level whilst overall responsibility is maintained by the Head of Department. For example the objective to "do a

complete defence review for presentation to Parliament by (date)" can be sub-divided and delegated to the Chief of Staff for Intelligence ("do a strategic intelligence appreciation"), the Chief of Staff for Policy-and-Planning ("do a strategic defence appreciation") and the Chief of Staff for Joint Operations ("do an operational appreciation of short-to medium-term defence commitments").

- Thirdly, the Head of Department may (and should) determine his or her own developmental objectives to ensure the continued improvement of the performance of the department. These could include objectives to improve the management processes of the department (delegated to Chief of Staff for Policy-and-Planning), to improve information technology systems (delegated to Chief of Staff for Joint Support) and to improve the command and leadership practises of the department (delegated to Chief of Staff for Joint Support).

The Force Employment Programme. The force employment programme will derive its objectives directly from the top-level defence commitments in the plan and will be co-ordinated at defence headquarters by the Chief of Staff for (Joint) Operations. This programme should also include sub-programmes for operational intelligence and counter intelligence, joint force preparation and command-and-control. Objectives for these sub-programmes are developed by the Chief of Staff for (Joint) Operations. Other than those objectives derived directly from defence commitments in the top-level plan, typical force employment objectives may include objectives to develop command-and-control skills through war-gaming and exercises, objectives to prepare and exercise joint formations through military exercises and objectives to ensure the intelligence for and security of operations.

The Force Provision Programmes. The three force provision programmes are the domain of the Chiefs of the Combat Services (Army, Air Force and Navy) who are responsible for the establishment, development, preparation and maintenance of combat ready forces as agreed upon in the approved force design. These programmes derive their objectives directly from the approved force design and structure and will include sub-programmes for each of the capability areas as defined in the approved force design as well as for service specific training and force preparation. Examples of these capability areas are; infantry, armour, artillery, anti-aircraft, engineering, special forces, fighter aircraft, air reconnaissance, helicopters, air transport, submarines, surface combat ships and sea mine warfare vessels.

The Joint Force Support Programme. The joint force support programme will identify those joint activities that are essential for the support of the defence administration, joint force employment and most importantly the force provision programmes of the services. This programme will be co-ordinated at defence headquarters by the Chief of Staff responsible for the co-ordination of the supporting functions. Most of the objectives for this programme will be derived through service agreements between the Chief of Staff for Joint Support and the other programme managers. This implies that, as certain functions can be executed more efficiently in a centralised manner, such functions should be identified and contracted to Joint Support by the Service Chiefs and other Divisional Chiefs by means of service agreements specifying the level of service required and the cost thereof. This programme should include sub-programmes for personnel management, logistic services including acquisition and procurement and military health services.

Typical joint force support objectives may be:

- Manage and execute the capital acquisition plan in support of the combat services.
- Manage and execute the departmental facilities plan.
- Provide and manage a personnel administration system for the department.
- Provide military health services in support of the combat services and defence commitments.

Resource Allocation to the Defence Programmes. The defence programmes provide the basis for performance agreements between the Head of Department and the Chiefs of Staff of the Combat Services and Headquarters Staff Divisions.

Performance agreements basically consist of the objectives to be achieved with timeframe and standards, the associated level of resource allocation and the required delegations of powers. Furthermore these programmes include the service agreements negotiated directly between programme managers. Service agreements similarly consist of the objectives to be achieved with timeframe and standards, the associated level of resource allocation and the required delegations of powers where applicable. As such, these programmes are the product of negotiations between the Head of Department and subordinate Chiefs as well as directly between programme managers. This process of negotiation is iterative in that each objective must be evaluated for cost and then be either agreed upon or changed as is required. Changes could be the increase of resources or the downscaling of the objective. To ensure efficiency the Head of Department (and other clients) must demand that programme managers accurately determine the cost for the achievement of set objectives and provide proof that all efficiency improvements had been considered. Benchmarking the cost of all activities should be done regularly. Only when the Head of Department is convinced that the objective is being pursued in the most efficient way possible should he/she consider increasing resources or downscaling the requirement.

The defence programmes, in the final instance, provide the starting point for the detailed development of the defence budget down to unit level.

THE DEFENCE PLAN

The defence plan is essentially the document that specifies the measurable outputs that defence will produce in pursuit of Government's objectives against the identified financial allocation within the Medium Term Expenditure Framework (MTEF) of three (to five) years. It incorporates the strategic plan, the defence programmes and the budget. The plan should also cover longer periods (up to 30 years) for matters such as capital acquisition, infrastructure and personnel planning. The defence plan provides the framework for the performance agreement between the Minister of Defence (the political head) and the Head of Department.

The defence plan provides

The performance agreement should be a written document that clearly specifies the outputs required from the department, the associated resource allocations and the performance measurements that will be employed. This serves as the contract between the Minister and the Head of Department. It must of necessity be a product of negotiation between these two individuals. The performance agreement is an important management tool and enhances transparency and accountability in defence management.

The primary outputs that must be specified in the defence plan are:

- Defence Administration. The top-level administrative outputs required for the management of the defence function. This includes the provision of defence policy, strategy, plans, programme and budgets.
- Defence Commitments. The identified short to medium term operational force employment tasks and objectives.
- Defence Capabilities. The Force Design with required readiness states as well as the supporting force structure. (Note: Defence Capabilities are the main cost-drivers of defence.)

The determination of the first two outputs are relatively simple and are based mostly on present and short-to medium-term future requirements. The determination of defence capabilities is however much more complex and long-term in nature.

Defence administration. Defence administration outputs are determined by an appreciation of the legislative, policy and management framework within which defence must function. It will be strongly influenced by the demands and requirements of government, specifically the Minister of Defence and other national departments such as the departments of finance and public service and administration. This programme function will identify specific objectives to be reached within a one to three year timescale. Some examples of such objectives are:

- Revise the defence act to be in line with the Constitution for presentation to Parliament by (date).
- Do a complete defence review for presentation to Parliament by (date).
- Develop an updated personnel policy for the Defence Force for presentation to the Minister of Defence by (date).
- Develop the defence plan for fiscal years (XXXX) to (YYYY) for presentation to the Minister of Defence by (date).
- Develop the defence budget for fiscal years (XXXX) to (YYYY) for presentation to the Department of Finance by (date).

These objectives are mostly determined, managed and co-ordinated by the policy-and-planning, finance and other staff divisions at the defence ministry/headquarters. The resources allocated to these activities are relatively small and are mostly associated with the personnel costs of the associated staff divisions, administrative costs and the costs for professional services.

Defence Commitments. Short-to medium-term defence commitments or operational outputs are determined through a military operational appreciation. It rests heavily on the intelligence forecasts of the internal and external security environment for the short-to medium-term. It will also be heavily influenced by the objectives of the departments of foreign affairs and internal safety and security. This programme function will identify specific objectives to be reached within a one to three year timescale. Some examples of such objectives are:

- Provide a force of battalion strength with tactical air transport and medical support to the peace mission in (X) from (date) to (date).
- Support the Police in crime prevention in (area) from (date) to (date).
- Do border control operations in (area) in support of the Police from (date) to (date).
- Do maritime patrols to monitor infringements of territorial waters in (area) from (date) to (date).

These activities are mostly determined, managed and co-ordinated by the (joint) operations division at defence headquarters. The resources allocated to these activities are dependant on their scale, duration and intensity. These should include all employment costs such as increased maintenance, fuel, ammunition, rations and operational allowances amongst others.

Defence Capabilities. The determination of defence capabilities. The establishment, development, preparation and maintenance of defence capabilities constitute the main cost-element of defence and the determination of the force design and structure is thus the prime area of debate between defence planners and political decision makers. In the defence plan the determined force design and structure of the Defence Force must be clearly stated in terms of quantity (number of units) and quality (readiness states and preparedness). The development and maintenance of this force design and structure constitute a specific objective for the department.

The staff work for the determination of this objective is primarily done and coordinated by the policy-and-planning and (joint) operations divisions at the defence ministry/ headquarters.

Summary of the Elements of the Defence Plan. The defence plan, which should be a stable but flexible document over time, should include the following elements:

- The strategic profile of the Defence Force consisting of its mission, vision, critical success factors and value system.

- The analysis and critical assumptions underlying the strategic plan.
- A clear statement of the required defence capabilities (force design and readiness state) of the Armed Forces.
- A clear statement of the required supporting force structure.
- The supportive capital acquisition plan, the facilities plan and the personnel plan.
- The administrative outputs required for the management of the defence function including the provision of defence policy, strategy, plans, programme and budgets.
- The identified short to medium term operational force employment tasks of the Armed Forces.

DEFENCE PLANNING, PROGRAMMING AND BUDGETING PROCESS

It should be clear that the defence planning, programming and budgeting process is an iterative process involving negotiation between all levels of defence management. Planning is largely top-down based on an analysis of requirements and environmental factors as well as an estimate of available resources. As it goes down in the organisation, through performance agreements between superiors and their subordinates, more and more accurate costing is done until, at unit level, accurate zero base budgeting can be done. These unit level budgets, in turn, are added from bottom-up to constitute the total defence budget. This obviously entails many iterations to "make ends meet resources".

DETERMINATION OF OPTIMAL DEFENCE CAPABILITIES

The determination of optimal defence capabilities to be developed and maintained as well as the associated readiness states is the major challenge to the defence planner. This is so because it is premised on an uncertain future, is severely constrained by the availability of resources, will always be contested by sectional interests within the defence establishment and is extremely difficult to motivate to a populace concerned with more immediate social and personal security issues. Furthermore the potential consequences of being wrong are enormous in their implications for the future security and well-being of the state.

The development and maintenance of defence capabilities are also the main cost-drivers of defence. The solution of the defence capabilities equation, therefore, requires the major effort in the defence planning process. It is also the prime area of debate between the defence planner and political decision makers. Political decision makers cannot be expected to simply decide on the ends and ways of defence without major inputs regarding the implications of their decisions especially the implications for the security of the state and the financial implications.

This poses the challenge to the defence planner to find a rationale for the determination of the requirement for defence capabilities that will elicit the understanding and support of political decision makers and civil society. Obviously such a rationale must be based on the need for efficiency in defence expenditure.

Defence Value

If it is accepted that the primary object of the defence force is to defend and protect the state, its territorial integrity and its people through the provision of contingency ready military forces and that this is to be done within given financial restrictions then, as already stated, the most efficient solution must be sought.

Efficiency implies the most optimal output for any given input or simply put the best value for money. This raises the question of how to determine defence value. As defence is concerned with possible future events or threats (defence contingencies), each of which carries an implied risk to the state, defence value should be equated to risk reduction. Each defence contingency carries with it an associated risk. If, therefore, the relative risk value of such contingencies can be determined, this will allow for the development of a system of determining relative defence value.

Defence Contingencies

The first step in this process is the determination of defence contingencies. This entails describing in some detail the possible future events that the defence force might have to counter. In this process there are no limits and the more contingencies accurately described the better. This list should not be restricted to probability, as that is the next step, but to as many possible defence contingencies as can be imagined. Examples are:

- Invasion of the national territory by a foreign power.
- Punitive military action against the state.
- Coercive military action against the state.
- Disruption of national sea lines of communication and trade.
- Military naval, air and land blockades.
- Border violations and trans-border crime.
- Natural and other disasters beyond the scope of civil society.
- Peace missions in alignment with international and regional obligations.

Risk

Defence is mostly concerned with possible future events (defence contingencies) and the preparation for successfully countering them when they occur. For each such contingency a statistical probability of occurrence can be determined as well as the potential impact that the occurrence of such contingency might have on the country. Obviously contingencies of high probability and major impact carry more risk to the state than contingencies of low probability and minor impact.

It can therefore be stated that risk is a function of probability and impact. High-risk contingencies have high probability of occurrence and the potential for grave impact and vice-versa. Risk is therefore proportional to the probability of occurrence and potential impact.

RISK IS PROPORTIONAL TO PROBABILITY AND IMPACT

The Determination of Probability. The determination of probability is the most difficult exercise in defence planning, as it is the most subjective and somewhat akin to crystal ball gazing. It cannot be an exact science as it deals with an uncertain and ever-changing future. However, without applying the mind to this factor it is extremely difficult to plan for the future and to determine priorities for defence capabilities to be maintained and developed. An exact formula for determining probability, but gives guidance regarding some factors to be considered. In "real life" the determination of the probability of occurrence of a contingency rests mostly with the intelligence community consisting of national

intelligence, foreign affairs and military intelligence and strategists. Pointers to the determination of probability are:

- Evaluate the historic (both international and national) frequency of occurrence over a very long period.
- Use a wide spread of probability over a range nearer 0,001 to 1 than 0,1 to 1. This ensures greater discrimination in the calculation of probability. As an example the probability of an invasion could be nearer 0,001 than 0,1.
- Absolute probability is nearly impossible to calculate. It is therefore recommended the effort should concentrate on the determination of relative probability between the likelihood of the occurrence of contingencies. The involvement of politicians, academics and civil society organisations in this exercise will greatly enhance the quality of the product.

The Determination of Impact. The determination of impact is less subjective that that of probability. Nonetheless this is not an easy exercise and the involvement of civil society and academics in particular in this endeavour is once again strongly recommended. The potential impact of a contingency, that cannot be successfully countered, can be calculated using the following parameters:

- The potential loss of life.

- The potential loss of infrastructure.
- The potential loss of economic production and trade.
- The relative loss of sovereignty.
- The relative loss of national image and prestige.
- The relative loss of international confidence.
- The effect on national morale.

Once the list of contingencies and their relative risk value (probability and impact) have been determined, the value part of the "value for money" formula has been established. What now remains to be done is to calculate the cost of dealing with these potential contingencies. This, once again, is a complex exercise.

CONCEPTS OF OPERATIONS AND FORCE DESIGN

For each of the defined contingencies the best operational concept to counter such an eventuality and the corresponding required capabilities (mini-force design) must be determined. War-gaming or simulation processes are the best tools for doing this. Once this has been done each mini-force design must be accurately costed. This is a major exercise that requires the full and honest participation of the combat services and units down to ground level as well as of financial experts. If this is not accurately done the basis for decision-making is seriously undermined.

Costing

Each element of the mini-force design must be fully costed over its life cycle to be able to determine cost/benefit ratios for optimisation. Annual operating cost is the full cost for the normal day-to-day running of the unit. This includes administrative expenses, transport, subsistence and travel, provisioning, day-to-day maintenance, fuel and professional and specialist services amongst others. Annualised capital cost is calculated by adding the full acquisition cost and the mid-life upgrade cost of capital equipment and dividing it through the expected operational life of such equipment. This shows the effect that the inclusion of such equipment in the force design will have on the annual budget. The emphasis on full life cycle cost is to ensure sustainability of the end result. If this is not done, it will lead to decisions being taken that will prove to be unaffordable in the future. This is the cause of many militaries in the third world having large inventories of unserviceable, unsupportable and unusable equipment.

Optimising

Once the list of contingencies, defence value calculations (relative risk reduction values) and the cost of the elements of the force design are available, calculations of best value for money can be done. This would probably provide the best results if computer support is used.

It must be emphasised that this process will not provide precise scientifically accurate answers, but it will provide insight into the defence planning problem and a good basis for discussion with decision makers. It removes the subjectivity of arguments by the individual combat services for prioritising their requirements. It provides a menu for decision-making where the services that can be ordered are shown against cost and from which the implications of decisions can be seen. It is also emphasised that the more inclusive the participation in this process (political decision makers, other government departments, academics and civil society organisations together with defence experts) the better and more credible the results will be.

Force Design And Supportive Planning

This process must lead to and culminate in the approval by Government of the Force Design of the Armed Forces. This also implies a clear commitment by Government to fund the Defence Department for the development, preparation and maintenance of such a force. Without this, no meaningful long-term planning or medium-term programming and budgeting can be done. The force design, together with the required support structures, will form the basis for the development of other long-term plans such as the Capital

Acquisition Plan, the Facilities or Infrastructure Plan and the Personnel Plan. These plans are long term plans providing for the acquisition of weapon systems, facilities and personnel and the development, preparation, maintenance and eventual disposal of such assets. All these plans should have a long-term horizon commensurate with the life cycles of these assets.

ACCOUNTABILITY IN DEFENCE RESOURCE MANAGEMENT

As foundation the need for efficiency, transparency and accountability in defence resource allocation and management. It is to achieve this that the importance of an inclusive defence planning, programming and budgeting process is put forward. To the same end, the process of performance and service agreements is stressed. Some further important guidelines for the achievement of efficiency, transparency and accountability in defence resource allocation and management.

Efficiency

Sustainability. If the defence plan and programmes are not sustainable over time, this will lead to the non-maintainability and ineffectiveness of capabilities. Sustainability will only be achieved if Government commits itself to the approved defence plan, all planning is done on full life cycle costing and the defence budget is expended in the most efficient manner possible. Care must also be taken in planning to accurately evaluate the effect of currency fluctuations on the life cycle cost of capital equipment.

The Funding of Operations. It is not possible or desirable to budget for the execution of military operations other than routine operations that can be foreseen and accurately planned well ahead of time. Most military operations come at short notice and in the running financial year for which the budget had been developed and approved many months ago. Examples are peace support missions, major disaster relief missions and even limited war. It is submitted that trying to budget for the unforeseeable will result in a misappropriation of funds. The only way to handle this problem is by the existence of a central contingency fund managed by the Department of Finance. For large-scale contingencies, exceeding the capacity of such a contingency fund, Government will have to revise the total budget both regarding departmental allocations and income.

Tooth-to-Tail Ratios. All possible effort must be made to ensure the optimal tooth-to-tail ratio of the Defence Force and the department of Defence. All too often supporting structures are bloated at the cost of operational capabilities. Determination of the size and capacity of support structures can only be done once the Force Design has been determined. Modern business process re-engineering (BPR) techniques can assist in the solution of this problem but will only be effective if top-management is committed to this cause and ruthless in its application. Direct Client/Supplier Relationships. In many defence forces certain structures exist through historic reasons only. The client (e.g. a Combat Service) is forced through organisational culture or other interests to make use of the services of such an organisation and not allowed to "shop for this service" elsewhere. This is bad practise and entrenches inefficiency. Accordingly clients for services should be allowed freedom of choice and to establish direct client/supplier relationships.

Other potential solutions for the improvement of efficiency are indicate and include outsourcing and public-private partnerships, improved "jointery" between services, improved management information through the use of better information technology, use of reserves, the better use of civilians in defence departments and improved management and leadership through education, training and development. Of these the improvement of management information through the use of better information technology might be the most crucial aspect to the improvement of efficiency in defence organisations.

TRANSPARENCY AND ACCOUNTABILITY

Transparency and accountability are crucial issues in the

allocation and management of defence resources for all levels of planning, programming and budgeting. If defence resources allocation and management are not transparent, defence will never be able to achieve public support or the co-operation and support of broader government. If not accountable to government and the people, defence becomes a cause onto its own and will not be aligned with national interests and priorities. It will easily be corrupted and decision-making will be easily manipulated towards self-interests. Civil involvement and control of overall budget decisions, as well as careful auditing at all levels, can help ensure that resources are actually used to accomplish policy objectives. Nevertheless, the most effective solution to this problem is a commitment at all levels to national interests and objectives and the development of clear and transparent planning, programming and budgetary processes and systems to implement them. These processes must of necessity be aligned with the national management framework.

Transparency and accountability are enhanced through the system of performance agreements as this relies on the definition of clear output objectives and performance standards and the agreement as to the required resources. The system is also based on negotiation, ensuring better insight, understanding and co-operation.

The planning, programming and budgeting process is the central feature of defence management for providing resources to the defence force to ensure "the defence and protection of the state, its territorial integrity and its people" in alignment with national security and defence policy. The process rests on the rationale that defence budgets should be the result of good short-, medium-and long-term plans that are based on open and clear defence and national security policy. All plans, programmes and budgets should be driven by clearly defined and agreed upon outputs.

The defence planning, programming and budgeting process should clearly be aligned to and integrated with the national public expenditure management process and therefore the principles applied to defence management should not differ markedly from those applicable to other activities of government.

The quality of these processes is crucial for ensuring the national defence and security whilst not making the opportunity cost of defence too high in terms of other social and developmental priorities. Inefficiency and imprudent use of scarce resources will undermine security and the broader national interest.

In the final instance, defence planning, programming and budgeting must be based on modern management practises, principles and procedures and on accurate research, analysis and strategic assumptions. It must have a long-term focus and be the product of an inclusive process. It must be innovative and ensure permanent efficiency improvements in order to make defence affordable. Whilst the nature of planning, programming and budgeting systems may vary widely internationally, the basic processes, techniques and principles put forward in this paper should assist in ensuring the effectiveness and efficiency of defence as well as greater transparency and accountability in defence resources allocation and management.

STRATEGIC DEFENCE PLANNING

Too often the defence debate is dominated by short-term views on security, based on snapshot views of the world, and the cost of defence. The argument is "there is no threat, so why spend?" As has already been stated, strategic situations change rapidly whilst the building of defence capabilities and expertise takes time. All strategic defence planning must therefore take the long-term view. To do so it is necessary to understand the major variables in defence planning. These are the ends, ways and means of defence. Government and defence planners share the responsibilities for the determination of these ends, ways and means.

This scale indicates that what Government requires from defence (Ends), taking into consideration the approved defence posture (Ways), must be balanced by defence capabilities (Means) and that this requires a determined amount of resources. The scale can be brought into balance by either reducing ends, adapting the defence posture (moving the pivot left or right) or by increasing means and thus resources. If there is an imbalance or inconsistency between ends, ways and means this will result in a strategic gap between what needs to be done and what can be done. This strategic gap must be managed as a risk by Government.

Ends of Defence. Defence Ends are the required defence outputs in support of Government's goals and objectives that include peace, security, stability and public safety. The primary responsibility for determining the ends of defence rests with Government (Parliament and Cabinet).

Examples of defence outputs (ends) are:

- Provision of deterrence through the existence of mission ready forces.
- Meeting international obligations such as search-and-rescue and disaster relief.
- Participation in peace missions.
- Peace-time border control and protection against non-military threats.
- Support to the Police.
- Support to Civil Authority.

Ways of Defence. The ways of defence are military strategic and operational concepts and are influenced by Government's national security and foreign policy as well as Government's strategic defence posture. The responsibility for determining the ways of defence is a dual Government/Military responsibility with the Military primarily responsible for expert advice to Government.

Examples of strategic and operational defence concepts (ways) are:

- Non-offensive defence or forward mobile defence concepts.
- A strategic defensive or offensive posture.

- Defence through regional defence co-operation and alliances or self-defence.

Means of Defence. The means of defence are essentially the operational capabilities of the defence force. This is expressed in the Force Design of the force. The determination of the defence means (Force Design) is primarily the responsibility of the defence planners in alignment with the ends and ways as prescribed by policy.

Examples of force design elements (means) are:

- Infantry units.
- Armour units.
- Artillery units.
- Naval surface combatants.
- Naval sub-surface combatants.
- Air Force fighter squadrons.
- Air Force transport squadrons.
- Air Force helicopter squadrons.
- Operational medical units.
- Military Attaches.

These defence means (Force Design) are the real cost drivers of defence. The creation, maintenance and development of these capabilities are the primary consumers of defence resources.

9

India's Defence Industry in the 21st Century

India's defence industry entered a new phase of self-reliance on the eve of the 21st century. Since the mid-1990s, several initiatives have been undertaken by the government to effect changes in the defence industry. Soon after the liberalisation of the economy was announced in 1990/91, the defence industry started realising the importance of civil-military interaction in the industrial sector. The private industries in India, which were thus far debarred from entering into defence production and whose role in the defence sector was limited to supplying spare parts and other minor contributions, started demanding a share in defence production. In 1994, the then Defence Minister founded six Task Forces on major areas of defence modernisation, of which reforms in defence industry was an important part. This was carried out by the government in consultation with institutions like the Confederation of Indian Industries (CII). The CII, on its part was instrumental in bringing out a series of proposals in the broad field of private participation in the defence sector and armed forces–industry co-operation. Soon after this, the government initiated a programme called 'Army-Industry Partnership', under the auspices of CII which highlighted the importance of co-operative arrangements between the armed forces, defence industry and the government.

After India's nuclear tests, various sanctions were imposed on India, of which sanctions related to the import of military and dual-use goods and technologies were considered the most important. Sanctions were imposed on more than 150 items, which affected the progress of many defence products. However, the impact of sanctions on military technology was taken up as a another phase of challenge for the defence scientists as they had faced similar sanctions after the test in 1974. At that time they had faced more difficulties as the defence industry was not in a position to withstand such severe cuts which had resulted in delays in many major programmes. This time around, the defence industry had made significant progress to be able to withstand sanctions. After the Kargil conflict in mid-1999, the government started looking into security gaps and founded a committee under Mr K. Subrahmanyam.

He brought out a major report on this conflict, which is known as the 'Kargil Committee Report'. This report, among other recommendations, highlighted the importance of reforms in higher defence management and reforms in institutional processes in the security sector. The Government also founded a Group of Ministers' committee to look into major aspects of the overall security management of the country. The committee submitted its report to the government, which is known as GoM Report on 'Reforming the National Security System. This report highlighted the importance of self-reliance in India's defence industry and recommended several steps to introduce institutional changes into the system. Coupled with changes at institutional and organisational levels, India's defence industry entered an entirely new era after the Government announced a major change in policy by outlining codes of conduct for and inviting private participation in the defence industry. This is seen as by far the most important policy shift in the defence-industrial sector in the last fifty years. By doing so, the Government, through an official notification No. 5(37)/2001-FCI, allowed private sector participation up to 100 percent and permitted foreign direct investment (FDI) up to 26 percent. This decision has been hailed by both the private industry and the government-owned defence industry. Institutions like CII and FICCI, which represent interests and views of the private sector, have been instrumental in influencing such a marked change in policies. According to Mr Sushanto Sen, the Director General of CII, such a policy change is certainly going to benefit both the defence industry and the private sector.

In tune with the stated objectives of India's defence industry to achieve a higher degree of self-reliance and a desire to make its flagship units globally competitive, thus entering into competitive defence markets, the Government has also introduced some institutional changes that are expected to smoothen operations both at structural and organisational levels. Earlier, procurement procedures were considered cumbersome, and there were overlaps in organisational responsibilities of respective organs responsible for procurement. Under the new system, the Services Headquarters were integrated into the Ministry of Defence to provide closer interaction. The procurement structure is now a three-tier structure with the recent establishment of the Defence Acquisition Council (DAC) at the apex. Its primary role will be to accord in-principle-approval of long-term perspective plans (15-20 years), acceptance of necessity for the capital acquisition plan (5 years), identify 'Make', 'Buy' and 'Make and Buy' projects and monitor progress of the three Boards under it – the Defence Procurement Board, Defence Production Board and the Defence R&D Board. The Defence Procurement Board under the Defence Secretary will have the primary role of capital procurements and co-ordination. The Defence Production Board will be headed by the Secretary Defence Production and Supplies and will oversee all activities related to indigenous manufacture, progress in 'make' projects and will provide support to DAC. The Defence R&D Board will be headed by the Secretary Defence R&D and will oversee progress, monitor and report on all R&D proposals in consultation with the user service and production board. Other measures at institutional level include direct linkages between the armed forces and the

Ministry of Defence through integrated headquarters, which include respective perspective planning branches. In sum, organisational and institutional changes brought about recently seem to complement policy changes.

Problems and Prospects: An Assessment

India's quest for self-reliance has produced mixed results. Some of the lessons that India has learnt in the past fifty years are worth noting here. First, a combination of factors have led to the indigenous design and development component of self-reliance slowing down to almost zero for over a quarter of a century after 1962. This has led not only to a huge technology gap but also contributed to severe difficulties in technology assimilation in the industrial sector. However, since the mid-1980s, activities toward achieving a greater degree of self-reliance have taken up momentum. The technology gap also widened the scope for acquisition of production technology rather than design technology from foreign sources. This in turn has created a license production regime at the cost of indigenous production. During the 1990s, the activities to encourage joint ventures and co-production in the defence-industrial sector is largely seen as a step to reduce license regime and boost indigenous industrial capabilities. How far this will achieve desired results are yet to be seen as such activities are only of recent origin and they need lead time to prove themselves. For example, the market for Brahmos missiles is estimated to be large, but it depends on how much is it likely to penetrate the cruise missile market at a global level. Success of this kind will not only validate India's defence-industrial capabilities to meet domestic demands but also increase its confidence in many ways.

Second, private participation in the defence-industrial sector has started after a long delay. This is attributable to several factors, ranging from the socialist and protective nature of the defence sector to fears of what is called 'security diffusion'. The latter especially relates to a fear of below-expectation performance by the private sector as it is hardly specialised to meet strict high military standards, hence compromising security standards. This kind of fear has been criticised by many who argue that private participation is essential in the defence sector which is primarily technology driven and capital intensive. The recent opening up of the defence sector for private participation has generated a lot of interest in the country. Institutions like CII caution that while such initiatives are always welcome, the government should come out with a clear 'road-map' for the private sector participants in defence so as to enable them to prepare themselves for the new reality. Fears regarding the ability of the private sector to match expectations of the country in the highly demanding and technology-dominated industrial sector are countered by industrialists like Atul Kirloskar (Chairman of Committee on National Defence, CII), who claim to have absolute faith in their abilities. Many also claim that given a chance, the secondary role of the private sector can be turned into a primary one in a short period of time. Some of the leading industrialists even claim that they have or intend to possess capabilities to produce complete weapons systems. Several companies like Mahindras and Mahindras (M&M), the Tata Group, Kirloskar Brothers, Larsen and Toubro (L&T), and many others have already jumped into the fray to obtain orders from the defence industry. Since 2002, the Government has received more than ten applications from the private sector to manufacture weapons systems. It has recently awarded five licenses to L&T and M&M to produce military vehicles and some weapons systems.

Third, the government has emphasised measures to enhance the defence industry to cope with future challenges. Such measures are carried out by both OFs and DPSUs, apart from respective branches of the Government and the armed forces. Digitalisation, strict quality control, performance-related benefits, professional management systems, allowing the private sector to carry out R&D activities in the government-owned laboratories, are some of the measures which have come up in recent years and are likely to impinge the defence-industrial landscape. A simplification of production and procurement rules promise better buyer-seller relations. There were some protests coming from employees' unions of OFs and DPSUs against privatisation. The Government has assured these unions that employees' interests will be borne in mind but that it will give priority to performance. In one instance, the Defence Minister is reported to have appealed to the workers in one DPSU to not to worry about possible relocations due to privatisation and assured them to take effective steps to safeguard their interests. It seems that rationalisation of the defence industry is on the cards which might bring some unrest in the form of reduction of employment in the defence-industrial sector. There are even rumours that some of the units, especially from the ordnance sector might be closed down. The private sector participants are, however, optimistic. They argue that their factories can effectively be converted into profit making civilian units. In several rounds of interviews with senior officers and industry analysts by the author, it seems that some of the industrial units may come under close scrutiny. Conversion to civilian production in their cases is not ruled out. In brief, significant rationalisation, diversification and closer private participation are coming and are likely to influence India's defence industry in many ways.

INDIA'S DEFENCE POLICY CHALLENGES IN THE 21ST CENTURY

The first macro problem that must be resolved, if India is to rise as a great power, is achieving higher rates of economic growth. The reason for that is simple. A competent military costs money and modern defense capabilities, which are sophisticated and effective, are priced in numbers that boggle the imagination. For a country like India, which has to deal not simply with questions of defense but also questions of development simultaneously, high economic growth becomes the only solution especially in those situations when India cannot choose between the objectives of defense and development.

When one begins to think of the revolution in military affairs — the kind of capabilities today that characterize the military forces of the great powers — it is simply impossible for India to acquire such capabilities without sustaining economic growth of at least 7 to 9 per cent per annum consistently. China is a good example. A country that has experienced close to double-digit growth for more than twenty years since 1978, still finds it hard to develop the kinds of sophisticated military capabilities it seeks to acquire across the board. Therefore, one must be prepared for the fact that even if the Indian economy were to grow between 7 and 9 per cent consistently for the next twenty years, the best India would be able to do in the area of cutting edge defense technology is to acquire niche capabilities. But those niche capabilities may be enough for the specific strategic circumstances that it faces.

The second macro problem that India needs to engage and satisfy is the development of an appropriate national vision and appropriate institutions designed to manage the acquisition of great power capabilities. What substantive goals, defined in terms of national interest, does India really seek to service? The answer to this question cannot be defined in terms of platitudes like a "just world order." That is a useful phrase for a political campaign. It is a terrible criterion for defense planning and force structuring. The other aspect of this question of defining India's goals and creating the appropriate institutions pertains to the issue of whether India will be able to achieve the right balance between state control and societal autonomy. It is very important to realize that successful states in the modern era have been those that have maintained this balance in the most creative way possible.

The third macro challenge that I would highlight for your consideration is whether India is capable of exploiting the existing structure of the international system to its advantage. In this context, I think India should get rid of the notion of a multipolar world order as a practical outcome in the relevant future. Pursuing chimerical goals like multipolarity does not make for good policy. The international system, for all practical purposes, is going to remain a unipolar system for at least the next half century. By all indicators, if you define power in terms of comprehensive national strength, it is unlikely that the United States will face serious peer competitors for at least another fifty years.

Consequently, the challenge for India becomes, can it develop a viable strategic partnership with the United States that serves both mutual interests and India's own unilateral interests? Can India develop a relationship with the United States that helps it enhance and magnify its own power? This is not to suggest that the United States is the only power in the international system. Clearly not — there are many others. This is also not to suggest that India's goals ought to consist solely of developing a relationship with the United States, or that India somehow is constrained solely to develop a relationship with the United States and no other. Not true. India has the flexibility to maneuver within the interstices of the international system. But at the end of the day, there is one eight hundred pound gorilla that has to be engaged. And that is the United States. That gorilla is not going to go away. That gorilla has already put its nose for the first time in modern history, into the physical environment of the subcontinent. And it is in India's national interest, and important for its capacity to generate and magnify its power, to develop a productive and a collaborative relationship with the United States that enhances the interests of the two countries.

First, India has to deal with the challenge of neutering internal security threats without undermining its capacity for effective external defense. This is harder to do than is sometimes imagined. It is unfortunate that the principal security threat that India is going to have to deal with on a day-to-day basis is the threat to internal security. There is no running away from this problem. Historically, India dealt with this challenge by essentially throwing manpower at the threat instead of technology. And the reason it did this was simply because it enjoyed a surfeit of manpower and a deficit of technology.

There were two consequences to this strategy. One was that its approach to preserving internal defense was probably not as effective as it could be, because technology could provide that valuable supplement which was not available to India. The second consequence was that preserving internal security became extremely expensive and has now come at the cost of being able to acquire the new technologies required to raise a modern military force. It is a myth that India's manpower is cheap. Maintaining the size and kind of forces that India does, if maintained over the secular period, will undercut its ability to acquire the kind of RMA capabilities that wins modern wars. And this is going to require India to make very painful choices — painful choices about reducing its manpower strength and changing the inter-service budgetary balances, choices that it cannot make today because of the gravity, importance, and burdens of its internal security commitments.

The next micro issue is the need to preserve effective external defense, now in a nuclear shadowed environment. This brings us face to face with the vexed question of whether India has the capacity to successfully prosecute a limited war. Most commentary so far has focused on the issue of limited war as an example of Indian recklessness. People have chastised the Defense Minister, Mr. George Fernandes, for arguing that limited war in fact represents a solution to India's external security problems. My take on the issue is somewhat different. I believe that limited war should be viewed not as a product of the proclivities of the state, but rather as a predicament resulting from a specific set of structural circumstances. The transparent presence of nuclear weapons in the subcontinent for the first time makes unlimited wars untenable as a matter of state policy. This is not simply India's choice — it actually represents a dilemma of the nuclear age. And it is a challenge that faces India both with respect to Pakistan and with respect to China. In both cases, unlimited war is not feasible. There is also no guarantee that war is obsolete. And therefore the challenge of limited war confronts India squarely, both with respect to its northern and its western borders.

What does limited war mean for Indian defense policy? It means that India is now confronted with the task of being required to hit hard and effectively enough to punish an adversary, but not hit so hard or so effectively as to cause inadvertent escalation. This in turn leads to questions like "how do you avoid escalation?" Most commentaries have focused on this aspect of the problem. But there is another aspect to the problem, which has largely escaped attention. Because it is going to demand of India a new style of war fighting that New Delhi traditionally has been uncomfortable with and which historically it has been relatively incapable of. It is a style of war fighting that puts a premium on achieving very speedy decision on the battlefield and then terminating offensive action either before the international community intervenes or before the conflict degenerates into unavoidable attrition. Getting the Indian military to successfully prosecute a fast paced war that generates quick decisions is something that we have not seen in fifty years of India's independence. It is also the kind of war that traditionally the United States was not very good at. We preferred wars that allowed us plenty of time to mobilize, plenty of time to deploy, and then plenty of time to be able to grind down the adversary at our convenience. If India is to be able to prosecute the opposite kind of war, as the United States is now proficient at — fast, decisive, and yet limited — it is going to require an investment in new technologies and new operating skills apart from new doctrines and new concepts of operation.

Third, if India is to become a great power of the sort that it seeks to become, it also has to become a net provider of regional security, both in the sub-continental and in the extra sub-continental arenas. This is easier said than done; yet at one level it is the quintessential part of the definition of a great power. After all, what is the meaning of having great power capabilities if at the end of the day you cannot extend net security to others? And yet any Indian attempt to provide the kind of regional security that I am talking of, even in the sub-continental arena, is fraught with hazards because it risks deepening intra-regional rivalries and it risks deepening the suspicions India's weaker neighbours have of its capabilities and its intentions. Finally, will India develop the organizational structures that are required to maintain and operate these capabilities if it seeks to provide the kind of regional security that is to be expected of a great power?

The fourth micro problem pertains to whether India can acquire an effective nuclear deterrent without breaking the bank. My view is that nuclear weapons are important for India's security in some limited sense, but it is also essential to remember that they are actually relatively obsolescent technologies. Nuclear weapons are now over fifty years old and they are generally unusable as instruments of international politics.

NATIONAL SECURITY, DEFENCE POLICY AND PLANNING

It is generally acknowledged that the approach to national security requires a comprehensive view of various political, social, economic, technological and strategic aspects. National security implies not only safeguarding territorial boundaries but also that the nation is able to build a cohesive, egalitarian, technologically efficient and progressive society with a good quality of life. Compared with national security, defence policy is more focused, concerned with the protection of the state and its citizens from direct and indirect (proxy) military threats and actions of other states. In defence planning, the emphasis shifts to national security concerns that are mainly military in nature. There are two concepts at this level: deterrence (including coercive diplomacy) and defence (dissuasion).

Deterrence refers to policies designed to discourage the adversary from taking direct or proxy military action, by raising the cost so that it outweighs the gains that he may wish to attain. Defence (dissuasion) policies are designed to reduce the capability of the adversary to cause damage—and own costs and risks—in the event deterrence fails. Deterrence and defence are two interwoven strands of defence policy. Defence planning involves the conceptualisation of plans and decisions for the execution of defence policy. Long-term planning for defence is essential for the following reasons:

(a) The existence of a highly fluid strategic environment, which results in continuous shifts and changing profiles of threat and power equations.

(b) To ensure judicious allocation of resources and cost effective utilisation.

(c) Revolution in Military Affairs (RMA), i.e. advances in technology, which result in weapons and equipment systems becoming obsolete at a fast rate.

(d) Lead time required to raise and prepare defence units; to produce or acquire and introduce new weapons and equipment systems.

(e) The changing nature of conflict and reduced reaction time.

(f) Coordination problems between defence, economic, science and technology, infrastructure and industrial activities, as well as among the Defence Forces.

The defence planning process attempts to match the budgetary resources likely to be made available for the requirement to establish the defence capability necessary to face the threats and challenges. This exercise is undertaken in two phases: (a) What should be the proportion allocated to the defence effort as against other areas of national security concerns and economic growth? This exercise involves a 'visionary' analysis of external and internal security threats (often linked) and challenges. In order to minimise adverse affects of high military expenditure on socioeconomic development, it is necessary to harmonise national development planning with defence planning. (b) Optimisation of allocated resources, i.e. distribution of resources within the Ministry of Defence (MoD) based on Force planning (Force and weapons mix, command and control, logistics and human resources management) by the Defence Services to combat current and future threats, and development of required capabilities by the Defence Research and Development Organisation (DRDO), defence production and other agencies concerned. The quantum of indigenous production and the requirements to be procured from outside are decided in this phase. The objective is to achieve maximum defence capability from the given resources. Both allocation and distribution are closely linked. They need to be reviewed periodically but not so frequently that the planning process becomes ad hoc. In India's case, this is done at five-year intervals.

DEFENCE PLANNING AND SERVICES

Before independence, the defence services worked on a system of contract budget. Defence expenditure was pegged at Rs 55 crore per year, which was more than half of the Central Government's revenue. There was no serious threat from outside (except during World War II, when a fresh agreement was signed) and this amount was more than adequate to maintain the establishment.

The savings were not allowed to lapse but put away in the Defence Reserve Fund that was utilised to finance measures for re-equipment of the Defence Services, thus freeing the Government from having to provide fund money greater than the contract amount. Expenditure on defence rose steeply soon after independence. However, there was no planned effort and defence programmes consisted mainly of outright purchases from abroad, drawing heavily on available Sterling reserves. In the late 1950s, some efforts were made to initiate domestic weapons production by the Ministry of Defence when Mr. Krishna Menon was the Defence Minister. The Sino-Indian conflict in 1962 aroused a new defence consciousness in the country. After taking care of immediate postwar requirements, systematic defence planning started in 1964. Defence requirements were assessed on a five-year basis and the First Five Year Defence Plan (1964-69) was drawn up. This plan took into account the resources available and assistance which could be expected from friendly foreign countries. The plan was primarily based on an expansion and modernisation programme considered necessary by each Service in the light of the respective threat perception assessed. It also proposed a defence production base that would gradually reduce the country's external dependence, provide for improvements in border roads and communications, and a modest expansion of DRDO. The Government recognised the imperative need to synergise 'defence' and 'development' instead of planning each on a separate and unrelated level. The MoD emphasised the "inevitable need to harness all resources of the country for the country's defence and for the defence effort to derive full sustenance from the country's economic development plans".

Thereafter, the National Development Council authorised the Chairman of the Planning Commission to review the needs of both development and defence. A Planning Cell was established in 1965 in the Ministry of Defence 'to deal with the wider aspects of defence planning'. The new system was intended to facilitate medium and long-term defence planning and to maintain constant liaison with the Planning Commission and other ministries. It was expected that the MoD would derive maximum advantage from the development effort by being able to place its priorities for consideration along with the overall economic and industrial plans drawn up by the Planning Commission. The experience of the First Five Year Defence Plan showed that the development of weapons and equipment was a long drawn out process. The Government realised that there could be no forward movement in attaining self-sufficiency in weapons and equipment unless these requirements were planned over a reasonably long period, long enough to cover the span of development and production of new weapons systems and other fighting tools.

The inadequacy of foreign exchange reserves was another hindrance in planning and implementation. In order to mitigate some of these drawbacks, the Second Five Year Defence Plan (1969-74) was instituted on a "roll-on" basis. After a year, an additional year was added so that the Defence Services would have before them a revised and updated five-year plan. In this context, the MoD commented: "Opportunity is taken by this annual exercise to take note of and reflect the change in priorities, the shifts in emphasis and the latest concepts and programmes to reorient the plan within the scheme of resources so that the aims and means are most effectively balanced." This system was expected to facilitate the planning of projects that took five years or more and to revise or eliminate projects, depending on the prevailing foreign exchange situation and availability of domestic resources.

For a period of five years, firm assurances were to be given on the availability of resources. This, unfortunately, never happened. In 1971, it was impossible to adhere to the discipline and the pattern of the roll-on plan. Instead of roll-on annual revisions, immediate requirements dominated the Government's attention that pre-empted plan efforts. In its 1971-72 Annual Report, the MoD acknowledged that having a Planning Cell in the ministry was an insufficient and unsatisfactory method of meeting a crisis.

The Planning Cell was not taken seriously in the crucial stages of economic planning and the argument that defence needs would be adjusted in the over-all allocation of resources was proved wrong. In 1974, an Apex Group headed by the Union Minister for Planning again suggested that steady long-term defence programmes would be more cost effective and economical rather than fluctuating allocations due to periodic economic and security crises. In order to integrate defence planning with the overall economic planning effort, defence and economic development plans were made co-terminus.

Defence Planning Machinery

Most of the defence planning machinery and planning methodology was developed in the decade 1964-74. The Joint Intelligence Committee (JIC) was established in the Cabinet Secretariat to provide external and internal threat assessments. Inputs for this purpose were to be provided by all Intelligence agencies of the Government. The Service Chiefs were to assess the broad military aims and a strategy, coordinated in the Chiefs of Staff Committee, was to be approved by the Defence Minister. However, this was seldom done. Each Service ended up planning its own force level, choice of weapons and equipment, and build-up of infrastructure. In 1977, the Government formed a Committee for Defence Planning (CDP) to "undertake regular assessments relevant to defence planning in the light of all factors having a bearing on national security and defence". However, this committee could not function smoothly nor meet the desired goals.

Planning units were also established in the Department of Defence Production and DRDO. A Planning and Coordination Cell was created in the MoD to coordinate and compile various plans into a 'Defence Plan' for Cabinet approval. As the bureaucrats in the ministry had no professional knowledge or background, this cell could only compile different requirements without any analysis. In Army Headquarters, the Deputy Chief of Army Staff was made responsible for preparing the Army plan. A Perspective Planning Directorate was established in the late 1970s. Naval and Air plans were prepared in the respective Planning Directorates. Financial considerations, nonexistent at this level earlier, were introduced through Finance Planning Sections attached to these Directorates. In 1986, the Directorate General of Defence Planning Staff (DGDPS), comprising officers from the three Services, DRDO, and Ministries of Defence and External Affairs, was established under the Chiefs of Staff Committee (COSC) to coordinate and harmonise defence planning. Civilian officers from the Ministries probably did not find the job professionally satisfying and were gradually withdrawn, thus leaving the DGDPS a tri-Service set up.

All these measures enabled each Service headquarters to prepare defence plans in a more rational manner. But due to lack of clear political direction and each Service primarily planning for itself, joint planning, coordination between Services and other departmental plans of the MoD, were largely ignored. After the Kargil conflict in 1999, the Group of Ministers (GoM) and later the Cabinet Committee on Security (CCS) approved several reforms. An Integrated Defence Headquarters (IDH) was established and the DGDPS was merged with it. The creation of the post of Chief of Defence Staff (CDS), whose tasks would include ensuring intra and inter-Services prioritisation of defence plans and improvement in joint functioning of the Defence Services, was recommended. The reforms also included establishment of a Defence Intelligence Agency and creation of Defence Equipment Production, Research and Planning councils in the IDH and MoD, respectively. Unfortunately, the CDS, who would be the cornerstone of integrated operational planning for defence, has not been appointed.

Analysis of the Planning System

Despite several years of planning efforts, defence planning in India is characterised by seesaw bouts of frenzied activity followed by long periods of relative inaction. Five-year defence plans have rarely been formally approved before commencement. The Tenth Defence Plan, now in its third year, is yet to be accorded formal government approval. Adhocism is the order of the day, leading to knee-jerk responses and haphazard planning, making India a reactive rather than proactive nation in matters pertaining to national security. Whenever India's major adversaries plan a big defence purchase, there is an outcry for similar acquisitions, resulting in piecemeal decisions regardless of long-term impact and overall requirements. The Defence Forces are forced to follow "a case-by-case" approach to modernisation and procurement of arms, ammunition and equipment to replace obsolescent items, in many cases long after their life cycle is over and they cannot be maintained in a cost effective manner. The Army's Vijayanta tanks, MiG-21s of the IAF, and IL-38 maritime reconnaissance aircraft of the Navy are some examples. Weapons development, procurement and absorption are complex processes. A lead-time of 15-20 years is required to plan and execute major projects. Despite this, for several years, a large amount of the capital acquisition budget has been surrendered. In the prevailing era of strategic uncertainty, the changing nature of warfare demands a judicious mix of threat and capabilities-based forces that can operate efficiently as combined arms, joint Services teams and components of multinational coalition forces.

CONCEPT OF NATIONAL SECURITY POLICY AND STRATEGY

The concept of national security rests mainly on the proposition that many foreign and domestic political, economic and military issues are interrelated, each with implications on the other. In India's case, this has been highlighted by insurgencies and other political events, particularly in border-states, and other outside pressures, which are brought to bear on the country's economy and technological progress from time to time.

A response to this type of environment calls for a highly focused national security policy and strategy. Effective guidance on national security and defence policy objectives is fundamental to the defence planning process. National security is a relative matter without a firm criteria but unless firm national security objectives are set and a defence policy evolved, there can be no military doctrine or balancing of defence effort with other national objectives and priorities such as maintaining a viable economy and supporting development of society. The lack of a cohesive national security strategy and defence policy has many implications. First, it results in the absence of clear political direction regarding politico-military objectives, which is the very basis of sound defence planning. Secondly, there is inadequate coordination of defence plans and economic development. Finally, science and technology policies for defence, general industrialisation and other development programmes are not coordinated properly to achieve security goals and objectives.

Defence Perspective and Integrated Planning

A Defence Plan has to be prepared on the basis of a 15-year long perspective planning system, such that the first five years of the plan are very firm (Definitive Plan), the second five years less firm (Indicative Plan) and the third five-year term tentative (Vision Plan). There has to be a reasonably firm allocation of financial resources for the first five years and an indicative allocation for the subsequent period. Perspective planning needs to be done in the Integrated Defence Headquarters, where military, technical and R&D

experts take an integrated view of future threats and challenges. This has to be based on future battlefield scenarios, and array of forecasts, evaluation of strategic options and force mixes, and analysis of potential technical and industrial capabilities. Based on this, the respective Service should work on their perspective plans and the R&D and Defence Production/Supplies experts should spell out their requirements in terms of effort, technology and indigenous production. As stated earlier, the CDS, who would be the cornerstone of integrated operational planning for defence, has not been appointed. India's defence planning, therefore, continues to be Service based. Often, the threat perception of one Service is at variance with that of another Service. What emerges is essentially a sum of total of Service or department wise programmes. The focus is not on overall goals or priorities but on what is required by a particular Service. In its endeavour to lay the groundwork for an increased share of the budget, each Service tends to exercise its own priorities, favouring its own plans to the detriment of joint plans.

Subjects like surveillance, air defence, electronic warfare, and amphibious operations, which relate to more than one Service, do not get adequate attention. Integrated planning for defence is essential for creating balanced force structures and for the successful execution of all military missions.

In fact, it is the most effective manner of ensuring effective defence. According to Charles Hitch, "the revolution in military technology has not only changed the character of our military programmes, it has also to a significant degree blurred the lines of demarcation among various Services". Most major military missions today require the participation of more than one military service. Therefore, the principal concern now must be centred on what is required by the defence establishment as a whole to perform a particular mission—not what is required by a particular Service to perform its individual part of that 'mission'. The areas of commonality in modern weapon systems are immense and growing rapidly. Communications, guidance systems, missiles, radars, lasers—

even traditional equipment such as guns, fuses, ammunition and vehicles are common. Integrated defence planning is necessary in view of escalating costs of these weapons and equipment.

Self-reliance in Defence Technology

The DRDO has a network of 51 laboratories and establishments. The Scientific Advisor (SA) to the Raksha Mantri (RM) is the Secretary of this Department. The DRDO has a staff of 30,000, including 6,800 scientists and engineers. It receives approximately four to six per cent of the defence budget annually. The DRDO is engaged in the pursuit of self-reliance in critical technologies relevant to defence. It formulates and executes a programme of scientific research, design and development for the induction into the Armed Forces of state-of-the-art weapons and other equipments.

In April 1984, the DRDO envisaged a programme "to transform the Department into a leader of international class with the mission to capture and retain commanding heights in critical technologies". A 'mission mode' organisational structure and approach was approved by the Government with a view to increasing the element of self-reliance from the current 30 per cent to 70 per cent by 2005. This goal, however, is nowhere in sight. The Department has developed more than 1,100 items of weapon systems and equipment with a production value of over Rs 6,000 crore. But it has not been able to make any major contribution to the state-of-art weapons and equipment. Most of its programmes, like Prithvi (sea borne version), Trishul (short-range surface to air missile), Akash (medium-range surface to air missile), Nag (anti-tank missile), Light Combat Aircraft with Kaveri engine, Pinaka (multiple-barrel rocket system), MBT Arjun, Electronic Warfare equipment, new radio sets for the Army, Sonar system for Navy, and many other items, are way behind schedule.

BUDGETING INDIA'S MILITARY MODERNISATION WITH MYOPIA

Armed Forces are not meant to parade on the Raj Path

on Republic Day displaying their might to impress the domestic and international audience. They are the vital instrument of implementing a nation's will both in peace and war. To this end, the nation's military represents the ultimate and final arbiter in projecting "National Will". This calls for planned growth over the years based on a sound modernisation plan. This is a must to ensure that the forces retain their edge and win India's wars and serve as a credible deterrence during peace.

It can be proved without doubt that India's past two wars of 1965 and 1971 were actually two front wars with China managing to tie down India forces by its pro Pakistan stance. This relation ship has only grown stronger over the years. Add to this Chinese theory of "String of Pearls" and the picture is complete.

A country which faces threats on a two and a half fronts cannot but strengthen this instrument of state'sComprehensive National Power. This, apart from keeping the military current and potent through tough training, requires pragmatic investments in its arming. Economics plays a crucial role here. When the potential adversaries are spending to the tune of $150 Billion on their militaries, the current Indian defence budget, which promises a mere Rs 60,000 crores for product acquisition, is grossly inadequate. If we study the numbers, we come to the conclusion that the capital budget of Rs 60,000 leaves only about one third or so for new acquisitions. The remainder being used to service the existing commitments.

For a nation with a periphery of contradictions, this is grossly inadequate. We want the military to be wired, lethal and light. This calls for right investments to be made across the three services to develop capability and threat based forces.

Our neighbours and potential adversaries merit a look here. As General Ashok Mehta comments, "IfIndia-China relations are at the lowest today, China-Pakistan relations have climbed to new heights and there will be more than menacing sounds in the event of conflict. The speed of Chinese defence modernisation is in sharp contrast to India's lethargic response. The PLA's first aircraft carrier, Shi Lang, will take to sea four years ahead of schedule at the end of the year and five more will follow in a decade. China's submarine fleet will reach 100 vessels in the next three to five years and its stealth fighter has been tested. A new anti-ship missile is also reported operational. Technology and fire power at the disposal of the PLA have grown fast and thanks to the Chinese economic miracle, the Defence Budget has been boosted five-fold in the last decade, touching nearly $90 billion though the actual figure could be as high as $150 billion. China has sent a general warning to keep off South China Sea, Taiwan and Tibet".

Can India sharpen the Look East Policy to counter the String of Pearls? This would take the sheen off the string and enable India to concentrate on Public Diplomacy to meet its ends on this front. It will require a commitment borne out of a high degree of pragmatic application of India's politico military diplomacy. Are we ready to use this instrument? This notwithstanding, Indian military needs to modernise despite a counter to the string of pearls through public diplomacy. A respected analyst argues:-

Cant we puzzle China by creating a counter pearl necklace around it? They seem to be becoming aware that we just might do that and are worried. Cultivate all the ASEAN countries, join them; invest in them financially, commercially, educationally, culturally, socially and you will have created a huge problem/alternative for SEAC which wasn't there earlier. That would be exposition of Indian jugad at its best.

This is one area where the Defence forces, MEA, Finance, Education, Oil, Industry, Commerce, Culture ministries all have a stake.

The trouble is that we have given no credence to military diplomacy else countries like Bangladesh, Myanmar, Vietnam and Indonesia would have been helping our string of pearls. Bhutan and some African countries are examples of our successful military diplomacy through organisations such as IMTRAT. The Look East is a must and we have written adequately on it but who is listening. Else Bangladesh and Myanmar would have been our friends with strong military to military contacts.

This notwithstanding, the "why" of modernising the military has unfortunately still not sunk in completely. In our earlier article we had argued for a military commission to be set up to ensure modernisation of the military lest we continue to arm without aiming. History has it that the Indian Military was found wanting in previous incidents of using hard power to meet the national interests due to its 'unpreparedness'. Even today the situation has not changed much.

To that end, this is a populist budget and "more will be made available when needed" proves our willingness and compulsions to follow knee jerk responses to National Security.

To put the record straight, our China threat has only multiplied over the years while Pakistan continues to poke a finger at us through incidents like Kargil. Recent assertions of being capable of managing the India threat after Exercise Azm e Nau are not new. Together, the two pose a strong case for a credible military capability under the nuclear shadow. The "half front" of a full blown insurgency and naxalism requires a "third force" capable of handling threats to internal security. This article in rediff.com calls for serious introspection, "China lends us; we give to Pak; Pak makes nukes". All the tears we expend; all the railing we do will not change the main lack/lacunae in our military thinking that we gain nothing by ruing China's military reach over us. It has always been there; will always be there.

However, the nation has to modernise the armed forces in tune with its threats it faces and is likely to face over the next decade, China not withstanding.

Restructuring and modernising the armed forces will require political courage, military astuteness, a non parochial approach and a singularity of purpose.

With India's defence budget now pegged at less than 2.0 per cent of the GDP, the funds available for modernisation of the armed forces are grossly inadequate. Or do we need to restructure the formula to a threat based dispensation. This way we would have the luxury to be ostrich like in relegating threats to national security. Then there is the need to build capabilities to keep India secure. Whatever the formula, the need to keep the military capable of dealing with any exigency is paramount.

The essence therefore is in instituting pragmatic approach based on our capability to meet all the threats with suitable capabilities. Till that is comprehended as a sub set of Comprehensive National Power, we shall evolve all wrong formulae with requisite myopia in place.

Bibliography

Ajey Lele: *Strategic Technologies for the Military : Breaking New Frontiers*, Sage, Delhi, 2009.

Amitabh Sikdar: *India and China : Strategic Energy Management and Security*, Manas, Delhi, 2009.

Anil, K.C.: *Military and Democracy in South Asia : Challenges, Politics and Power*, Sumit Enterprises, Delhi, 2009.

Arend, A.: *International Law and the Use of Military*, London, Routledge, 1993.

Benoit, E.: *Defence and Economic Growth in Developing Countries*, Lexington MA: Lexington Books, 1973.

Bhaskara Rao: *Military Conversion : Impact on Science and Technology*, Discovery, Delhi, 2003.

Bhat, T.P. : *India and China : Trade Complementarities and Competitiveness*, Bookwell, Delhi, 2008.

Brauer, J. and J.P. Dunne : *Arms Trade and Economic Development: Theory Policy and Cases in Arms trade Offsets*, London and New York: Routledge, 1973.

Cathy Solheim: *Military Economics: Issues, Policies, and Solutions*, Washington, D.C., Island Press, 1995.

Damrosch, L.F.: *Law and Force in the New International Order*, Boulder, Westview Press, 1991.

Deepak, B R : *India and China : 1904-2004 : A Century of Peace and Conflict*, Manak, Delhi, 2005.

Dixit, Prabla: *Defence Budget: A Struggle for Power*, New Delhi, Orient Longman, 1981.

Dunne, J. P. and Brauer, J.: *Arms Trade and Economic Development: Theory, Policy*, Routledge, London, 2004.

Gautam, P.K. : *Environmental Security : New Challenges and Role of Military*, Shipra, Delhi, 2010.

Gupta, Asha: *Military Rule and Democratization : Changing Perspectives*, Deep & Deep, Delhi, 2003.

Hewitt, D.: *Military Expenditure – Econometric Testing of Economic and Political Influences: Working Paper*, Washington DC: IMF, 1991.

Huntington, S.P.: *The China Modernisation Military and the State*, N.Y., Vintage Books, 1964.

John M. Seidl: *Politics American Style: Race, Environment and Central Cities*, New York, Prentice-Hall, 1972.

Jones, W.H.: *Government and Politics of India Military Budget*, London, Hutchinson, 1971.

Juvale, R.P. : *Military Strategy and Diplomacy*, Cyber Tech Publications, Delhi, 2010.

Kapur, C.K. : *Chinese Military Budgeting*, Manas, Delhi, 2003.

Leena Parmar: *Military Budgeting: Global Perspectives*, Rawat, Delhi, 1999.

Mauro, P.: *The Effects of Corruption on Growth, Investment, and Government Expenditure: Working Paper*, Washington, DC: IMF, 1996.

Omitoogun, W. and E. Hutchful : *Budgeting for the Military Sector in Africa: The Processes and Mechanisms of Control*, Oxford: Oxford University Press, 2006

Posen, B.R.: *The Sources of Indian Military Doctrine*, Ithaca, 1984, Cornell Univ. Press.

Radhakrishna: *Handbook of Military and Defence Budgeting*, Sumit Enterprises, Delhi, 2009.

Rita Raj: *Global Encyclopaedia of Military Education and Training*, Global Vision, Delhi, 2010.

Roeber, J.: *Parallel Markets: Corruption in the International Arms Trade*', London: Campaign Against Arms Trade, 2005.

Rosen, P.: *Societies and Military Power: India and its Armies*, Ithaca, Cornell University Press, 1996.

Sutton, J., *Technology and Defence Market Structure*, MIT Press, Delhi, 1998.

Index

M

N

P

R

S

□□□